BLOOM'S TAXONOMY
A Forty-year Retrospective

BLOOM'S TAXONOMY
A Forty-year Retrospective

Ninety-third Yearbook of the
National Society for the Study of Education

PART II

Edited by
LORIN W. ANDERSON AND LAUREN A. SOSNIAK

Editor for the Society
KENNETH J. REHAGE

19 | NSSE | 94

Distributed by THE UNIVERSITY OF CHICAGO PRESS   ●   CHICAGO, ILLINOIS

The National Society for the Study of Education

Founded in 1901 as successor to the National Herbart Society, the National Society for the Study of Education has provided a means by which the results of serious study of educational issues could become a basis for informed discussion of those issues. The Society's two-volume yearbooks, now in their ninety-third year of publication, reflect the thoughtful attention given to a wide range of educational problems during those years. In 1971 the Society inaugurated a series of substantial publications on Contemporary Educational Issues to supplement the yearbooks. Each year the Society's publications contain contributions to the literature of education from more than a hundred scholars and practitioners who are doing significant work in their respective fields.

An elected Board of Directors selects the subjects with which volumes in the yearbook series are to deal and appoints committees to oversee the preparation of manuscripts. A special committee created by the Board performs similar functions for the series on Contemporary Educational Issues.

The Society's publications are distributed each year without charge to members in the United States, Canada, and elsewhere throughout the world. The Society welcomes as members all individuals who desire to receive its publications. Information about current dues may be found in the back pages of this volume.

This volume, *Bloom's Taxonomy: A Forty-year Retrospective*, is Part II of the Ninety-third Yearbook of the Society. Part I, published at the same time, is entitled *Teacher Research and Educational Reform*.

A listing of the Society's publications still available for purchase may be found in the back pages of this volume.

Library of Congress Catalog Number: 92-063306
ISSN: 0077-5762

Published 1994 by
THE NATIONAL SOCIETY FOR THE STUDY OF EDUCATION

5835 Kimbark Avenue, Chicago, Illinois 60637
© 1994 by the National Society for the Study of Education

First Printing

Printed in the United States of America

v

Acknowledgments

The contributors to this volume assess the impact of Bloom's well-known Taxonomy of objectives for the cognitive domain. Some of the authors participated in the development of the Taxonomy more than forty years ago. They reflect on its use (and misuse) since its publication in 1956. Some recall the numerous studies that have sought to validate claims made for the Taxonomy, for example, that it is "neutral," that it has a "cumulative-hierarchical" structure, that distinctions can be made between "lower-order" and "higher-order" objectives. Others recount experiences with the use of the Taxonomy in the United States and abroad.

The editors, Lorin W. Anderson and Lauren A. Sosniak, obtained the assistance of a distinguished list of authors to participate in this retrospective analysis of the Taxonomy and to reflect upon its contributions to educational thought and practice. The National Society for the Study of Education is grateful to the editors and to each of the contributors for the time and effort that made this book possible.

Margaret Early, formerly a member of the Society's Board of Directors and a professor at the University of Florida, has again provided superb assistance in the editing of this volume, as she has with several other recent NSSE Yearbooks. Christopher Shinn has done the painstaking work required to prepare the name index.

KENNETH J. REHAGE
Editor for the Society

Preface

Arguably, one of the most influential educational monographs of the past half century is the *Taxonomy of Educational Objectives, The Classification of Educational Goals, Handbook I: Cognitive Domain*. Nearly forty years after its publication in 1956 the volume remains a standard reference for discussions of testing and evaluation, curriculum development, and teaching and teacher education. A search of the most recent *Social Science Citation Index* (1992) revealed more than 150 citations to the *Handbook*. At a recent meeting of approximately 200 administrators and teachers, the senior editor of this volume asked for a show of hands in response to the question, "How many of you have heard of Bloom's Taxonomy?" Virtually every hand in the audience was raised. Few education publications have enjoyed such overwhelming recognition for so long.

The purpose of this volume is not to honor or glorify the Taxonomy. In our opinion, such an effort is neither necessary nor worthwhile. Rather, our purpose is to present a critical analysis and evaluation of a recognized classic in American education. The author of each chapter was asked to (1) examine the Taxonomy in the context of the primary topic(s) of his or her chapter, (2) present a balanced discussion of the strengths and weaknesses of the Taxonomy relative to those topic(s), and (3) interpret the Taxonomy in terms of the historical period in which it was developed, of the present educational milieu, and of the likely future of education in the United States and throughout the world. As the reader will see, the authors adhered quite closely to these criteria.

Some readers, recalling the 1956 publication date so widely cited for the *Handbook*, may wonder about the title of this volume. In fact, it has been more than forty years since the inception of the Taxonomy. Initial meetings of the committee responsible for the development of the Taxonomy and the publication of the *Handbook* began in 1949 and a preliminary draft of the *Handbook* was published in 1954.

In this preface, as well as throughout this volume, we differentiate between the *Handbook* and the Taxonomy. The term "Taxonomy" is

vii

used when we or the authors of the various chapters refer to the classification system itself. The term *"Handbook"* is used when the reference is to the publication in which the classification system appears.

We would like to extend our appreciation to all of the chapter authors. They were prompt and professional, and they produced chapters of the highest quality. In addition, we are extremely proud of the fact that the authors of three of the chapters are themselves co-editors of the *Handbook*. Their remembrances and reflections lend credibility to our work.

We owe a debt of gratitude to the Bloom of Bloom's Taxonomy. Early in our careers, Benjamin Bloom served as our mentor. Over time, he has become our friend and colleague.

Finally, we wish to express our appreciation to the thirty-four participants who contributed to the development of the Taxonomy through attending one or more of the conferences from 1949 to 1953. Their group effort has made a contribution far beyond what anyone could have imagined.

In a field marked by wide pendulum swings, the likelihood of finding an idea, concept, or point of view that has remained constant in its acceptance and application is small indeed. Without doubt, the Taxonomy is one of these rarities. Our hope is that this volume will help educators understand our legacy and its meaning for the problems of today.

LORIN W. ANDERSON
LAUREN A. SOSNIAK
January, 1994

Table of Contents

X   TABLE OF CONTENTS

CHAPTER I

Reflections on the Development and Use of the Taxonomy

BENJAMIN S. BLOOM

The *Taxonomy of Educational Objectives, Handbook 1: Cognitive Domain*, a small volume developed to assist college and university examiners, has been transformed into a basic reference for all educators worldwide. Unexpectedly, it has been used by curriculum planners, administrators, researchers, and classroom teachers at all levels of education.

The committee that met to develop the Taxonomy initially disputed the use of the term "taxonomy." However, I believed that the term was quite distinctive and descriptive. Eventually, the committee agreed that the term would be used and it has become commonplace not only in education but in other fields as well.

The phenomenal growth of the use of the Taxonomy can only be explained by the fact that it filled a void; it met a previously unmet need for basic, fundamental planning in education. For the first time, educators were able to evaluate the learning of students systematically. As they did so, they became aware that too much emphasis was being placed on the lowest level of the Taxonomy—"Knowledge." Frequently as much as 90 percent of the instructional time was spent at this level, with very little time spent on the higher mental processes that would enable students to apply their knowledge creatively. With the explosion of knowledge that has taken place during the past forty years, the ability to use higher mental processes has assumed prime importance.

The Origins of the Taxonomy

Under President Robert Hutchins's General Education Plan, the undergraduate division of the University of Chicago was organized

---

Benjamin S. Bloom is the Charles H. Swift Professor Emeritus, Department of Education, University of Chicago.

around interdisciplinary core courses and comprehensive examinations. Faculty members wrote the examinations, which were to emphasize higher mental processes, for a Board of Examiners. Many of the examinations were "open book" and students were free to bring books and notes to the examinations. During the years from 1948 to 1956 I was first College Examiner and then University Examiner with the Board of Examiners. It should be obvious why the development of the Taxonomy was of special importance to the faculty and to me.

The idea for the Taxonomy was first discussed at an informal meeting of college and university examiners who attended the 1948 American Psychological Association convention in Boston. The group believed that some common framework used by all college and university examiners could do much to promote the exchange of test materials and ideas for testing. They also believed that such a framework could be useful in stimulating research on examinations and on the relation between examinations and education. After considerable discussion, there was agreement that the framework might best be obtained through a system of classifying the *goals* of the educational process using educational objectives.

This meeting was the first in a series of informal annual meetings of college and university examiners. (See table 1 for a list of the individuals who attended one or more of these meetings.) Gathering at a different university each year and with some changes in membership, the group considered the problems involved in developing a classification of educational objectives. It also considered many other problems of examining students and conducting educational research.

The original plans called for a complete taxonomy in three parts— the cognitive, affective, and psychomotor domains. It was decided that the cognitive domain, which includes those objectives pertaining to the recall or recognition of knowledge and the development of intellectual skills and abilities, would be the first to be published. The reason for this choice was quite simple. The cognitive domain was the domain most central to much of the test development work at that time. It was also the domain in which most of the work in curriculum development had taken place and where the clearest definitions of objectives as *descriptions of student behavior* were to be found.

To overcome the problem of classifying objectives which could not be observed or manipulated as directly as those in the physical and biological sciences, the group decided that virtually all educational

TABLE 1

Participants in One or More of the Conferences
on the Taxonomy between 1949 and 1953

Anderson, Gordon V., University of Texas
Bloom, Benjamin S., University of Chicago
Churchill, Ruth, Antioch College
Cronbach, Lee J., University of Illinois
Dahnke, Harold L., Jr., Michigan State University
Detchen, Lily, Pennsylvania College for Women
Dressel, Paul L., Michigan State University
Dyer, Henry S., Educational Testing Service
Ebel, Robert L., University of Iowa
Engelhart, Max, Chicago Public Schools
Findley, Warren, Educational Testing Service
Furst, Edward J., University of Michigan
Gage, Nathaniel L., University of Illinois
Harris, Chester W., University of Wisconsin
Hastings, J. Thomas, University of Illinois
Heil, Louis M., Brooklyn College
Hill, Walker H., Michigan State University
Horton, Clark W., Dartmouth College
Krathwohl, David R., Michigan State University
Loree, M. Ray, Louisiana State University
Mayhew, Louis B., Michigan State University
McGuire, Christine, University of Chicago
McQuitty, John V., University of Florida
Morris, John B., University of Mississippi
Pace, C. Robert, Syracuse University
Plumlee, Lynnette, Educational Testing Service
Remmers, H. H., Purdue University
Stern, George G., Syracuse University
Sutton, Robert B., Ohio State University
Thiede, Wilson, University of Wisconsin
Travers, Robert M., Human Resources Research Center, San Antonio, Texas
Tyler, Ralph W., Center for Advanced Study in the Behavioral Sciences, Stanford,
    California
Warrington, Willard G., Michigan State University
Watt, Rex, University of Southern California

objectives when stated in behavioral form have their counterparts in student behavior. These behaviors, then, could be observed and described, and the descriptions could be classified.

Some fear was expressed that the Taxonomy might lead to a fragmentation and atomization of educational purposes such that the parts and pieces finally placed into the classification might be different from the more complete objective with which one started. Although this was recognized as a very real danger, one solution to this potential problem appeared to be establishing the categories at a level of generality where the loss of fragmentation would not be too great.

Furthermore, the hierarchical relations among the categories would enable the users of the Taxonomy to understand more clearly the place of a particular objective in relation to other objectives.

It was further agreed that every effort should be made to avoid value judgments about objectives and behaviors. Neutrality with respect to educational principles and philosophies was to be achieved by constructing a system which, insofar as possible, would permit the inclusion of objectives from a wide range of educational orientations. Thus, it should be possible to classify any and all objectives which were stated as descriptions of student behavior.

The Development of the Handbook

After completing a draft of the *Handbook*, we naturally were hesitant about publishing it without securing as widespread comment and criticism as possible. Members of the committee had discussed the Taxonomy with colleagues in their own institutions, with graduate students in curriculum and testing, and with other groups of teachers and educational specialists. Whenever possible, the criticisms and suggestions were incorporated into a revision of the draft.

A somewhat more formal presentation was made in a symposium at the American Psychological Association convention held in Chicago in 1951. The symposium, chaired by H. H. Remmers, included a presentation that I made on the cognitive domain and a presentation by David Krathwohl on the affective domain. Oscar K. Buros, O. H. Mowrer, and John Stalnaker served as discussants.

Despite these various reviews and reactions, we still felt the need for the comments, suggestions, and criticisms of a larger and more representative group of educators and researchers. Thus, we were pleased when Longmans, Green and Company agreed to print a preliminary edition of 1000 copies of the *Handbook*. This preliminary edition was sent to a group of professors, teachers, administrators, curriculum directors, and educational researchers. They were asked to read the preliminary edition carefully and offer criticisms and suggestions, as well as additional illustrations of objectives and test materials. They responded very generously and the final version of the *Handbook* included many of their ideas. We were truly appreciative of the time and thought they gave to this work.

The development of the *Handbook* was truly a group project. It was the direct outgrowth of the thinking of more than thirty persons who attended the various meetings at which the idea of a taxonomy was discussed. It was based on the work of countless test developers, curriculum workers, and teachers. Several hundred readers of the preliminary edition contributed criticisms, suggestions, and illustrative materials. The committee which assumed responsibility for the actual writing hoped that the *Handbook* justified the enormous amount of time and effort devoted to it by the many persons involved. We regarded the work as well worth the effort if the *Handbook* was found to be of value as a means of communication within the field of education. We submitted it in the hope that it would stimulate thought and research on problems of curriculum and testing.

Experiences with Applications of the Taxonomy

It has been both stimulating and gratifying to assist educators in countries throughout the world in exploring ways of effectively using the Taxonomy in their educational systems. Since its publication in 1956, the *Handbook* has been translated, either totally or partially, into at least eighteen languages (see chapter 9). I have had several experiences with the use of the Taxonomy outside the United States. I briefly summarize here three of these experiences.

The Gränna seminar. In 1970 I went to South America for the purpose of selecting teams of educators to participate in the historic seminar on curriculum development which was to be held in Gränna, Sweden, in 1971. I was surprised to discover that in every country I visited, the Taxonomy (which had come to be known as "Bloom's Taxonomy") was well known, thanks to the Spanish translation. As a consequence, educators in these countries were eager to be selected to participate in the Gränna seminar.

The Gränna seminar was attended by teams of six subject specialists from each of twenty-three countries located on five continents: Africa, Asia, Europe, North and South America. Politically, the Middle East was represented by Israel and Iran and the then Iron Curtain countries were represented by Hungary and Poland. Following the seminar, each six-person team was to return to their own country and establish curriculum research centers.

The seminar was led by an international faculty of outstanding educators and featured Ralph Tyler. A basic text used by the seminar participants was the newly published (1971) *Handbook of Formative and Summative Evaluation of Student Learning.*[1] Based on the Taxonomy, it brought together the best techniques available for evaluating the *improvement* of student learning. The major assumption was that "education must be increasingly concerned about the fullest development of all children and youth, and it will be the responsibility of the schools to seek learning conditions which will enable each individual to reach the highest level of learning possible."[2] To this end, applications of the Taxonomy in eleven major subject fields were illustrated and ways in which evaluation can be used to help students attain mastery in these subject fields were detailed. The Gränna seminar resulted in the establishment of Curriculum Research Centers—all based on the Taxonomy—in many of the participating countries.

The IEA studies. Since 1967, the International Association for the Evaluation of Educational Achievement (IEA) has published the results of a series of comparative studies. Achievement has been studied in a variety of subject areas (e.g., mathematics, science, literature, second languages, civics). In all cases, the Taxonomy, or some modification thereof, has been the basis for developing the achievement tests.

These comparative studies have not only been used to describe the relative standing of countries on tests of both lower and higher mental processes, but have also identified factors related to higher achievement. These factors have enabled educators in the various countries to consider ways in which their educational systems could benefit from the most successful educational practices and techniques. For example, the excellent results in mathematics in Japan became a standard by which mathematics programs can be judged and have provided an incentive for self-examination worldwide.

The China experience. In 1986, I was invited by Lin Fu Nian, Honorary President of East China Normal University in Shanghai, to be an exchange scholar. One of my primary responsibilities was to conduct a series of seminars. During these seminars, the Taxonomy was described and discussed. Lin Fu Nian was so impressed with the *Handbook* that he had it translated into Chinese and distributed a million copies to educators throughout China. The magnitude of this effort is truly mind-boggling.

Reactions to the Taxonomy

One of the primary reactions to the Taxonomy on the part of educators was a shift from a concern about teachers' actions to a concern for what students learned from those actions. As a result of this shift, there was a need to define clearly the intended learning outcomes in terms of changes in students' overt behavior.

Using the Taxonomy as a prototype, educators rapidly developed subject-specific taxonomies in a wide variety of fields. By the time the *Handbook of Formative and Summative Evaluation of Student Learning* was published in 1971, subject-specific taxonomies had been developed in fields ranging from the traditional academic disciplines of mathematics, biology, and history to areas such as aesthetics education, creative dramatics, art education, music, and medicine. In addition, the Taxonomy has become one of the most frequently cited sources for educational research. Each year the *Social Science Citation Index* includes over a hundred articles referencing the Taxonomy.

Criticisms of the Taxonomy have been many and varied. Some have felt that only those behaviors which could be tested were included. Others have argued that the use of behavioral objectives would impose constraints upon teacher behavior leading to a military training paradigm that could be tedious and stultifying. Still others believed it would lead to the training of children analogous to human engineering.

The Taxonomy does not impose a set of teaching procedures, nor does it view objectives as so detailed and restrictive that a single teaching method is implied. Rather, a teacher has a wide range of choices in making instructional decisions related to objectives associated with each level of the Taxonomy.

The Taxonomy does emphasize the need for teachers to help students learn to apply their knowledge to problems arising in their own experiences and to be able to deal effectively with problems that are not familiar to them. This emphasis alone should guard against the rote learning of ready-made solutions. It is obvious, at least to me, that many of the criticisms directed toward the Taxonomy have resulted from very narrow interpretations of both the Taxonomy and its proper application.

Concluding Remarks

Major changes in curriculum, testing, research, and educational psychology have occurred in the forty years since the Taxonomy was developed and the preliminary draft of the *Handbook* was published. These changes obviously have had a profound impact on the use of the Taxonomy in education. In the late 1940s, the prevalent view was that education was to serve a selection function; that is, the purpose of education was to determine which students should be dropped at each stage of the educational process and which merited and were fitted by nature or nurture for the rigors of more advanced education.

8 DEVELOPING AND USING THE TAXONOMY

The more modern view of the learner is that his or her ability is neither permanent nor highly stable; rather, it is highly *alterable* when proper stimulation and experience are provided. Furthermore, the teaching of higher mental processes need not be limited to the gifted or otherwise "deserving." Finally, recent research in the area of cognitive psychology will likely enhance our understanding of higher mental processes. Past research has demonstrated that as higher mental processes are emphasized and taught, lower level skills can be learned concomitantly.

In closing, I am gratified that Lorin Anderson and Lauren Sosniak have undertaken to edit this book. It is my sincere desire that it will help to promote a greater understanding and more effective use of the Taxonomy.

NOTES

1. Benjamin S. Bloom, J. Thomas Hastings, and George F. Madaus, *Handbook on Formative and Summative Evaluation of Student Learning* (New York: McGraw-Hill, 1971).

2. Ibid., p. 6.

CHAPTER II

Excerpts from the "Taxonomy of Educational Objectives, The Classification of Educational Goals, Handbook I: Cognitive Domain"

SELECTED BY

LORIN W. ANDERSON AND LAUREN A. SOSNIAK

EDITORS' NOTE. Benjamin Bloom once told the senior editor of this volume that the *Handbook* was one of the most widely cited yet least read books in American education. Thus, as we were developing the idea for this "Retrospective" we decided to include a chapter containing excerpts from the *Handbook* for those who may have heard about it but have never read it.

For those who have never read the *Handbook* in its entirety it is instructive to point out that it contains two parts. The first part, "Introduction and Explanation," includes chapters on the nature and development of the Taxonomy, educational objectives and curriculum development, and the problems of classifying educational objectives and test exercises. The second part, "The Taxonomy and Illustrative Materials," contains descriptions and examples of the category system itself. It is this second part with which educators are most familiar. As a consequence, the excerpts included in this chapter are taken primarily from the first part, with the exception of the bulk of the material included in the section we call "Translating Plan into Action: Filling in the Details."

Before beginning with the excerpts two points must be made. First, excerpts related to the discussion of the history of the development of the Taxonomy are not included. Bloom reviews this history in the previous chapter. Second, we have organized the excerpts into six sections, the headings for which are ours. These sections are related to, but distinct from, the chapters included in the *Handbook*. The organizational scheme we have used in this chapter is intended to remove some of the redundancy from the *Handbook* and to represent the flow of events from the initial vision of the developers of the Taxonomy through its educational applications. The page references given are the numbers of the pages of the *Handbook* on which the excerpt can be found. These references will enable the reader to connect our organizational scheme with the *Handbook* itself.

9

The Vision

You are reading about an attempt to build a taxonomy of educational objectives. It is intended to provide for classification of the goals of our educational system. It is expected to be of general help to all teachers, administrators, professional specialists, and research workers who deal with curricular and evaluation problems. It is especially intended to help them discuss these problems with greater precision (p. 1).

Teachers building a curriculum should find here a range of possible educational goals or outcomes in the cognitive area ("cognitive" is used to include activities such as remembering and recalling knowledge, thinking, problem solving, creating). Comparing the goals of their present curriculum with the range of possible outcomes may suggest additional goals they may wish to include (pp. 1-2).

Use of the taxonomy can also help one gain a perspective on the emphasis given to certain behaviors by a particular set of educational plans. Thus, a teacher, in classifying the goals of a teaching unit, may find that they all fall within the taxonomy category of recalling or remembering knowledge. Looking at the taxonomy categories may suggest to him that, for example, he could include some goals dealing with the application of this knowledge and with the analysis of the situations in which the knowledge is used (p. 2).

Curriculum builders should find the taxonomy helps them to specify objectives so that it becomes easier to plan learning experiences and prepare evaluation devices. . . . Once they have classified the objectives they wish to measure, teachers and testers working on evaluation problems may refer to the discussions of the problems of measuring such objectives (pp. 2-3).

Some research workers have found the categories of use as a framework for viewing the educational process and analyzing its workings. . . . But any of these uses demands a clear understanding of the structure of the taxonomy, its principles of construction, and its organization (p. 3).

The major purpose in constructing a taxonomy of educational objectives is to facilitate communication. In our original consideration

These excerpts from Benjamin S. Bloom et al., *Taxonomy of Educational Objectives, The Classification of Educational Goals, Handbook I: Cognitive Domain* (New York: David McKay, 1956, © 1956, Longman Publishing Group), are reprinted here with permission of the Longman Publishing Group.

of the project we conceived of it as a method of improving the exchange of ideas and materials among test workers, as well as other persons concerned with educational research and curriculum development (p. 10).

Set at this level, the task of producing a taxonomy, that is, a classification of education outcomes, is quite analogous to the development of a plan for classifying books in a library. Or, put more abstractly, it is like establishing symbols for designating classes of objects where the members of a class have something in common (p. 10).

The major task in setting up any kind of taxonomy is that of selecting appropriate symbols, giving them precise and usable definitions, and securing the consensus of the group which is to use them. Similarly, developing a classification of educational objectives requires the selection of an appropriate list of symbols to represent all the major types of educational outcomes. Next, there is the task of defining these symbols with sufficient precision to permit and facilitate communication about these phenomena among teachers, administrators, curriculum workers, testers, educational research workers, and others who are likely to use the taxonomy. Finally, there is the task of trying the classification and securing the consensus of the educational workers who wish to use the taxonomy (p. 11).

As achievement testers and educational research workers, the major phenomena with which we are concerned are the changes produced in individuals as a result of educational experiences. Such changes may be represented by the global statements of the educational objectives of an educational unit, or they may be represented by the actual description of the student behaviors which are regarded as appropriate or relevant to the objectives. Objectives may also be inferred from the tasks, problems, and observations used to test or evaluate the presence of these behaviors (pp. 11-12).

We are of the opinion that although the objectives and test materials and techniques may be specified in an almost unlimited number of ways, the student behaviors involved in these objectives can be represented by a relatively small number of classes. Therefore, this taxonomy is designed to be a classification of the student behaviors which represent the intended outcomes of the educational process. It is assumed that essentially the same classes of behavior may be observed in the usual range of subject-matter content, at different levels of education (elementary, high school, college), and in different schools. Thus, a single set of classifications should be applicable in all these instances (p. 12).

Guiding Principles

In discussing the principles by which a taxonomy might be developed, it was agreed that the taxonomy should be an educational-logical-psychological classification system. The terms in this order express the emphasis placed on the different principles by which the taxonomy could be developed (p. 6).

It was further agreed that in constructing the taxonomy every effort should be made to avoid value judgments about objectives and behaviors. Neutrality with respect to educational principles and philosophies was to be achieved by constructing a system which, insofar as possible, would permit the inclusion of objectives from all educational orientations. Thus, it should be possible to classify all objectives which can be stated as descriptions of student behavior (pp. 6-7).

Since the determination of classes and their titles is in some ways arbitrary, there could be an almost infinite number of ways of dividing and naming the domains of educational outcomes. To guide us in our selection of a single classification system and to make the product more readily understood and used, we established certain guiding principles. First, since the taxonomy is to be used in regard to existing educational units and programs, we are of the opinion that the major distinctions between classes should reflect, in large part, the distinctions teachers make among student behaviors (p. 13).

A second principle is that the taxonomy should be logically developed and internally consistent. Thus, each term should be defined and used in a consistent way throughout the taxonomy. In addition, each category should permit logical subdivisions which can be clearly defined and further subdivided to the extent that appears necessary and useful (p. 14).

A third principle is that the taxonomy should be consistent with our present understanding of psychological phenomena. Those distinctions which are psychologically untenable, even though regularly made by teachers, would be avoided. Further, distinctions which seem psychologically important, even though not frequently made in educational objectives, would be favorably considered for inclusion. Perhaps it should be reiterated that, since the taxonomy deals only with educationally intended behavior, it falls considerably short of being a classification scheme for all psychological phenomena (p. 14).

A fourth principle is that the classification should be a purely descriptive scheme in which every type of educational goal can be represented in a relatively neutral fashion. To avoid partiality to one view of education as opposed to another, we have attempted to make the taxonomy neutral by avoiding terms which implicitly convey value judgments and by making the taxonomy as inclusive as possible. This means that the kinds of behavioral changes emphasized by *any* institution, educational unit, or educational philosophy can be represented in the classification. Another way of saying this is that any objective which describes an intended behavior should be classifiable in this system (p. 14).

In one sense, however, the taxonomy is not completely neutral. This stems from the already noted fact that it is a classification of intended behaviors. It cannot be used to classify educational plans which are made in such a way that either the student behaviors cannot be specified or only a single (unanalyzed) term or phrase such as "understanding," or "desirable citizen," is used to describe the outcomes. Only those educational programs which can be specified in terms of intended student behaviors can be classified (p. 15).

We have so far used the terms "classification" and "taxonomy" more or less interchangeably. It is necessary, however, that we examine the relationship between these terms because, strictly speaking, they are not interchangeable. Taxonomies, particularly Aristotelian taxonomies, have certain structural rules which exceed in complexity the rules of a classification system. While a classification scheme may have many arbitrary elements, a taxonomy scheme may not. A taxonomy must be so constructed that the order of the terms must correspond to some "real" order among the phenomena represented by the terms. A classification scheme may be validated by reference to the criteria of communicability, usefulness, and suggestiveness, while a taxonomy must be validated by demonstrating its consistency with the theoretical views in research findings of the field it attempts to order (p. 17).

Early Concerns

One of the first problems raised in our discussions was whether or not educational objectives could be classified. It was pointed out that we were attempting to classify phenomena which could not be observed or manipulated in the same concrete form as the phenomena of such fields as the physical and biological sciences, where taxonomies of a very high order have already been developed. Nevertheless,

it was the view of the group that educational objectives stated in behavioral form have their counterparts in the behavior of individuals.
Such behavior can be observed and described, and these descriptive
statements can be classified (p. 5).

There was some concern expressed in the early meetings that the
availability of the taxonomy might tend to abort the thinking and
planning of teachers with regard to curriculum, particularly if teachers
merely selected what they believed to be desirable objectives from the
list provided in the taxonomy (p. 5).

Some fear was expressed that the taxonomy might lead to
fragmentation and atomization of educational purposes such that the
parts and pieces finally placed into the classification might be very
different from the more complete objective with which one started
(pp. 5-6).

It is recognized that the *actual behaviors* of the students after they
have completed the unit of instruction may differ in degree as well as
kind from the *intended behaviors* specified by the objectives. That is,
the effects of instruction may be such that the students do not learn a
given skill to the desired level of perfection; or, for that matter, they
may not develop the intended skill to any degree. This is a matter of
grading or evaluating the goodness of the performance. The emphasis
in the *Handbook* is on obtaining evidence on the extent to which
desired and intended behaviors have been learned by the student
(pp. 12-13).

We need a method of ordering phenomena such that the method of
ordering reveals significant relationships among the phenomena. This
is the basic problem of a taxonomy—to order phenomena in ways
which will reveal some of their essential properties as well as the
interrelationships among them. Members of the taxonomy group
spent considerable time in attempting to find a psychological theory
which would provide a sound basis for ordering the categories of the
taxonomy. We reviewed theories of personality and learning but were
unable to find a single view which, in our opinion, accounted for the
varieties of behaviors represented in the educational objectives we
attempted to classify. We were reluctantly forced to agree with Hilgard that each theory of learning accounts for some phenomena very
well but is less adequate in accounting for others. What is needed is a
larger synthetic theory of learning than at present seems to be available. We are of the opinion that our method of ordering educational
outcomes will make it possible to define the range of phenomena for
which such a theory must account (pp. 17-18).

Turning Plan into Action: The Big Picture

Keeping in mind the aforementioned principles, we began work by gathering a large list of educational objectives from our own institutions and the literature. We determined which part of the objective stated the behavior intended and which stated the content or object of the behavior. We then attempted to find divisions or groups into which the behaviors could be placed. We initially limited ourselves to those objectives commonly referred to as knowledge, intellectual abilities, and intellectual skills. (This area, which we named the cognitive domain, may also be described as including the following behaviors: remembering, reasoning, problem solving; concept formation; and, to a limited extent, creative thinking.) We proceeded to divide the cognitive objectives into subdivisions from the simplest behavior to the most complex. We then attempted to find ways of defining these subdivisions in such a way that all of us working with the material could communicate with each other about the specific objectives as well as the testing procedures to be included (p. 15).

Our attempt to arrange educational behaviors from simple to complex was based on the idea that a particular simple behavior may become integrated with other equally simple behaviors to form a more complex behavior. Thus our classifications may be said to be in the form where behaviors of type A form one class, behaviors of type AB form another class, while behaviors of type ABC form still another class (p. 18).

As the taxonomy is now organized, it contains six major classes:

1.00 Knowledge
2.00 Comprehension
3.00 Application
4.00 Analysis
5.00 Synthesis
6.00 Evaluation

Although it is possible to conceive of these major classes in several different arrangements, the present one appears to us to represent something of the hierarchical order of the different classes of objectives. As we have defined them, the objectives in one class are likely to make use of and be built on the behaviors found in the preceding classes on the list (p. 18).

Probably the most common educational objective in American education is the acquisition of knowledge or information. That is, it is desired that as the result of completing an educational unit, the student will be changed with respect to the amount and kind of knowledge he possesses. Frequently knowledge is the primary, sometimes almost the sole kind of educational objective in a curriculum. In almost every course it is an important or basic one. By knowledge, we mean that the student can give evidence that he remembers, either by recalling or by recognizing, some idea or phenomenon with which he has had experience in the educational process. For our taxonomy purposes, we are defining knowledge as little more than the remembering of the idea or phenomenon in a form very close to that in which it was originally encountered (pp. 28-29).

Knowledge or information may be justified as an important objective or outcome of learning in many ways. Perhaps the most common justification is that with increases in knowledge or information there is a development of one's acquaintance with reality (p. 32).

Another justification for the teaching of knowledge is that it is quite frequently regarded as basic to all the other ends or purposes of education. Problem solving or thinking cannot be carried out in a vacuum, but must be based upon knowledge of some of the "realities." The intellectual abilities represented in the taxonomy assume knowledge as a prerequisite (p. 33).

Still another justification for the development of knowledge as an objective of education arises from the status of knowledge in our own culture. Many workers assume a positive relationship between increase in knowledge and increase in maturity (p. 34).

Many teachers and educators prize knowledge to some extent because of the simplicity with which it can be taught or learned. Mass methods, such as lectures, audio-visual methods, printed material, and the like, can be readily used for the acquisition of information (p. 34).

Although information or knowledge is recognized as an important outcome of education, very few teachers would be satisfied to regard this as the primary or the sole outcome of instruction. What is needed is some evidence that the students can do something with their knowledge, that is, that they can apply the information to new situations and problems. It is also expected that students will acquire generalized techniques for dealing with new problems and new materials. Thus, it is expected that when the student encounters a new problem or situation, he will select an appropriate technique for attacking it and will bring to bear the necessary information, both facts and principles. This has been labeled "critical thinking" by some, "reflective thinking" by Dewey and others, and "problem solving" by still others. In the taxonomy we have used the term "intellectual abilities and skills." The most general operational definition of these abilities and skills is that the individual can find appropriate information and techniques in his previous experience to bring to bear on new problems and situations. This requires some analysis or understanding of the new situation; it requires a background of knowledge or methods which can be readily utilized; and it also requires some facility in discerning the appropriate relations between previous experience and the new situation (p. 38).

Justification for the development of intellectual abilities and skills can readily be derived from a consideration of the nature of the society and culture in which we live, the knowledge that is available to us, and the kind of citizen the schools seek to develop. Further justification may be derived from what is known in educational psychology about the permanence of various kinds of learning and the extent to which various kinds of learning can be transferred to new situations (p. 39).

It is very clear that in the middle of the 20th century we find ourselves in a rapidly changing and unpredictable culture. It seems almost impossible to foresee the particular ways in which it will change in the near future or the particular problems which will be paramount in five or ten years. Under these conditions, much emphasis must be placed . . . on the development of generalized ways of attacking problems and on knowledge which can be applied to a wide range of situations (p. 40).

The importance of the intellectual abilities and skills is further illustrated by our recognition of the individual's ability to independently attack his problems as a desirable sign of maturity. Individuals are expected, as they mature, to solve problems on their own and to make decisions wisely on the basis of their own thinking. Further, . . . it is recognized that unless the individual can do his own problem solving he cannot maintain his integrity as an independent personality (p. 41).

As we have defined intellectual abilities and skills, they are more widely applicable than knowledge. If we are concerned with the problem of transfer of training, by definition we would select intellectual abilities and skills as having greater transfer value (p. 42).

[Furthermore,] from psychological theory (e.g., reinforcement theory) it would seem reasonable to expect greater permanence of learning for those outcomes of education which can be generalized and applied in a number of different situations throughout the individual's formal educational experience than for those outcomes which are so specific that they are likely to be encountered only once or at the most a few times throughout the educational program (p. 42).

Translating Plan into Action: Filling in the Details

The taxonomy *Handbook* in its present form defines a class or subclass of educational objectives in three ways. The first and major type of definition is represented by a verbal description or definition of each class and subclass. . . . A second type of definition is provided by the list of educational objectives which are included under each subclass of the taxonomy. . . . The third type of definition attempts to make clear the behavior appropriate to each category by illustrations of the examination questions and problems which are regarded as appropriate (p. 44).

1.00 KNOWLEDGE

Knowledge as defined here includes those behaviors and test situations which emphasize the remembering, either by recognition or recall, of ideas, material, or phenomena. The behavior expected of a student in the recall situation is very similar to the behavior he was expected to have during the original learning situation. In the learning situation the student is expected to store in his mind certain information, and the behavior expected later is the remembering of this information. Although some alterations may be expected in the material to be remembered, this is a relatively minor part of the knowledge behavior or test. The process of relating and judging is also involved to the extent that the student is expected to answer questions or problems which are posed in a different form in the test situation than in the original learning situation (p. 62).

In the classification of the knowledge objectives, the arrangement is from the specific and relatively concrete types of behaviors to the more complex and abstract ones. Thus, the knowledge of specifics refers to types of information or knowledge which can be isolated and remembered separately, while the knowledge of universals and abstractions emphasizes the interrelations and patterns in which information can be organized and structured (p. 62).

While it is recognized that knowledge is involved in the more complex major categories of the taxonomy (2.00 to 6.00), the knowledge category differs from the others in that remembering is the major psychological process involved here, while in the other categories the remembering is only one part of a much more complex process of relating, judging, and reorganizing (p. 62).

2.00 COMPREHENSION

Probably the largest general class of intellectual abilities and skills emphasized in schools and colleges are those which involve *comprehension*. That is, when students are confronted with a communication, they are expected to know what is being communicated and to be able to make some use of the materials or ideas contained in it. The communication may be in oral or written form, in verbal or symbolic form, or, if we allow a relatively broad use of the term "communication," it may refer to material in concrete form as well as material embodied on paper. For instance, we commonly expect comprehension of a physics demonstration, a geologic formation viewed on a field trip, a building illustrating a particular architectural feature, a musical work played by an orchestra (p. 89).

Although the term "comprehension" has been frequently associated with reading, e.g., reading comprehension, the use to which it is being put here is a somewhat broader one in that it is related to a greater variety of communications than that encompassed by written verbal materials. In another sense, the use of the term here is somewhat more limited than usual, since comprehension is not made synonymous with complete understanding or even with the fullest grasp of a message. Here we are using the term "comprehension" to include those *objectives, behaviors,* or *responses* which represent an understanding of the literal message contained in a communication. In reaching such understanding, the student may change the communication in his mind or in his overt responses to some parallel form more meaningful to him. There may also be responses which represent simple extensions beyond what is given in the communication itself (p. 89).

Three types of comprehension behavior are considered here. The first is *translation* which means that an individual can put a communication into other language, into other terms, or into another form of communication. It will usually involve the giving of meaning to the various parts of a communication, taken in isolation, although such meanings may in part be determined by the context in which the ideas appear (p. 89).

The second type of behavior is *interpretation* which involves dealing with a communication as a configuration of ideas whose comprehension may require a reordering of the ideas into a new configuration in the mind of the individual. This also includes thinking about the relative importance of the ideas, their interrelationships, and their relevance to generalizations implied or described in the original communication. Evidence of interpretation behavior may be found in the inferences, generalizations, or summarizations produced by the individual (p. 90).

The third type of behavior to be considered under comprehension is *extrapolation*. It includes the making of estimates or predictions based on understanding of the trends, tendencies, or conditions described in the communication. It may also involve the making of inferences with respect to implications, consequences, corollaries and effects which are in accordance with the conditions described in the communication. It differs from application, however, in that the thinking is based on what is given rather than on some abstraction brought from the other experiences to the situation, such as a general principle or rule of procedure. Extrapolation may include judgments with respect to a universe where the communication characterizes a sample, or conversely with respect to a sample where the communication describes a universe. For the purpose of classification, interpolation may be regarded as a type of extrapolation in that judgments with respect to intervals within a sequence of data presented in a communication are similar to judgments going beyond the data in the usual sense of extrapolation (p. 90).

3.00 APPLICATION

The whole cognitive domain of the taxonomy is arranged in a hierarchy, that is, each classification within it demands the skills and abilities which are lower in the classification order. The application category follows this rule in that to apply something requires "comprehension" of the method, theory, principle, or abstraction applied. Teachers frequently say, "If a student really comprehends something, then he can apply it." To make the distinction between the "Comprehension" and "Application" categories clear, we have described it in two ways (p. 120).

One way of looking at the distinction is this. A problem in the comprehension category requires the student to know an abstraction well enough that he can correctly demonstrate its use when specifically asked to do so. "Application," however, requires a step beyond this. Given a problem new to the student, he will apply the appropriate abstraction without having to be prompted as to which abstraction is correct or without having to be shown how to use it in that situation. A demonstration of "Comprehension" shows that the student can use the abstraction when its use is specified. A demonstration of "Application" shows that he will use it correctly, given an appropriate situation in which no mode of solution is specified (p. 120).

A second way of looking at this is demonstrated in figure 1. It shows in diagrammatic form the problem-solving process of answering questions classified in the "Application" category. In the complete solution of an "Application" problem, all six steps are involved. Whether the process more closely resembles the left or right side of the chain at steps 1 and 2 would depend upon the student's familiarity with the problem. Steps 1 through 4 are part of "Application" but not of "Comprehension." Comprehension is best represented by a problem which starts with step 5, steps 1-4 being unnecessary because of the structuring of the problem situation (p. 120).

4.00 ANALYSIS

At a somewhat more advanced level than the skills of comprehension and application are those involved in analysis. In *comprehension* the emphasis is on the grasp of the meaning and intent of the material. In *application* it is on remembering and bringing to bear upon given material the appropriate generalizations or principles. *Analysis* emphasizes the breakdown of the material into its constituent parts and detection of the relationships of the parts and of the way they are organized. It may also be directed at the techniques and devices used to convey the meaning or to establish the conclusion of a communication (p. 144).

Although analysis may be conducted merely as an exercise in detecting the organization and structure of a communication and may therefore become its own end, it is probably more defensible educationally to consider analysis as an aid to fuller comprehension or as a prelude to an evaluation of the material (p. 144).

Skill in analysis may be found as an objective of any field of study. It is frequently expressed as one of their important objectives by teachers of science, social studies, philosophy, and the arts. They wish, for example, to develop in students the ability to distinguish fact from hypothesis in a communication, to identify conclusions and supporting statements, to distinguish relevant from extraneous material, to note how one idea relates to another, to see what unstated assumptions are involved in what is said, to distinguish dominant from

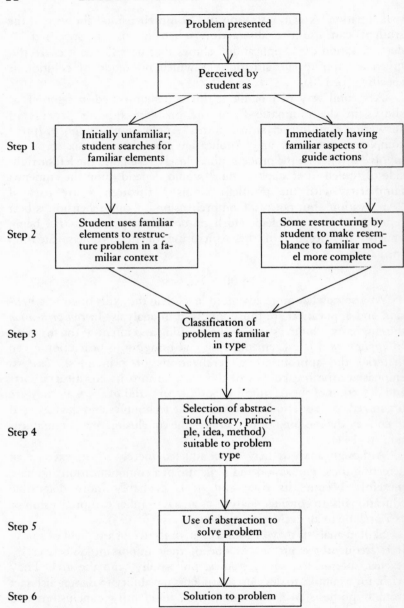

Fig. 1. The problem-solving process in answering
questions in the "Application" category.

subordinate ideas or themes in poetry or music, to find evidence of the author's techniques and purposes, etc. (p. 144).

No entirely clear lines can be drawn between analysis and comprehension at one end or between analysis and evaluation at the other. Comprehension deals with the content of material, analysis with both content and form. One may speak of "analyzing" the *meaning* of a communication, but this usually refers to a more complex level of ability than "understanding" or "comprehending" the meaning—and that is the intention of the use of "analysis" here. It is true also that analysis shades into evaluation, especially when we think of "critical analysis." As one analyzes the relationships of elements of an argument, he may be judging how well the argument hangs together. In analyzing the form of a communication, or the techniques used, one may express opinions about how well the communication serves its purpose (pp. 144-145).

And yet the type of ability we call analysis may be abstracted, and usefully. One who comprehends the meaning of a communication may not be able to analyze it at all effectively, and one who is skillful in the analysis of material may evaluate it badly (p. 145).

Analysis, as an objective, may be divided into three types or levels. At one level the student is expected to break down the material into its constituent parts, to identify or classify the *elements* of the communication. At a second level he is required to make explicit the *relationships* among the elements, to determine their connections and interactions. A third level involves recognition of the *organizational principles*, the arrangement and structure, which hold together the communication as a whole (p. 145).

5.00 SYNTHESIS

Synthesis is here defined as putting together of elements and parts so as to form a whole. This is a process of working with elements, parts, etc., and combining them in such a way as to constitute a pattern or structure not clearly there before. Generally this would involve a recombination of parts of previous experience with new material, reconstructed into a new and more or less well-integrated whole. This is the category in the cognitive domain which most clearly provides for creative behavior on the part of the learner. However, it should be emphasized that this is not completely free creative expression since generally the student is expected to work within the limits set by particular problems, materials, or some theoretical and methodological framework (p. 162).

Comprehension, application, and analysis also involve the putting together of elements and the construction of meanings, but these tend to be more partial and less complete than synthesis in the magnitude of the task. Also there is less emphasis upon uniqueness and originality in these other classes than in the one under discussion here. Perhaps the main difference between these categories and synthesis lies in the possibility that they involve working with a *given* set of materials or elements which constitutes a whole in itself. They involve studying a whole in order to understand it better. In synthesis, on the other hand, the student must draw upon elements from many sources and put these together into a structure or pattern not clearly there before (p. 162).

We recognize the difficulty of classifying essay questions. The tendency is to place them in the synthesis category. For example, if the student writes out his comprehension or analysis of a reading selection, does such a form of response constitute synthesis as we have defined it? If his essay involves analysis in terms of underlying elements and the like, perhaps not, since he has not come out with a product substantially different from that which he is studying. If we accept this point of view, then we would not regard every act of writing as an act of synthesis. We would assume that writing as such is primarily a skill in expression, much of which represents the remembering of ideas, the interpretation of given materials, and the translation of ideas into writing (pp. 162-163).

For the present, it seems best to distinguish between different kinds of synthesis primarily on the basis of the product. Such an approach does permit classification into three relatively distinct divisions which have some practical significance. . . . In the first subcategory, one may view the product or performance as essentially *a unique communication.* . . . In the second subcategory, one may view the product as *a plan or proposed set of operations* to be carried out. . . . In the third subcategory, one may view the product of synthesis as primarily *a set of abstract relations* (pp. 163-164).

6.00 EVALUATION

Evaluation is defined as the making of judgments about the value, for some purpose, of ideas, works, solutions, methods, material, etc. It involves the use of criteria as well as standards for appraising the extent to which particulars are accurate, effective, economical, or satisfying. The judgments may be either quantitative or qualitative, and the criteria may be either those determined by the student or those which are given to him (p. 185).

Evaluation represents not only an end process in dealing with cognitive behaviors, but also a major link with the affective behaviors where values, liking, and enjoying (and their absence or contraries) are the central processes involved. However, the emphasis here is still largely cognitive rather than emotive (p. 185).

Although Evaluation is placed last in the cognitive domain because it is regarded as requiring to some extent all the other categories of behavior, it is not necessarily the last step in thinking or problem solving. It is quite possible that the evaluative process will in some cases be the prelude to the acquisition of new knowledge, a new attempt at comprehension or application, or a new analysis or synthesis (p. 185).

For the most part, the evaluations customarily made by an individual are quick decisions not preceded by very careful consideration of the various aspects of the object, idea, or activity being judged. These might more properly be termed *opinions* rather than *judgments*. Customarily, opinions are made at less than a fully conscious level and the individual may not be fully aware of the clues or bases on which he is forming his appraisals. For purposes of classification, only those evaluations which are or can be made with distinct criteria in mind are considered. Such evaluations are highly conscious and ordinarily are based on a relatively adequate comprehension and analysis of the phenomena to be appraised (p. 186).

One type of evaluation can be made largely on the basis of internal standards of criticism. Such internal standards are for the most part concerned with tests of the accuracy of the work as judged by consistency, logical accuracy, and the absence of internal flaws. . . . A second type of evaluation may be based on the use of external standards or criteria derived from a consideration of the *ends* to be served and the appropriateness of specific means for achieving these ends. Such evaluations are primarily based on considerations of efficiency, economy, or utility of specific means for particular ends (pp. 186-187).

The Taxonomy: Its Use and Usefulness

This *Handbook* is truly a group product. It is the direct outgrowth of the thinking of over thirty persons who attended the taxonomy conferences. It is based on the work of countless test constructors, curriculum workers, and teachers. Several hundred readers of the preliminary edition have contributed criticisms, suggestions, and illustrative materials. The committee which took responsibility for the actual writing hope that this *Handbook* justifies the enormous amount of time and effort devoted to it by the many persons involved. We regard the work as well worth the effort if the taxonomy is found of value as a means of communicating within the field of education. We submit it in the hope that it will help to stimulate thought and research on educational problems (p. 9).

We have subjected this classification scheme to a series of checks, primarily of communicability and comprehensiveness. A major check of communicability was to determine whether a number of workers could agree in their classification of specific educational objectives and test materials (p. 20).

One of the major problems in the classification of test items which this study revealed is that it is necessary in all cases to know or assume the nature of the examinees' prior educational experiences. Thus, a test problem could require a very complex type of problem-solving behavior if it is a new situation, while it may require little more than a simple kind of recall if the individual has had previous learning experiences in which this very problem was analyzed and discussed. This suggests that, in general, test material can be satisfactorily classified by means of the taxonomy only when the context in which the test problems were used is known or assumed (p. 20).

Comprehensiveness, of course, is never finally determined. We have repeatedly taken lists of objectives found in courses of study and other educational literature and have attempted to classify them. As yet, in the cognitive domain we have encountered few statements of student behaviors which could not be placed within the classification scheme (p. 21).

Properly used, a taxonomy should provide a very suggestive source of ideas and materials for each worker and should result in many economies in effort.... Altogether, the taxonomy is suggestive in pointing to a large number of problems in the field of education and testing. If the taxonomy could do nothing more than this, it would be useful. Although there are dangers in devising a classification scheme which might tend to rigidify our thinking about education, the relatively chaotic nature of our field at present and the great emphasis on persuasive skills rather than on research findings for claims in the field of education justify some procedure such as this for ordering the phenomena with which we deal (pp. 21, 23-24).

A final criterion is that the taxonomy must be accepted and used by the workers in the field if it is to be regarded as a useful and effective tool. Whether or not it meets this criterion can be determined only after a sufficient amount of time has elapsed (p. 24).

CHAPTER III

Bloom's Taxonomy:
Philosophical and Educational Issues

EDWARD J. FURST

The purpose of this review is to deal with philosophical criticism of the Taxonomy. I will concentrate on the properties of neutrality, comprehensiveness, and cumulative hierarchical structure.

Neutrality

Philosophy of education and values. One of the guiding principles of the Taxonomy was that it be a purely descriptive scheme in which every kind of goal could be represented in a relatively neutral way.[1] By neutrality was meant impartiality with respect to source, such as educational unit or philosophy of education, and with respect to the relative worth of goals. It did not, however, mean impartiality with respect to the concept of educational objectives, for here the authors ruled out goals that were not specified as intended student behaviors or could not readily be specified as changes of that sort.[2] By this very delimitation, then, the Taxonomy could not be neutral with respect to philosophy of education, for it ignored those philosophies that shunned specification of such intended changes.

That any classification of educational objectives can be wholly free of questions of values, and thus be a purely technical matter, is not possible.[3] Classifications tend to throw emphasis on certain qualities and, in turn, to diminish the apparent significance of other qualities.

Edward J. Furst, Professor Emeritus of Education in the College of Education, University of Arkansas, was a member of the Committee of College and University Examiners that wrote the *Taxonomy of Educational Objectives, Handbook 1: Cognitive Domain.* This chapter reprints a substantial portion of Professor Furst's article, "Bloom's Taxonomy of Educational Objectives for the Cognitive Domain: Philosophical and Educational Issues," which appeared in *Review of Educational Research* 51, no. 4 (Winter, 1981): 441-453. It is reprinted here with the permission of the American Educational Research Association and of the author.

Questions of epistemology. However descriptive and neutral the intentions behind the Taxonomy, the focus on student behaviors does create serious difficulties which call into question the epistemology upon which the scheme operates.[4]

First of all, the use of behavioral-specified goals runs the much discussed risk of confusing the objective with its indicator. The Taxonomy seems open to this risk, inasmuch as the authors had adopted Ralph W. Tyler's idea of an educational objective as a change in behavior: ways of acting, thinking, and feeling. Clearly, this is a broader concept than the usual (overt) behavioral one, because it includes covert as well as overt states and responses. But covert processes and states are unobservable, confronting us with an impasse. At this point we can turn to public evidence (empirical data) and equate the objective with its indicator. But confusing the observable correlates, what Wittgenstein called the criteria for a state of mind, with that state is to succumb to a logical confusion.[5] At the other extreme, we can regard the evidence as but a sign of the attainment or change, and examine in detail the relationship of the empirical description to the proposition about the educational objective. The more that such propositions approximate descriptions of overt behavior, the greater the need to examine the difficulties in translating propositions about the mind into descriptions of what can be observed.[6] Now it is important to recognize that such an examination would be essentially a philosophical analysis, and it is one that the authors of the Taxonomy had not pursued to any appreciable extent.[7] Instead they placed much of the burden of defining educational goals and cognitive levels upon test items, the correct response to which was taken as the necessary evidence of the attainment at issue. Thus, the authors took as the only viable alternative the operational definition in which the intended student behavior was implicit.[8] They did recognize, however, that operational definition was not sufficient; one also had to know or assume the nature of the student's educational experience.[9]

A second and related difficulty arising from the use of behavioral-specified goals, no matter what the scheme, is the neglect of important goals that do not yield readily to precise specification. The most serious omissions are those that provide a basis for rational action. Green made the distinction clearly when he argued that the goal of teaching is not to change students' behavior, but to transform behavior (which was defined as reiterative and habitual) into action (which, in contrast, is rule guided or principled).[10] In other words, the goal is the capability, competence, or understanding that makes rational action possible. A few critics have argued that the Taxonomy erred in excluding a broad category of "understanding" as one of the prime goals of education.[11] Also, closely akin to "understanding" is the tacit knowledge students acquire by transforming the details of formal instruction into interpretive schemata or categories. If we insist on total explicitness of "objectivity" as well as overt behavioral statements, Broudy has argued, we fail to recognize this kind of learning so important in the "life uses" of schooling: "When school learnings are used interpretively, they are used to think and feel *with.*"[12]

Further difficulties of a philosophical nature stem from the possible distinction between behavioral and substantive (content) elements in statements of educational objectives. This distinction on which the Taxonomy rests came from Tyler's model of curriculum planning, itself an example of the "ideal model of the Rational Curriculum Plan."[13] Though Tyler had held that a statement of objectives should indicate both the kind of behavior and the area of content or of life to be useful for planning instruction, the authors chose to classify objectives on the basis of intended behaviors, more or less disregarding the particular content.[14]

That a distinction between process and content is artificial was not unknown to the authors, the idea having been voiced often by psychologists, semanticists, and philosophers. It seemed to the authors that the advantages of a classification of cognitive processes transcending particular content would far outweigh any limitation from such abstracting. But opposition to the whole notion of abstracting or describing cognitive processes is strong, perhaps most forcefully embodied in the work of Wittgenstein and his followers.[15] Wittgenstein would shun the quest for general categories based on "common essences" and instead insist on close study of the facts: the circumstances surrounding particular behaviors. His philosophical analysis is incisive, profound, and compelling; one must turn to it to get the full import of his argument.

Critics of the Taxonomy, whose writings show the influence of Wittgenstein's philosophy, hold that such a classification cannot convey the full nature of educational objectives. Sockett took as an example the so-called process of "remembering":

"[R]emembering" is unintelligible just as a psychological process (even if we lay aside its counterpart—forgetting) for we remember *something*, cases of remembering are cases of being *right* about what was or is the case. We cannot posit remembering in any sense *apart* from content. If remembering is thought of as content-free we have an empty concept which could not be even part of an educational objective.[16]

In a companion article, Pring also used remembering as an example:

It would seem that the isolation of "behaviors" (for example, "remembering") from the learning experiences through which they are to be learned is not possible where the ends and means are logically, not contingently, related.[17]

Somewhat later Hirst argued in a like vein, taking as examples knowing a simple fact, learning an intellectual skill as deduction, and developing an ability to solve problems. He noted that we usually think of deduction as a psychological process and (following Wittgenstein) that this misleads us to look for a sequence of events in the mind. Are there any actual psychological processes necessary to deducing?

The prime example of deduction is perhaps a mathematical theorem, so how do mathematicians work out theorems? Do they go down a ladder of reasoning, working strictly in a given order? Generally speaking, no mathematician does that. . . . What the sequence of his thought is does not in fact matter, for his processes of thought are not the deduction; the deduction is the pattern of the end achievement that he establishes. To teach children to deduce is not to teach them to think along particular psychological channels, it is to teach them, whatever channels or psychological processes they use, to produce certain patterns of statements in the end.[18]

A fourth critic, Ormell, also found the process-content distinction on which the Taxonomy is based epistemologically naive:

The point here is that the process-content distinction implies a clear-cut boundary between that which one cannot influence (content) and that which one can (process). This overlooks the fact that behaviors falling under the higher objectives must—if they are to make sense—be based on *true* mappings (comprehension), *true* laws (application), *true* dissections (analysis), *etc.* In other words, the principles and rules of "process" which we hope our students will learn to use, must also reflect "what is the case."[19]

Hirst argued further that the Taxonomy in treating objectives as isolated ends fails to bring out logical interrelations—the central objective of education as "elements within integrated developing structures of understanding."[20] In this view, items of knowledge such as concepts, facts, norms, principles, and so on, instead of being detached from each other, form distinctive networks of relationships. A proposition becomes meaningful because the concepts are used in a particular way in a given domain. But the acquisition of knowledge in a given domain involves not only the mastery of such networks of concepts (with their rules of relationships), but also of operations with these, and of particular criteria of truth or validity associated with these concepts, as well as more general criteria of reasoning.

Hirst's prescription implies some combination of subject matter (i.e., "content") analysis and performance analysis. Content analysis could map out relational networks of concepts and the like. Performance analysis could specify, in behavior, the instructional objectives associated with particular content, but go beyond to identify the competencies necessary (at least implicitly) to perform the behavior and to derive learning hierarchies of prerequisite competencies. However, a simple combination of these two analyses will not do; major limitations remain. To overcome these, Scandura has proposed a structural/algorithmic method of analysis representing knowledge/content as rules and sets thereof.[21] This method can accommodate propositional and algorithmic knowledge as both can be represented formally in terms of rules.

No discussion of epistemological questions would be complete without bringing in the distinction between cognitive and affective domains. One can reasonably argue that the cognitive and feeling sides of mental life can neither be conceptually nor practically separated.[22] Of course, the authors saw the distinction as artificial and saw the need to bring the two domains together after the analysis. Nonetheless, the distinction creates educational and philosophical problems by separating the world of knowledge from the world of values.[23]

If these various critics are right, and so it seems, the Taxonomy is not neutral with respect to a theory of knowledge. In fact, in their view it rests upon an epistemology that is inadequate to the task: it provokes rather than answers questions about the nature and structure of educational objectives.[24] The categorization does not really define the achievements enough nor tell how one kind relates to another. The Taxonomy may well be a classification of cognitive processes but whether it can then serve as a classification of educational objectives is a further question.[25]

Comprehensiveness

As a scheme, does the Taxonomy allow nearly all of the cognitive objectives to be classified? This is the question of its comprehensiveness. A qualified answer is that, while no one would consider it perfect, most users generally have been satisfied with it.[26]

One qualification comes from certain investigators who have tried to use the Taxonomy for classifying oral questions in the classroom and found it somewhat incomplete.[27] This is understandable because the scheme is aimed more at the outcomes of instruction than at the language moves a teacher might undertake to probe meanings, opinions, and preferences and otherwise to facilitate discussion.

Rather more serious are those omissions that stem from artificial separation of the cognitive from the affective and psychomotor domains. By virtue of this separation, certain desired outcomes such as receptivity and sensitivity,[28] skill in observing and data gathering,[29] certain activities labeled as "perceptual" or "motor,"[30] group-procedure skills,[31] moral concepts,[32] basic democratic values,[33] rationality,[34] and the continual reconstruction of experience, that is, education as its own end,[35] would not be readily encompassed within the cognitive scheme. Some of these, it is true, would be captured in part through the categories of knowledge and comprehension, but perhaps not enough to avoid the objection of serious distortion.

The most serious omission according to Ormell is the central goal of "understanding."[36] He did not accept the argument that the Taxonomy provided for "understanding" by breaking it into its constituents, nor the argument for omitting it as a major heading because it was not precise. Ormell believes that a general behavioral definition is possible and to that end has begun major research. His tentative definition stresses the imaginative use of information in recreating relations. The test for understanding is whether the student can answer a connected range of "if . . . then . . ." questions about some situation, preferably a hypothetical one. Thus, a student who "understood the differential of a car" would be able to imagine the relative motion of the parts, and so forth, and so be able, in principle, to answer an indefinite number of questions about what happens.[37] It remains to be seen whether "understanding" will emerge as a major category. Nonetheless, there is support from authorities, such as Nedelsky and Hirst,[38] who set forth "progress in rational understanding" as the overriding development, with the "acquisition of knowledge and rational beliefs" as the most central goals.

So, in a way, by following a wholly process-oriented approach to the objectives of education, we have supposedly lost the essential characteristics of an educated person: that he or she possesses a rational, connected view of the world. This is also to say that content is underrepresented in the Taxonomy. Where content does come out is in the categorized objects of the various mental operations and as specifics in the illustrative test items and questions. To include content as another dimension, of course, is to complicate the business of classification enormously and virtually to disclaim a general scheme of this sort. In contrast, the authors of the Taxonomy had assumed that the categories and subcategories would be points of departure for the fleshing out of particular objectives and content in curriculum planning.

Cumulative Hierarchical Structure

Of all the properties of the Taxonomy, that of cumulative hierarchy seems most central to the theory. It was postulated that the several levels show an order from simple to complex; also, that the successive levels are cumulative in the higher, building upon and incorporating the lower.

The linear assumption. The notion of a cumulative hierarchy, ordered on a single dimension of simple-to-complex behavior, has provoked strong philosophical criticism. But no matter what the hierarchical scheme, the linear assumption is suspect on general philosophical grounds. Phillips and Kelly saw it as too simplistic when applied to theories of development in biology, education, and psychology.[39] They singled out the theories of Piaget on cognitive development, Jensen on mental abilities, Gagné on learning hierarchies, and Kohlberg on moral development. Although Phillips and Kelly did not mention the Taxonomy, their criticism would seem to apply to it with equal force, inasmuch as it too posits a straightforward sequence.

A like criticism has come from educators.[40] In his attempt to apply the Taxonomy, Ormell found contradictions in the frequent inversion of various objectives and tasks. For instance, certain demands for Knowledge are more complex than certain demands for Analysis or Evaluation. To make the Taxonomy a more effective classificatory device, he would abandon any pretence of a single principle of organization by complexity and would split it into six parallel taxonomic categories. This would recognize, as the Taxonomy roughly does now for category 1.00, Knowledge, several levels within each category. Ormell would also introduce other distinctions, such as "weight," to recognize the emphasis to be given in a problem or a curriculum to each of the levels of complexity within each of the main categories, and "visibility," to recognize that instances of general rules are rarely equally visible or evident. Although these further distinctions were no doubt prompted by Ormell's interest in mathematical education, they nonetheless seem of wider import.

Certain philosophers of education have also taken the linear assumption to task, particularly on the separation of Knowledge from the intellectual abilities: Comprehension, Application, and so forth. Essentially the argument is that to know in any important sense presupposes certain intellectual skills. This connection is seen clearly when abstract or formal material such as mathematics is taught using reflective thinking, in which elements are not presented as meaningless statements to be learned at the level of Knowledge (1.00), but where emphasis is on the "why" of each point.[41] Thus, the student may not know what a principle means until understanding occurs at least at the next level (2.00, Comprehension). But even under knowledge of specifics there is necessarily embedded a variety of intellectual abilities and skills.[42] For instance:

[F]or something to be recognized as a fact requires some comprehension of the concepts employed and thus of the conceptual framework within which the concepts operate. Similarly with regard to the knowledge of terminology, it does not make sense to talk of the knowledge of terms or of symbols in isolation from the *working* knowledge of these terms or symbols, that is, from a comprehension of them and thus an ability to apply them.[43]

A further implication is that the notion of a fact is not a "logically primitive educational objective," for it is impossible to learn facts, to know them as such, without acquiring related concepts and the criteria for truth involved.[44] Whether knowledge of specifics, as narrowly defined in the Taxonomy, should even be considered a proper goal can be questioned. Ormell thought a minimum change would be to define Knowledge in terms of "awareness of what is the case."[45] We know what is the case "where what we know is expressed in a true statement or proposition—usually referred to as 'knowledge-that'."[46]

The proposition that intellectual skills and abilities cannot be kept out of any meaningful definition of knowledge can be extended.

Certain writers on education have suggested that activities (instructional as well as testing) aimed at a lower level in the Taxonomy may activate mental operations placed in the higher categories. Pring has argued that comprehension of principles must include the ability to apply principles to new situations.[47] Orlandi implied that meaningful comprehension in the social studies must be accompanied with or preceded by analysis.[48] Purves took a similar view with respect to the field of English literature.[49] Working in elementary language arts, Moore and Kennedy took the position that some analysis must be undertaken before application can be carried out.[50] Several authorities have considered evaluation inherent in synthesis and, therefore, not superordinate.[51] Empirical evidence also suggests that Evaluation should not be placed higher than Synthesis in the Taxonomy, but at best, parallel with it.[52]

Altogether, these various exceptions suggest that dissecting the cognitive domain into distinct, linearly ordered categories has drawbacks. Inversions occur and there is frequent overlap between and within categories. Bloom et al. did acknowledge that it was not possible to make as clear-cut distinctions as one would like.[53]

With respect to the definition of knowledge as a category and the epistemological criticism of it, the authors of the Taxonomy would doubtless readily grant that an element of comprehension most often enters instances of recall or recognition. But they would tend to see that as an enabling ability auxiliary to the principal ability at issue. At the same time they would assert that statements of objectives and their operational counterparts in test items do indeed often use "knowledge" in a much more limited sense than philosophers might prefer. Finding a place for these more limited intentions does, after all, meet two of the guiding principles of the Taxonomy: namely, neutrality and comprehensiveness. It is not difficult to find support from highly competent authorities for such a limited category of knowledge.[54] Most teachers would most likely claim goals beyond knowledge in this narrow sense and still find assessment of it useful for diagnosis of difficulties in attaining higher-order learnings, or otherwise for formative as opposed to summative evaluation.

Other criticisms of a philosophical nature. Travers saw the scheme as falling short of a true taxonomy.[55] Although the major categories give the appearance of a continuum of complexity, this dimension is not clear and the classification is only a rough beginning. He regarded it as an inventory of educational customs. In this respect it lacks the theoretical underpinning of true taxonomies, such as those in chemistry and biology, as well as the usual features of bifurcation of classes, class hierarchies, and multidimensional system categorization.

Other authorities have raised questions about the basis on which various of the categories and subcategories had been formed. DeCorte has pointed out that the subcategories were not always based on the same principle of classification.[56] Thus, for Knowledge, Analysis, and Synthesis, the subcategories correspond to a scale of products; for Evaluation, to different kinds of criteria against which judgments are to be made. Gagné has also pointed out that some categories differ only in their content (as suggested by test items used as examples) and not by formal characteristics affecting their conditions of learning.[57]

Concluding Remarks

Inasmuch as each section of this chapter has consisted of a detailed and, it is hoped, balanced review of evidence and argument, the reader may perhaps best draw his or her own conclusions on each of the three properties. The writer, for his part, will close with some general observations.

The need for, or at least interest in, classification of cognitive operations and objectives persists, and distinctions continue to be made. Indeed, even where an educational specialist backs away from a classification, she or he backs into it another way, as in working out a guide for test-item development. Even those who might regard the conceptual analysis of a domain or discipline as the final answer find a need for distinctions when the inevitable question of evaluation of learning arises: How are knowledge and understanding to be manifested?

Not all who opt for a classification insist on one organized as a hierarchy; but for some, the notion of hierarchy has much appeal. And rightly so, for hierarchy is fundamental in the make-up of skills, abilities, and conceptual organizations of subject matter.[58]

Hierarchical schemes may consist of categories of mental operation but ultimately the referents of these must center on cognitive tasks and the products therefrom. This is true of the Taxonomy of Bloom et al. It would also be true of Piagetian analysis of the formal properties of knowledge, touted by Travers as an alternative to the earlier taxonomy.[59] In any event, operationalization of constructs in such schemes moves in the same direction.

Finally, if one accepts the premise that subject matter cannot be completely divorced from the development of taxonomies of educational objectives, a strong case can be made for a logical mapping of objectives in the several basic domains of knowledge.[60] In principle, such a mapping could take the form of rule-based analyses as advocated by Scandura in his structural/algorithmic approach to instruction.[61] Whatever the form of structural analysis undertaken, it seems certain that the elucidation would be in large part philosophical and that the time, effort, and resources required would be considerable. In the end, it is likely that no single scheme would emerge as an all-inclusive, all-purpose tool.

NOTES

1. Benjamin S. Bloom et al., *Taxonomy of Educational Objectives, Handbook 1: Cognitive Domain* (New York: McKay, 1956), p. 14.

2. Ibid., p. 15.

3. C. P. Ormell, "Bloom's Taxonomy and the Objectives of Education," *Educational Research* 17 (1974): 3.

4. Paul H. Hirst, *Knowledge and the Curriculum: A Collection of Philosophical Papers* (London: Routledge and Kegan Paul, 1974); Ormell, "Bloom's Taxonomy and the Objectives of Education"; R. Pring, "Bloom's Taxonomy: A Philosophical Critique," *Cambridge Journal of Education* 1 (1971): 83-91; Hugh Sockett, "Bloom's Taxonomy: A Philosophical Critique," *Cambridge Journal of Education* 1 (1971): 16-25; Robert L. Wilhoyte, "Problems of Meaning and Reference in Bloom's Taxonomy: Cognitive Domain" (Doctoral Diss., Indiana University, 1965).

5. Ludwig Wittgenstein, *Philosophical Investigations*, tr. by G. E. M. Anscombe (Oxford: Basil Blackwell, 1953); Hirst, *Knowledge and the Curriculum*, p. 21.

6. Pring, "Bloom's Taxonomy," p. 84.

7. Pring, "Bloom's Taxonomy"; Wilhoyte, "Problems of Meaning and Reference in Bloom's Taxonomy."

8. Wilhoyte, "Problems of Meaning and Reference in Bloom's Taxonomy," p. 34.

9. Bloom et al., *Taxonomy of Educational Objectives*, pp. 15-16, 20-21.

10. Thomas F. Green, "Teaching, Acting, and Behaving," *Harvard Educational Review* 34 (1964): 507-524.

11. Hirst, *Knowledge and the Curriculum*; Ormell, "Bloom's Taxonomy and the Objectives of Education."

12. Harry S. Broudy, "Can Research Escape the Dogma of Behavioral Objectives?" *School Review* 79 (1970): 54.

13. Sockett, "Bloom's Taxonomy: A Philosophical Critique," p. 17.

14. Bloom et al., *Taxonomy of Educational Objectives*, p. 12.

15. Wittgenstein, *Philosophical Investigations*; Norman Malcolm, "The Myth of Cognitive Processes and Structures," in *Cognitive Development and Epistemology*, edited by Theodore Mischel (New York: Academic Press, 1971); George Pitcher, *The Philosophy of Wittgenstein* (Englewood Cliffs, NJ: Prentice-Hall, 1964).

16. Sockett, "Bloom's Taxonomy: A Philosophical Critique," p. 20.

17. Pring, "Bloom's Taxonomy: A Philosophical Critique," p. 83.

18. Hirst, *Knowledge and the Curriculum*, pp. 19-20.

19. Ormell, "Bloom's Taxonomy and the Objectives of Education," p. 11.

20. Hirst, *Knowledge and the Curriculum*, p. 26.

21. Joseph M. Scandura, "Structural Approach to Instructional Problems," *American Psychologist* 32 (1977): 33-53.

22. Pring, "Bloom's Taxonomy: A Philosophical Critique."

23. Leon Apt, "Behavioral Objectives and History," *Intellect* 101 (1973): 445-447.

24. Hirst, *Knowledge and the Curriculum*, p. 27.

25. Sockett, "Bloom's Taxonomy: A Philosophical Critique," p. 23.

26. Viviane DeLandsheere, "On Defining Educational Objectives," *Evaluation in Education* 1 (1977): 73-150.

27. Meredith Gall, "The Use of Questions in Teaching," *Review of Educational Research* 40 (1970): 707-721; Stephen R. Mills et al., "The Correspondence between Teachers' Questions and Student Answers in Classroom Discourse," *Journal of Experimental Education* 48 (1980): 194-209; Rodney P. Riegle, "Classifying Classroom Questions," *Journal of Teacher Education* 27 (1976): 156-161.

28. Ormell, "Bloom's Taxonomy and the Objectives of Education."

29. Leopold E. Klopfer, "Evaluation of Learning in Science," in Benjamin S. Bloom, J. Thomas Hastings, and George F. Madaus, *Handbook on Formative and Summative Evaluation of Student Learning* (New York: McGraw-Hill, 1971); Louis E. Raths et al., *Teaching for Thinking: Theory and Application* (Columbus, OH: Charles E. Merrill, 1967).

30. Constance K. Kamii, "Evaluation of Learning in Preschool Education: Socio-emotional, Perceptual-motor, Cognitive Development," in Benjamin S. Bloom et al., *Handbook on Formative and Summative Evaluation of Student Learning* (New York: McGraw-Hill, 1971).

31. Lisanio R. Orlandi, "Evaluation of Learning in Secondary School Social Studies," in Benjamin S. Bloom et al., *Handbook on Formative and Summative Evaluation of Student Learning* (New York: McGraw-Hill, 1971).

32. Apt, "Behavioral Objectives and History."

33. Orlandi, "Evaluation of Learning in Secondary School Social Studies."

34. Hirst, *Knowledge and the Curriculum*.

35. Wilhoyte, "Problems of Meaning and Reference in Bloom's Taxonomy."

36. Ormell, "Bloom's Taxonomy and the Objectives of Education"; idem, "The Problem of Analyzing Understanding," *Educational Research* 22 (1979): 32-38.

37. Ormell, "Bloom's Taxonomy and the Objectives of Education," pp. 13-15.

38. Leo Nedelsky, *Science Teaching and Testing* (New York: Harcourt, Brace and World, 1965); Hirst, *Knowledge and the Curriculum*, p. 22.

39. Denis C. Phillips and Mavis E. Kelly, "Hierarchical Theories of Development in Education and Psychology," *Harvard Educational Review* 45 (1975): 351-375.

40. Apt, "Behavioral Objectives and History"; Ormell, "Bloom's Taxonomy and the Objectives of Education."

41. Wilhoyte, "Problems of Meaning and Reference in Bloom's Taxonomy," p. 121.

42. Pring, "Bloom's Taxonomy: A Philosophical Critique"; Sockett, "Bloom's Taxonomy: A Philosophical Critique."

43. Pring, "Bloom's Taxonomy: A Philosophical Critique," p. 90.

44. Hirst, *Knowledge and the Curriculum*, pp. 18-19.

45. Ormell, "Bloom's Taxonomy and the Objectives of Education."

46. Hirst, *Knowledge and the Curriculum*, p. 57.

40 PHILOSOPHICAL AND EDUCATIONAL ISSUES

47. Pring, "Bloom's Taxonomy: A Philosophical Critique."

48. Orlandi, "Evaluation of Learning in Secondary School Social Studies."

49. Alan C. Purves, "Evaluation of Learning in Literature," in Benjamin S. Bloom et al., *Handbook on Formative and Summative Evaluation of Student Learning* (New York: McGraw-Hill, 1971).

50. Walter J. Moore and Larry D. Kennedy, "Evaluation of Learning in the Language Arts," in Benjamin S. Bloom et al., *Handbook on Formative and Summative Evaluation of Student Learning* (New York: McGraw-Hill, 1971).

51. See chapters by Joseph J. Foley ("Evaluation of Learning in Writing") and Brent G. Wilson ("Evaluation of Learning in Art Education") both in Benjamin S. Bloom et al., *Handbook on Formative and Summative Evaluation of Student Learning* (New York: McGraw-Hill, 1971). See also, Christine McGuire, "Research in the Process Approach to the Construction and Analysis of Medical Examinations," in the *Twentieth Yearbook* of the National Council on Measurement in Education (Washington, DC: National Council on Measurement in Education, 1963), and Ormell, "Bloom's Taxonomy and the Objectives of Education."

52. Russell P. Kropp and Howard W. Stoker, *The Construction and Validation of Tests of the Cognitive Processes Described in the "Taxonomy of Educational Objectives"* Cooperative Research Project No. 2117 (Washington, DC: U.S. Office of Education, 1966); George Madaus, Elinor M. Woods, and Ronald L. Nuttall, "A Causal Model Analysis of Bloom's Taxonomy," *American Educational Research Journal* 10 (1973): 253-262.

53. Bloom et al., *Taxonomy of Educational Objectives*, pp. 15, 144-145.

54. For example, see Nedelsky, *Science Teaching and Testing*, and Michael Scriven, "The Methodology of Evaluation," in *Perspectives of Curriculum Evaluation*, edited by Ralph W. Tyler, Robert M. Gagné, and Michael Scriven (Chicago: Rand McNally, 1967).

55. Robert M. W. Travers, "Taxonomies of Educational Objectives and Theories of Classification," *Educational Evaluation and Policy Analysis* 2 (1980): 5-23.

56. E. DeCorte, as cited in DeLandsheere, "On Defining Educational Objectives," p. 105.

57. Robert M. Gagné, "The Implications of Instructional Objectives for Learning," in *Defining Educational Objectives*, edited by C. M. Lindvall (Pittsburgh: University of Pittsburgh Press, 1964).

58. Phillips and Kelly, "Hierarchical Theories of Development in Education and Psychology."

59. Travers, "Taxonomies of Educational Objectives and Theories of Classification."

60. Hirst, *Knowledge and the Curriculum*.

61. Scandura, "Structural Approach to Instructional Problems."

CHAPTER IV

Psychological Perspectives

WILLIAM D. ROHWER, JR. AND KATHRYN SLOANE

When the *Taxonomy of Educational Objectives* was published in 1956, the psychology of learning and thinking was nearing a turning point. At that time, behaviorism dominated the theoretical scene. The theories propounded by its most influential proponents, such as Clark L. Hull and B. F. Skinner, explicitly excluded mental processes and aspired to explain all forms of learning in terms of two basic processes: classical and instrumental conditioning—and their extensions. But 1956 was also the year that Jerome Bruner has referred to as "the mythical birthday of the cognitive revolution."[1] In that year, a mentalistic upstart, cognitive psychology, made its first formal appearance on the American theoretical stage with the publication of *A Study of Thinking*.[2] By now, the upstart has matured. Cognitive psychology dominates the current theoretical scene, according mental processes a privileged explanatory role, and acknowledging a variety of kinds of learning and thinking.

This shift in dominant theoretical orientation, from the reign of behaviorism in the 1950s to the reign of cognitive psychology in the present, was punctuated by the emergence of a number of alternative theoretical conceptions of human learning and thinking, as well as of the development of these capacities. During the 1960s, the attempt within the behaviorist tradition to construct general theories had given way to local theories that were typically specific to particular classes of human performance. In the case of learning and memory, for example, Hullian theory was superseded by mediation theory and interference theory. Also in the behaviorist tradition, psychologists committed to the study of human development, such as Howard and Tracy Kendler, constructed a neo-behaviorist theory. Concurrently, relying heavily on information-processing approaches, cognitive

William D. Rohwer, Jr. is Professor of Education and Dean of the Graduate School of Education at the University of California at Berkeley. Kathryn Sloane is a Research Educator in the Graduate School of Education, University of California at Berkeley.

psychology continued to grow. This growth was accelerated by the publication in 1960 of Miller, Galanter, and Pribram's *Plans and the Structure of Behavior*.[3] Moreover, the cognitive developmental theory of Piaget was gradually gaining increasing influence in the United States, in part due to the interpretations provided by J. McVicker Hunt and by John Flavell,[4] and in part to transformed versions of Piaget's approach such as that constructed by Bruner and his colleagues in their book, *Studies in Cognitive Growth*.[5]

These trends continued into the 1970s, a decade marked by the growing influence of information-processing approaches on conceptions of both learning and development. Robert Gagné, for example, in the first edition of his book, *The Conditions of Learning*,[6] presented a model that explicitly distinguished a variety of hierarchically ordered different kinds of learning in terms of the conditions that fostered each kind and in terms of the kinds of performance each made possible. In that first edition, however, higher order varieties were built up of increasingly complex chains of primitive behaviorist units, that is, stimulus-response (S-R) connections. In contrast, in subsequent editions of his book, Gagné presented a significantly revised model that incorporated information-processing constructs and relegated S-R connections to a minor role. Similarly, neo-Piagetian psychologists were constructing theories of cognitive development that incorporated information-processing conceptions into Piagetian principles.

In the last decade or so, the march toward cognitive theories has become a stampede. Psychologists have joined with linguists, computer scientists, philosophers, neurologists, anthropologists, and others from a variety of disciplines to create the new field of cognitive science. Moreover, the development of this field, and of cognitive psychology itself, has been accompanied by a dramatic increase in the attention cognitive scientists have paid to education. Complex learning of the kinds that are intended to occur, and that sometimes actually do occur, in classrooms has become the focus of research for many cognitive scientists.[7]

While these revolutionary changes have been taking place in psychological theory during the years since 1956, the *Taxonomy of Educational Objectives* has itself exerted a powerful and continuing influence on both the theory and practice of education. Curiously, however, the psychologists responsible for the cognitive revolution, including those whose research focuses on education, have largely ignored the Taxonomy. Similarly, those who have relied heavily on the Taxonomy in conceiving and conducting their educational research have largely ignored the dramatic changes occurring in the psychology of learning and thinking.

Why, then, should an entire chapter in this volume be given over to an examination of the Taxonomy from psychological perspectives? The authors of the Taxonomy provided their own answers to this question, in references to psychological theories and perspectives, in three different contexts. First, the authors explicitly aimed for an "educational-logical-psychological" classification scheme in designing the Taxonomy. While placing educational considerations first, they stated quite clearly that "the taxonomy should be consistent with relevant and accepted psychological principles and theories" (p. 6).[8]

Second, the authors suggested that psychology of learning should be taken into account when applying the Taxonomy to the design of educational experiences and instruction:

[E]ducational objectives must be related to a psychology of learning. . . . The use of a psychology of learning enables the faculty to determine the appropriate placement of objectives in the learning sequence, helps them discover the learning conditions under which it is possible to attain an objective, and provides a way of determining the appropriate interrelationships among the objectives (p. 27).

We would add only that learning theories might provide guidance in the construction of educational objectives themselves, constraining the range of and relations among these objectives.

The third context in which the authors of the Taxonomy referred to the psychology of learning was in their discussion of the implications of constructing a taxonomy of educational objectives. They proposed that the Taxonomy could provide insights and direction for the further study of the process of student learning:

[T]he psychological relationships employed by the classification schemes are suggestive of psychological investigations which could further our understanding of the educational process and provide insight into the means by which the learner changes in a specified direction (p. 3).

Given this rationale for the existence of the present chapter, we shall examine the Taxonomy from several psychological perspectives on learning, including those extant at the time the Taxonomy was aborning and those that emerged in succeeding decades up to the present reign of cognitive science. In doing so, we will focus on features of the Taxonomy that appear to presuppose one or another theoretical proposition about human learning or thinking.

Presuppositions of the Taxonomy

Our reading of the Taxonomy suggests that its structure and principles depend on presuppositions about the nature of human learning and thinking that we have organized into six categories: (1) the relationship between learning and performance; (2) the existence of qualitatively different varieties of learning; (3) the hierarchical and cumulative nature of learning; (4) transfer of learning; (5) generalizability of higher-order skills and abilities; and (6) differences between novice and expert learning. For some of these presuppositions, the authors of the Taxonomy make explicit their reliance on propositions from learning theory. For others, the relationship is implicit.

LEARNING AND PERFORMANCE

The first presupposition is that the performance of students faithfully reflects what they have learned. This presupposition may seem unworthy of examination because it is so obviously essential in any effort to chart educational objectives. How else can the outcomes of learning be assessed except in terms of the behaviors exhibited by learners? Yet, on any given occasion, student performance may reflect less than what the student has learned. After all, when we forget what we have learned, for example, we are unable to display that learning in our performance.

The impression gained from the text of the Taxonomy is that such possibilities were not a part of the authors' conception of the relationship between learning and behavior. This impression begins to arise in reading about objectives and behavior in the introductory chapter of the *Handbook*:

[T]his Taxonomy is designed to be a classification of the student behaviors which represent the intended outcomes of the educational process (p. 12).

What we are classifying is the *intended behavior* of students—the ways in which individuals are to act, think, or feel as the result of participating in some unit of instruction (p. 12).

Only those educational programs which can be specified in terms of intended student behaviors can be classified (p. 15).

Moreover, the authors evidently embraced the proposition that how students behave corresponds to or, at the least, directly reflects what they have learned.

The emphasis in the *Handbook* is on obtaining evidence on the extent to which desired and intended behaviors have been learned by the student (p. 12);

If we view statements of educational objectives as intended behaviors which the student shall display at the end of some period of education, we can then view the process as one of change (p. 16).

They offered one caveat about the correspondence between learning and performance. An observer, they contended, cannot determine what kind of learning students have accomplished solely from the nature of the performances they give. The observer must also have information about prior learning opportunities.

One of the major problems in the classification of test items . . . is that it is necessary in all cases to know or assume the nature of the examinees' prior educational experiences. Thus, a test problem could require a very complex type of problem-solving behavior if it is a new situation, while it may require little more than a simple kind of recall if the individual has had previous learning experiences in which this very problem was analyzed and discussed (p. 21).

They also acknowledged explicitly that students may learn less than their teachers intend, or even nothing at all, from completing an instructional unit. But such shortfalls would be evident in the students' inability to perform on a criterion task.

What the authors did not acknowledge explicitly is the possibility that what students have learned may not be manifest in their performance. Yet, we find it implausible that they would have rejected this possibility. It seems more likely that they confined their attention to academic learning sufficient to endure over time, to resist interference and forgetting, and to manifest itself in behavior regardless of the incentives available for successful performance. Stated this way, we note the high probability that the Taxonomy authors share this focus with the majority of those who concern themselves with education.

VARIETIES OF LEARNING

In the Taxonomy, the authors decisively rejected the proposition that a single kind of learning accounts for the range of performances human beings are capable of attaining. Instead, they presupposed that a different variety of learning is responsible for each of the six distinct classes of educational objectives they delineated: knowledge and the five kinds of intellectual skills and abilities (comprehension, application, analysis, synthesis, and evaluation). In their explication of each class, they addressed the question: what is learned? They then identified the nature of the learning that is necessary to make possible the kinds of performances specified by the objectives.

Furthermore, in describing the kind of performance required to meet each category of objectives, the authors often also specified the kind of learning that was required, and the conditions that fostered such learning. In the case of the knowledge category, for example, performance is specified in this way: "By knowledge we mean that the student can give evidence that he remembers, either by recalling or by recognizing, some idea or phenomenon with which he has had experience in the educational process" (p. 28). They also described the conditions for promoting knowledge learning: "[W]e tend to think of knowledge as something which is learned as the result of simply presenting it to the learner in one form of communication or another" (p. 34). And in a metaphor, they described the learning involved: "It may be helpful in this case to think of knowledge as something filed or stored in the mind" (p. 29).

Furthermore, the authors implied the existence of distinctly different varieties of learning in their discussion of theories available at the time they constructed the Taxonomy:

We reviewed theories of personality and learning but were unable to find a single view which, in our opinion, accounted for the varieties of behaviors represented in the educational objectives we attempted to classify. We were reluctantly forced to agree with Hilgard that each theory of learning accounts for some phenomena very well but is less adequate in accounting for others.[9] What is needed is a larger synthetic theory of learning than at present seems to be available. We are of the opinion that our method of ordering educational outcomes will make it possible to define the range of phenomena for which such a theory must account (pp. 17-18).

Indeed, the last sentence of this excerpt can be interpreted to imply the existence of as many as six different varieties of learning, one for each of the classes of objectives in the Taxonomy.

HIERARCHICAL AND CUMULATIVE NATURE OF LEARNING

By taking the position that learning comes in distinctly different kinds, the authors of the Taxonomy take on the task of specifying how these different kinds are related. In this case, too, they assumed a definite position; they explicitly asserted that the classes in the Taxonomy are ordered hierarchically: "[T]he present [order of the levels] appears to us to represent something of the hierarchical order of the different classes of objectives. As we have defined them, the objectives in one class are likely to make use of and be built on the behaviors found in the preceding classes on this list" (p. 18). They also appear, at various points in the discussion, to have assumed implicitly that objectives within classes are ordered hierarchically as well, from simple to complex. Moreover, they explicitly claimed that learning (the "educational process") is cumulative:

One may take the Gestalt point of view that the complex behavior is more than the sum of the simpler behaviors, or one may view the complex behavior as being completely analyzable into simpler components. But either way, so long as the simpler behaviors may be viewed as components of the more complex behaviors, we can view the educational process as one of building on the simpler behavior (p. 16).

Counter to these strong and explicit claims about the structural character of the taxonomy are other statements that have contrary implications. One such implication is that the attainment of higher level objectives can affect the attainment of lower level ones. Another is that the attainment of the objectives may not always proceed in an invariant order from lower to higher ones. "[I]t is probably more defensible educationally to consider analysis as an aid to fuller comprehension [a lower level class] or as a prelude to an evaluation of the material" (p. 144).

The authors also acknowledged that the sequence of attainment may have a spiral or iterative character but, again, the sequence may not be invariant from lowest class to highest class:

Although Evaluation is placed last in the cognitive domain because it is regarded as requiring to some extent all the other categories of behavior, it is not necessarily the last step in thinking or problem solving. It is quite possible that the evaluation process will in some cases be the prelude to the acquisition of new knowledge, a new attempt at comprehension or application, or a new analysis and synthesis (p. 185).

The structure claimed for the hierarchy, then *resembles* a hierarchy, and the learning that makes possible the attainment of the objectives is *cumulative-like*.

VERTICAL AND HORIZONTAL TRANSFER OF LEARNING

The hierarchical nature of the Taxonomy implies that learning has transfer effects. The learning that leads to the attainment of lower-level objectives transfers to or facilitates the learning that leads to related higher-level objectives. The nature of the Taxonomy, then, presupposes that learning results in transfer up the hierarchy, a kind of transfer that might be thought of as *vertical*.

In addition, the authors of the Taxonomy explicitly affirmed the importance of *horizontal* transfer. They asserted that learning, especially the kind that leads to higher-level objectives, enables students to deal effectively with tasks they have not confronted before.

[Problem-solving skills] are more widely applicable than knowledge. If we are concerned with the problem of transfer of training, by definition we would select intellectual abilities and skills as having greater transfer value (p. 42).

The fact that most of what we learn is intended for application to problem situations in real life is indicative of the importance of application objectives in the general curriculum. . . . Those of you familiar with educational psychology will quickly recognize this as the age-old problem of transfer of training. Research studies have shown that comprehending the abstract does not certify that an individual will be able to apply it correctly (p. 122).

The authors left no doubt, then, that they believed transfer to be both an essential goal of education, and eminently achievable as well. In our view, they even went beyond this already bold position to claim that higher-order skills and abilities are broadly generalizable.

GENERALIZABILITY OF HIGHER-ORDER SKILLS AND ABILITIES

One of the great hopes of many educators and learning theorists alike has been that students can be assisted to acquire content-neutral, if not content-free, intellectual skills such as critical thinking skills or cognitive strategies. If so, students could apply these skills very broadly across a wide spectrum of domains. In current parlance, such skills are referred to as "domain-general." The authors of the Taxonomy plainly took the position that this hope could be transformed into reality:

[M]uch emphasis must be placed in schools on the development of generalized ways of attacking problems and on knowledge which can be applied to a wide range of new situations. That is, we have the task of preparing individuals for problems that cannot be foreseen in advance, and about all that can be done under such conditions is to help the student acquire generalized intellectual abilities and skills which will serve him well in many new situations (p. 40).

NOVICES AND EXPERTS

For educators and for many psychologists as well, the nature of intellectual expertise is of intrinsic interest. Furthermore, it is of potential pragmatic importance insofar as one of the goals of education is to assist student novices to move toward expertise. In this connection, the question arises whether novices should be provided direct instruction in acquiring the knowledge and skills that are characteristic of experts. The authors of the Taxonomy took positions on both of these issues, that is, on the nature of expertise and on the utility of expert characteristics in the teaching of novices.

One of the hallmarks of expertise is the capability of dealing effectively with complex problems. According to the authors of the Taxonomy, the more complex the objective to be attained, the more students, as novices in a field, are conscious of the intellectual activities they engage in during learning.

One of the major threads running through all the taxonomy appears to be a scale of consciousness or awareness. Thus, the behaviors in the cognitive domain are largely characterized by a rather high degree of consciousness on the part of the individual exhibiting the behavior. . . . Further, in the cognitive domain especially, it appears that as the behaviors become more complex, the individual is more aware of their existence (p. 19).

At the same time, however, the authors noted that the higher the level of expertise, the lower the level of consciousness or awareness:

If the level of consciousness can be demonstrated to be an important dimension in the classification of behavior, it would pose a great range of problems and point to a whole new set of relationships which would be of interest to researchers in the field of educational psychology. One might hope that it would provide a basis for explaining why behaviors which are initially displayed with a high level of consciousness become, after some time and repetition, automatic or are accompanied by a low level of consciousness (p. 20).

In addition to (a) the automaticity of their behavior, experts (b) have acquired more knowledge than novices, (c) have organized their knowledge differently, and (d) have more detailed and precise knowledge (pp. 36-37).

As for the issue of applying an understanding of expertise to the instruction of novices, the authors of the Taxonomy were evidently quite skeptical:

Some educators frequently assume that the knowledge which the expert or specialist needs to possess about a field or topic and the knowledge which the beginning student may reasonably be expected to learn are identical. Such an assumption tends to overestimate the student's ability to learn and retain information. . . . The decision to be made is whether to use an organization externally imposed by some authority or expert as compared with an organization that fits the internal state of the learner at his particular stage of development (pp. 36-37).

Evidently the position of the authors is that salutary educational provisions for novices differ from the expert's organization of knowledge: "As previously noted, the cases of the specialist and the student are not identical. The organization the specialist finds most useful is not necessarily the organization that provides the easiest learning path for the student" (p. 37).

In the remainder of the chapter, we examine these six presuppositions from five different theoretical perspectives: behaviorism, neo-behaviorism, information processing, cognitive developmental, and cognitive science. Moreover, we contend that the Taxonomy (a) in some respects presupposes propositions dominant at the time of its conception and publication, (b) in other respects presupposes propositions that would not gain currency in psychology for another decade or more, and (c) in still other respects presupposes propositions that were and are now incongruent with dominant contemporaneous psychological conceptions.

Behaviorist Perspectives

As we noted at the outset, behaviorist orientations dominated in American psychology during the period when the Taxonomy was being developed. Furthermore, one version of behaviorism gained considerable influence in education during the decade following the publication of the Taxonomy. Drawing on the reinforcement principles he had proffered, Skinner argued that effective learning could be fostered by means of "programmed instruction."[10] Given this aspect of the intellectual context of the time, we find it interesting that the Taxonomy was not built on behaviorist principles. Instead, a number of taxonomic presuppositions contrast with those principles. One of these contrasts involves the first presupposition about the relationship between learning and performance.

While behaviorist theories hold that learning is one factor that determines performance, they specify other factors as well. At least four other factors can be found in one or another of such theories:

1. *Response-produced inhibition* can be thought of as being like fatigue. The notion is that the more frequently a performance has been given in the recent past, the less a person will be inclined to give it again.

2. *Latent extinction* is motivational in nature; if one's experiences teach one that a performance is unlikely to result in reward, or even punishment instead, one is unlikely to give the performance.

3. *Response competition* has been used as one explanation for what can appear to an outside observer to be forgetting. This notion is that persons often learn to give two or more performances that are so similar that they compete or interfere with one another. A student might, for example, learn what the terms "stalactite" and "stalagmite" refer to, but due to their similarity be unable later to correctly identify the referents of either.

4. *Disuse* also has to do with forgetting. The principle is that the longer it has been since one has given a performance, the less likely one will be able to display it successfully. For example, many of us would be hard pressed to state much of the information we learned in elementary school, or even high school for that matter.

For a number of reasons, then, behaviorist theories run contrary to the proposition of a one-to-one correspondence between learning and performance. What would have been the consequences for the Taxonomy if the authors had relied on these theories? An extreme and implausible consequence: they might have scrapped the entire enterprise in despair of ever being able to assess students' learning through tests or observations of their behavior. More in keeping with the interpretation we offered at the outset, a more likely consequence is that the authors of the Taxonomy might have made more explicit their concern with learning that endures and that students exhibit even under nonsupportive motivational conditions.

The presuppositions of the authors of the Taxonomy about what is learned and the nature of learning constitute the central, and sharpest, contrast with behaviorist principles. In responding to the question, "What is learned?" behaviorist theories eschew terms that crowd the text of the Taxonomy, terms such as "knowledge," "principle," or "intellectual ability." Instead, they answer "connections (or associations) between stimuli (Ss) and responses (Rs)." Additionally, these theories hold that S-R connections (also called habits) are strengthened by repetition and especially by reinforcement, often in the form of rewards. Most behaviorists would, of course, hold that S-R connections are learned in either of two ways. One of these is by means of classical (Pavlovian) conditioning. The other is by means of instrumental conditioning.

Regardless of the particular form of conditioning involved, S-R connections constitute the content of learning. In contrast, then, to the taxonomic presupposition of qualitatively different categories of what human beings learn, the presupposition of the behaviorists is that the content of all learning is of a single kind. Despite this contrast, behaviorist theorists might well agree with Bloom and his colleagues that the performances set forth in the Taxonomy are worthy educational objectives. According to behaviorist theories, these complex performances are made possible by the learning of additional connections, ones between elemental S-R connections; that is, individual S-R connections, or habits, can themselves be connected to others to form chains or habit families that result in complex behavior.

Nevertheless, behaviorist theories needed to provide an account of the internal organization of S-R connections and of families of these habits. They met this need in ways that resemble, on the surface at least, the solution adopted by the authors of the Taxonomy, that is, by presuming that learning is cumulative and hierarchical. They posited that learning is cumulative, and that collections of habits that support common performances are compiled into *habit family hierarchies*. In these theories, however, the elements that compose a hierarchy are all of one kind, that is, S-R connections. Thus, the kinds of learning required for complex performances differ only quantitatively from the kind required for simple performances. In the Taxonomy, however, qualitatively different kinds of learning are related hierarchically such that the learning of knowledge, for example, is prerequisite to the learning of intellectual abilities and skills.

Behaviorist principles about transfer are also superficially similar to taxonomic presuppositions. Vertical transfer stems from the proposition that habit families consist of chains of linked S-R connections. Thus, the learning of a habit family is promoted by the prior learning of its constituent connections. Once again, however, the content of the learning that transfers (connections) contrasts sharply with the content presupposed by the Taxonomy (knowledge, intellectual skills and abilities). This contrast is also evident in the case of horizontal transfer, but another contrast is evident as well. This additional contrast stems from the behaviorist contention that horizontal transfer is limited to instances where a new performance task requires learning that contains some of the identical connections that have been learned previously.

The remaining two taxonomic presuppositions (generalizability of higher-order skills, and differences in novice and expert learning) fall outside the scope of behaviorist theories. Because these theories deny the existence of higher-order skills and abilities as such, the issue of their generalizability does not arise. Similarly, behaviorist theories deny the existence of consciousness, so that changes in awareness as a function of growing expertise is not a sensible issue.

Practically speaking, then, what would have been different about the Taxonomy if its authors had relied on behaviorist theories of learning in constructing it? As we have noted, the categories in the Taxonomy might well have remained nominally the same. The substance of the categories, however, would have changed dramatically. This change in substance would have resulted in equally dramatic changes in the implications of the Taxonomy for curriculum and instruction. In brief, curricula and instruction would have consisted of the presentation of carefully crafted sequences of elemental stimuli designed to elicit correct responses to the presentation of prompts to assemble elemental connections into chains of responses that would eventually have the appearance of ideas. Instruction would also have involved the delivery of rewards or reinforcers, for example, for uttering a sentence containing a component of a target "idea," and later for uttering a paragraph that conveyed this "idea" in its entirety. This is not so strange a scenario to those familiar with the devotion of some educators, at least at one time, to drill and practice.

Neobehaviorist Perspectives

The late 1950s and 1960s saw the rise of neobehaviorist and neo-associationist perspectives. Due to the lesser but still substantial rise of information processing and cognitive perspectives, these "neo" perspectives did not dominate their era as thoroughly as had their progenitors. They nevertheless attained a position of great influence and are

54   PSYCHOLOGICAL PERSPECTIVES

significant, for present purposes, for their introduction of the notion
of two qualitatively different kinds of learning: *direct* connections or
associations between stimuli and responses, and *mediated* connections
or associations.

We discussed direct connections, symbolized as S-R, in the
preceding section. The notion of mediated connections, symbolized as
S-r_m-s_m-R, is that one can make an implicit (almost but not quite
mental) response (r_m) to an external stimulus (S). This implicit
response itself produces an implicit stimulus (s_m) that elicits an overt
response (R). In this formulation, the notion of mediation is entirely
consistent with the earlier behaviorist perspectives as it merely
involves a chain of connections between stimuli and responses.
Indeed, this conception of mediation was introduced in the theories of
both Pavlov and Hull.

Influenced perhaps by Pavlovian theory, Vygotsky had introduced a distinction between two varieties of learning, elementary and
mediated, and in his theory the difference was definitely qualitative.[11]
Moreover, he theorized that a shift from the less mature to the more
mature mediated form of learning marked a milestone in human development. Vygotsky also emphasized the role of social activity in
bringing about this shift.

The theorizing of Kendler resembles that of Vygotsky, even
though her neobehaviorist approach is far more indebted to her
behaviorist forebears. Kendler gradually transformed the Hullian
notion of mediation to explain a decided change, especially between
the ages of five and seven years, in the learning capabilities of children.
This change consisted of a shift in children's tendencies, from
responding to the physical properties of stimuli to responding to
stimuli as members of classes. Loosely speaking, this shift marked the
development of the capability of learning concepts. Early versions of
Kendler's theory[12] remained consistent with her behaviorist conceptions, but later versions[13] contain the suggestion that mediated learning is qualitatively different from direct learning or, at the least that
mediated learning results in qualitatively different kinds of performance capabilities.

In the domain of verbal learning and memory during the late
1950s and through the 1960s, the growth of neoassociationist theories
also involved the notion of mediation. As in the evolution of Kendler's theory, neoassociationist conceptions were consistent with the
basic S-R approach. The learning of associations between words, for
example, was held either to be direct or to be mediated internally by

previously learned verbal associations. These conceptions, however, evolved into ones that posited that imagery, and even concepts, could serve a mediating function. At this point the specificity of internal r_m-s_m connections was left behind.[14] Eventually, these notions, too, evolved into the proto-cognitive proposition that human beings apply previously acquired knowledge to elaborate on and learn newly encountered information. Furthermore, developmental change in learning proficiency was attributed by some to differences in the propensity to engage in such elaborative activity.[15]

These evolutionary changes within, and eventually beyond, the behaviorist tradition brought that perspective closer to the presuppositions that informed the authors of the Taxonomy. That is to say, they anticipated by approximately a decade the evolution in the dominant view among American learning psychologists of the proposition that learning consists of qualitatively different varieties.

From Neobehaviorism to Information Processing

This proposition played its most prominent role on the stage of American psychology in the framework proposed by Robert Gagné in the first edition of his book, *Conditions of Learning*, published in 1965. In this first edition, Gagné drew heavily on the behaviorist heritage. Gradually, however, his basic perspective shifted so that the dominant approach in the 1977 edition was that of information processing.[16]

The framework Gagné proposed arguably represents the closest parallel to the presuppositions we have identified in the Taxonomy. Furthermore, Gagné explicitly acknowledges the "ingenious" contributions the authors of the Taxonomy made to the endeavor of assessing the attainment of educational objectives.

Like the authors of the Taxonomy, Gagné asserts that learning is manifest in behavior, and identifies objectives with performance:

The kind of change [in capability] called learning exhibits itself as a change in behavior, and the inference of learning is made by comparing what behavior was possible before the individual was placed in a learning situation and what behavior can be exhibited after such treatment (p. 5).

It is logical to suppose that the initial step in deciding on the conditions for learning is that of defining objectives. In terms of the system model, this means that . . . there needs to be a decision about the *nature of the change in behavior* sought (p. 241).

Gagné also adamantly endorses the proposition that learning comes in a number of qualitatively different varieties: "Throughout many years of experimental investigation of learning, there have been those who have contended that *all learning is basically the same*. . . . It should be perfectly clear from the present chapter that it is this viewpoint that is categorically rejected" (pp. 59-60).

In the 1965 edition of his book, Gagné distinguished eight varieties of learning, ranging from Pavlovian conditioning to problem solving. While these varieties do not correspond in one-to-one fashion with the categories of outcomes distinguished by the authors of the Taxonomy, the higher-level types match reasonably well with the categories included in the Taxonomy as intellectual abilities and skills.

This match with the taxonomic categories increased over time as the Gagné framework evolved. In the 1977 edition of *Conditions of Learning*, Gagné distinguished "five major categories of learning outcomes": intellectual skill, cognitive strategy, verbal information, motor skill, and attitude. His treatment of the categories of intellectual skill and cognitive strategy corresponds quite well with the treatment of intellectual abilities and skills in the Taxonomy. Similarly, Gagné's treatment of verbal information corresponds quite well with the treatment of knowledge in the Taxonomy. With regard to the proposition about varieties of learning, then, the 1977 version of the Gagné framework approximated that presented in the Taxonomy in 1956.

Gagné not only placed the proposition about varieties of learning at the forefront of his framework, initially he also held that all of these varieties are related hierarchically. He asserted that lower-level types of learning are prerequisites for higher-level types.In 1965, he wrote,

Problem Solving (type 8)
>   requires as prerequisites:
Principles (type 7),
>   which require as prerequisites:
Concepts (type 6),
>   which require as prerequisites:
Multiple discriminations (type 5).[17]

This conception of different classes of learning being related by virtue of the higher classes subsuming the lower squares quite well with the conception expressed by the Taxonomy authors:

Our attempt to arrange educational behaviors from simple to complex was based on the idea that a particular simple behavior may become integrated with other equally simple behaviors to form a more complex behavior. Thus . . . behaviors of type A form one class, behaviors of type AB form another class, while behaviors of type ABC form still another class.[18]

By 1977, Gagné asserted hierarchical relationships only among the sub-types of learning (discrimination, concrete concept, defined concept rule, higher-order rule) within the category of intellectual skills. For example, the learning of the rule that doubling a pint produces a quart depends on the prior learning of the component concepts, doubling, pint and quart. In contrast to the Taxonomy, however, Gagné still did not claim that such intellectual skills depend on the prior learning of verbal information.

The taxonomic presuppositions about vertical and horizontal transfer are reflected in Gagné's framework. In fact, Gagné himself wrote of the work of the authors of the Taxonomy: "These authors describe knowledge transfer objectives under the headings 'comprehension,' 'application,' 'analysis,' 'synthesis,' and 'evaluation'."[19] He goes on to present an example from the Taxonomy of an item that assesses the breadth of transfer, that is, horizontal transfer. In addition, he associates the taxonomic category of "synthesis" with vertical transfer. Similarly, Gagné emphasizes the importance of fostering the generalizability of knowledge and intellectual skills, and especially of the category he refers to as "cognitive strategies."

Plainly, then, the "conditions of learning" framework largely corresponds to the presuppositions identified in the Taxonomy. The degree of this correspondence is such that the Taxonomy would have been little different had Bloom and his colleagues had access to *Conditions of Learning* at the time they wrote the Taxonomy. The only two significant changes might have been the inclusion of the category of cognitive strategies and, perhaps, omission of the assertion that intellectual abilities and skills are hierarchically dependent on lower-level kinds of knowledge and information.

Cognitive Developmental Perspectives

In the 1960s, the structural theory of Jean Piaget came to exert a marked influence on developmental psychology in the United States. Although Piaget's theory and research had been available in published form for some thirty-five years, its impact on both psychological and educational thinking in the United States did not become widespread until the 1960s with the publication of Hunt's *Intelligence and Experience*, Flavell's *The Developmental Psychology of Jean Piaget*, and Bruner, Oliver, and Greenfield's *Studies in Cognitive Growth*.[20] At the present time, Piagetian theory has itself been eclipsed by neo-Piagetian sequelae, and for this reason, we rely more heavily on one of these contemporary perspectives, the theory promulgated by Case.[21]

Cognitive developmental theory offers a very different slant on the Taxonomy from any of the other perspectives we have reviewed. In all the preceding perspectives, the notion of learning has been the centerpiece. In contrast, in Piagetian theory and in the cognitive developmental perspectives that have succeeded it, the notion of development is the centerpiece. This difference has substantive consequences for the taxonomic presuppositions we are examining.

For example, from the cognitive-developmental perspective, what students learn and how they perform depend on their developmental status. Thus, the issue is not about the relationship between learning and performance, but rather about the relationship between development and performance. Nevertheless, the issue remains important, in that from the neo-Piagetian perspective, students' cognitive capabilities may not be manifest in their performances for a variety of reasons, including the affective meaning of the performance to them.

In prima facie agreement with the first taxonomic presupposition, from a neo-Piagetian perspective such as that proposed by Case, students can acquire or, better, construct a variety of qualitatively different kinds of capabilities. The differences among these capabilities, however, are not conceived to depend on the kind of learning involved, but on two other factors. First, the differences stem from the students' developmental stage. What students are capable of learning is conditioned by their developmental progress. How they learn remains constant across developmental levels. Second, the differences depend on the domain of the subject being learned. The strategies students learn for solving spatial reasoning problems will differ from the strategies they learn for solving scientific reasoning problems.

Similarly, whereas a neo-Piagetian perspective might resemble the Taxonomy in asserting that students' capabilities are related hierarchically, this assertion stems from the proposition that all students progress through the major developmental stages and their substages in the same order. It is the stages that are hierarchically related, not the kinds of learning that characterize the stages.

The specific terms "vertical" and "horizontal" appear verbatim in a neo-Piagetian formulation like Case's, but their meaning and significance are distinctive. Neither refers to transfer in the sense that the authors of the Taxonomy used these terms. Rather, "vertical" refers to the proposition that students' capabilities develop in an invariant sequence of stages. And "horizontal" refers to the proposition that within any one of these stages, students have attained comparable levels of capability across tasks within intellectual domains.

Again, a neo-Piagetian perspective such as Case's would agree that intellectual abilities and skills are generalizable. From this perspective, however, (developmentally) higher-order skills are no more nor less generalizable than (developmentally) lower-order skills. Moreover, at whatever level, generalizability is limited by the boundaries of the domains in which the students have constructed their capabilities. So, for example, skills developed in the domain of spatial reasoning would not be expected to generalize to the domain of scientific reasoning. From this perspective, then, higher-order skills and abilities are not domain general.

The theory offered by Case provides a specific perspective on the distinction between novices and experts. Experts within a domain are those who have consolidated, integrated, and elaborated their structures of both declarative and procedural knowledge so that the components of these structures are fully coordinated. This perspective is in agreement with the taxonomic presupposition that effective instruction for novices must be designed to bring them to the next natural level of attainment rather than to bring them immediately into conformity with expert ways of thinking and solving problems.

Had the authors relied on a neo-Piagetian perspective in constructing the Taxonomy, the notion of development would have been pivotal. Most importantly, educational objectives would have been keyed primarily to the developmental capabilities of students. Of almost equal importance, the educational objectives would have been delineated separately for the major different knowledge domains. In Case's conception, for example, these domains would include causal reasoning, spatial reasoning, verbal reasoning, mathematical reasoning, scientific reasoning, and social reasoning.

Cognitive Science Perspectives

At present, cognitive science does not constitute a univocal theoretical or methodological perspective. Those who work in this field come from a variety of disciplines, including linguistics, philosophy, computer science, and cognitive psychology. The methods used by this range of cognitive scientists include those of artificial intelligence and computer modeling, as well as ethnographic and experimental methods.

Despite this variety, some hallmarks distinguish the field.[22] First, cognitive scientists conduct research on cognition in knowledge-rich areas, focusing, for example, on problem solving in physics and the comprehension of extended text passages. Second, in agreement with cognitive developmental theorists, they assume that learners acquire new knowledge and skill by processes of active construction and that this construction is heavily conditioned by the structure and content of the knowledge they already possess. Third, they believe that knowledge and skill are structurally organized and domain specific. Fourth, for the most part, they accord substantial importance to students' knowledge of their own abilities and the monitoring of their own learning; in short, to metacognition.

With reference to the first in our list of taxonomic presuppositions, cognitive scientists would agree that learning or, better, knowledge can become manifest in students' performances. Most would insist, however, that the extent and structures of student knowledge can be assessed only by performance tasks that require extended work and explicit explanation on the part of the student. Timed tests consisting of multiple-choice questions are viewed as being of little value.

Cognitive scientists also would agree that learning comes in qualitatively different varieties. They trace these differences, however, not to the ways learning occurs but to the distinctive characteristics of various knowledge domains. Learning differs across domains because the structure and content of knowledge and skill vary across these domains. The nature of learning itself, however, is held to be constant across domains. Students learn by bringing their prior knowledge to bear in constructing new knowledge and new ways of solving problems.

From the preceding proposition, it follows that knowledge or learning is cumulative, to be sure, but may not be organized hierarchically. The organization of learning depends on the structure of the domain being learned. Similarly, the transfer of learning, and the generalizability of knowledge and skill is expected only within domains. Furthermore, transfer and generalizability will be determined by the structure of the knowledge and skill that students construct in the course of their learning.

Many of these features of the cognitive science perspective emerge in connection with the presupposition about expert-novice differences. The proposition that the knowledge structures that make for proficiency in a given intellectual domain are distinctive to that domain stems from expert/novice research. This research seems to indicate that experts differ from novices not only in the amount of knowledge they possess, but also in the organization and accessibility of that knowledge.[23] Differences between experts and novices in knowledge structures are of four principal kinds:

1. Whereas the knowledge of novices is structured around the main phenomena in a domain, that of experts represents these phenomena in relation to higher-order principles.

2. For the expert, these principles are represented in the form of problem-solving procedures as well as in the form of declarative knowledge.

3. Moreover, such procedural representations include specifications of the conditions under which the principles are applicable. Thus, the principles are connected with the phenomena to which they can be applied and even with the concrete components of the phenomena.

4. Experts' knowledge structures, in contrast to those of novices, also include understandings of the goals and structures of the domain.

These kinds of differences suggest that student proficiency can best be increased by instruction that facilitates the construction of knowledge bases that are comprehensive, structured in terms of higher-order principles, inclusive of problem-solving procedures and heuristics along with specifications of the conditions of their applicability, and framed by appreciation of the distinctive goals of the various domains.

A taxonomy of educational objectives designed in accord with the principles of cognitive science, then, would differ from the Taxonomy constructed by Bloom and his colleagues in three principal ways. First and most dramatically, there would be no single taxonomy. The principles of cognitive science would dictate the development of numerous taxonomies, one for each distinctive discipline. This necessity follows from the proposition that the character of essential knowledge and procedures varies from domain to domain. Therefore, the objectives of learning and instruction must also be domain specific. Second, because knowledge and skills are domain specific, productive transfer and generalizability could occur only within domains. Third, the objectives within some domains might be related hierarchically, whereas in others objectives might be related in quite different ways, depending on the structure of knowledge within each domain.

Conclusion

Having examined presuppositions in the Taxonomy from the perspective offered by each of five different psychological theories of cognition, we continue to find ourselves impressed by how bold and, in many ways, modern the authors were in the psychological presuppositions they made. Their boldness is evident in the marked clashes between each proposition and one or more of the theoretical perspectives that have dominated in psychology from the early 1950s to the present. Their modernity is evident in their anticipation of developments that occurred in psychological theory decades later.

We also find ourselves intrigued by the question of what psychological presuppositions the authors would make if they undertook to build the Taxonomy anew today. We doubt that their presuppositions would exhibit a docile adoption of the principles of cognitive science, despite the current dominance of that perspective. To be sure, they might well celebrate the emphasis of that perspective on higher-level learning and thinking as well as the proposition that the nature of assessment must be congruent with the nature of the learning to be assessed. Nevertheless, we believe that the authors of the Taxonomy would be no more inclined to temper their convictions to please the cognitive scientists today than they were to please the behaviorists when they were dominant. Instead, our bet is that the authors would now, as we believe they did then, make presuppositions consistent with their vision of what constitutes education for productive learning. What intrigues us is what those presuppositions would be and how far in the future they might make their appearance in psychological theory.

NOTES

1. Jerome S. Bruner, "Another Look at New Look 1," *American Psychologist* 47 (1992): 780-783.

2. Jerome S. Bruner, Jacqueline J. Goodnow, and George A. Austin, *A Study of Thinking* (New York: Wiley, 1956).

3. George A. Miller, Eugene Galanter, and Karl H. Pribram, *Plans and the Structure of Behavior* (New York: Holt, 1960).

4. J. McVicker Hunt, *Intelligence and Experience* (New York: Ronald, 1961); John Flavell, *The Developmental Psychology of Jean Piaget* (Princeton, NJ: Van Nostrand, 1963).

5. Jerome S. Bruner, Rose R. Oliver, and Patricia M. Greenfield, *Studies in Cognitive Growth* (New York: Wiley, 1966).

6. Robert M. Gagné, *The Conditions of Learning* (New York: Holt, Rinehart and Winston, 1965, 1977).

7. See, for example, Ann L. Brown, "Domain-Specific Principles Affect Learning and Transfer in Children," *Cognitive Science* 14 (1990): 107-133; Jill H. Larkin, "Understanding, Problem Representation, and Skill in Physics," in *Thinking and Learning Skills*, Vol. 2, edited by Judith W. Segal, Susan F. Chipman, and Robert Glaser (Hillsdale, NJ: Erlbaum, 1985); and Alan H. Schoenfeld, "GRAPHER: A Case Study in Educational Technology, Research, and Development," in *Toward a Scientific Practice of Science Education*, edited by Andrea diSessa, Marjorie Gardner, James Greeno, Frederick Reif, Alan Schoenfeld, and Elizabeth Stage (Hillsdale, NJ: Erlbaum, in press).

8. Benjamin S. Bloom et al., *Taxonomy of Educational Objectives, Handbook 1: Cognitive Domain* (New York: McKay, 1956), p. 6. Unless otherwise noted the page numbers for quoted passages in the following pages are for this volume by Bloom et al.

9. Ernest R. Hilgard, *Theories of Learning* (New York: Appleton-Century-Crofts, 1948).

10. B. F. Skinner, *The Technology of Teaching* (New York: Appleton-Century-Crofts, 1968).

11. Lev S. Vygotsky, *Mind in Society* (Cambridge, MA: Harvard University Press, 1978).

12. Tracy S. Kendler, Howard H. Kendler, and Beulah Learnard, "Mediated Responses to Size and Brightness as a Function of Age," *American Journal of Psychology* 75 (1962): 571-586.

13. Tracy S. Kendler, "Cross-sectional Research, Longitudinal Theory, and a Discriminative Transfer Ontogeny," *Human Development* 22 (1979): 235-254.

14. Allan Paivio, *Imagery and Verbal Processes* (New York: Holt, 1971).

15. William D. Rohwer, Jr. "An Elaborative Conception of Learner Differences," in *Aptitude, Learning, and Instruction*, Vol. 2: *Cognitive Process Analyses of Learning and Problem Solving*, edited by Richard Snow, Patrick Federico, and William Montague (Hillsdale, NJ: Erlbaum, 1980).

16. Gagné, *Conditions of Learning* (1977). Unless otherwise noted the page numbers for the quotations immediately following are from this volume.

17. Gagné, *Conditions of Learning* (1965), p. 60.

18. Bloom et al., *Taxonomy of Educational Objectives*, p. 18.

19. Gagné, *Conditions of Learning* (1965), p. 261.

20. Hunt, *Intelligence and Experience*; Flavell, *The Developmental Psychology of Jean Piaget*; Bruner et al., *Studies in Cognitive Growth*.

21. Robbie Case, *Intellectual Development* (New York: Academic Press, 1985).

22. William D. Rohwer, Jr., and John W. Thomas, "Domain-Specific Knowledge, Metacognition, and the Promise of Instructional Reform," in *Cognitive Strategy Research: From Basic Research to Educational Applications*, edited by Christine B. McCormick, Gloria Miller, and Michael Pressley (New York: Springer-Verlag, 1989).

23. Michelene T. H. Chi, Robert Glaser, and Ernest Rees, "Expertise in Problem Solving," in *Advances in the Psychology of Human Intelligence*, Vol. 1, edited by Robert J. Sternberg (Hillsdale, NJ: Erlbaum, 1982).

CHAPTER V

Empirical Investigations of the
Hierarchical Structure of the Taxonomy

AMELIA E. KREITZER AND GEORGE F. MADAUS

One is tempted to open a discussion of Bloom's taxonomy of educational objectives, as have many writers, with superlatives. Indeed, only the tersest, driest, or most academic writing concerning the Taxonomy fails to include a comment about its tremendous impact, utility, fame, publicity, or influence. Such comments are justified; after all, the Taxonomy has sold over a million copies and has been translated into several languages. (See chapter 9, this volume.) It receives treatment in virtually every textbook in general education and in measurement for prospective teachers. It has even been the subject of examination questions on teacher competency tests. In short, it has become part of the lore of educators.

The Taxonomy made its way into the pool of professional knowledge for educators despite criticism—sometimes quite harsh—on logical, philosophical, psychological, and empirical grounds. This last area is the subject of this chapter. Specifically, we review the empirical investigations of the hierarchical structure of the Taxonomy.

The organization of this review is as follows. First, we consider what the authors of the Taxonomy asserted about its structure. Then we briefly summarize the logical or philosophical concerns about the structure which are most relevant to the empirical evidence. Next, we discuss attempts to validate the cumulative hierarchical structure. Finally, we close with a consideration of the value and necessity of empirically validating the structure.

Amelia E. Kreitzer was a Research Associate in the Center for the Study of Testing, Evaluation, and Educational Policy (Boston College) while this chapter was being prepared. She now lives in Norway. George F. Madaus is Boisi Professor of Education and Public Policy at Boston College.

The authors wish to thank Michael Hallisy and Ann Jones for their timely and helpful research work on this chapter.

The Structure of the Taxonomy

The Taxonomy is, in its essence, the product of pragmatists. A group of college examiners, meeting informally, recognized the need for a framework that could make discussions about tests and testing more precise and mutually understandable. (See chapter 1.) The mission of the group eventually became the construction of a descriptive framework for classifying educational objectives, which they phrased in terms of the intended behavior of students. The initial goal of facilitating communication guided the development of the Taxonomy and kept it grounded firmly in the practical world of educators. Using the work of "countless test constructors, curriculum workers, and teachers,"[1] the framers attempted to capture the collective experience of practitioners. Their completed taxonomy described six progressively more complex categories of objectives that reflected "the distinctions teachers make among student behaviors" (p. 13), which they gleaned from teachers' plans, materials, and methods. Indeed, the very names of the categories—Knowledge, Comprehension, Application, Analysis, Synthesis, and Evaluation—were deliberately common terms likely to be familiar to potential users.

The authors of the Taxonomy made remarkably modest claims about it. They acknowledged, for example, that they had failed "in finding a method of classification which would permit complete and sharp distinctions among behaviors" (p. 15). They made no claims about its theoretical underpinnings; in fact, it was explicitly not theory-based, for the committee was "unable to find a single view which . . . accounted for the varieties of behaviors represented in the educational objectives we attempted to classify" (p. 17). At best, it seems, they hoped that their Taxonomy, by virtue of its comprehensiveness, would provide some clues to theory builders. The problem of the theory to be developed is extremely complex. Although that problem "has probably not been solved completely satisfactorily, it is the opinion of the writers that we have made some progress toward a solution" (p. 18).

Their "solution-in-progress" was an arrangement of six classes of behavioral objectives, ordered by presumed complexity of behavior.

Our attempt to arrange educational behaviors from simple to complex was based on the idea that a particular simple behavior may become integrated with other equally simple behaviors to form a more complex behavior. Thus our classifications may be said to be in the form where behaviors of type A form one class, behaviors of type AB form another class, while behaviors of type ABC form still another class (p. 18).

Thus, the essential structure of the Taxonomy was a cumulative hierarchy: hierarchy because the classes of objectives were arranged in order of increasing complexity, and cumulative because each class of behaviors was presumed to include all the behaviors of the less complex classes. While Bloom and his associates most often described their hierarchy of objectives as related to complexity, they also posited that "it should be related to an order of difficulty such that problems requiring behavior A alone should be answered correctly more frequently than problems requiring AB" (p. 18).

One other feature of the classification scheme is relevant here. The Taxonomy makes a special distinction between the lowest level, Knowledge, and the five higher levels. The Taxonomy's authors asserted that Knowledge involved "little more than the remembering of the idea or phenomenon in a form very close to that in which it was originally encountered" (pp. 28-29). In contrast, the higher levels of the Taxonomy were presumed to involve the exercise of intellectual skills and abilities on that knowledge:

Problem solving or thinking cannot be carried on in a vacuum, but must be based upon knowledge of some of the "realities." The intellectual abilities represented in the Taxonomy assume knowledge as a prerequisite. Knowledge . . . becomes the material with which the problem solving deals (p. 33).

The assertions above describe the essence of the structure of the Taxonomy. Its cumulative nature, its increasing order of complexity, its increasing order of difficulty, and the distinction between knowledge and intellectual skills are the properties that have been subject to empirical investigation in attempts to validate the taxonomic structure.

Logical and Philosophical Commentary on the Structure

Over the past three decades, objections have been raised to the Taxonomy for countless reasons,[2] many of which are discussed in chapter 3 of this volume. Among the Taxonomy's critics are those who have questioned the imputed structure of the classification scheme. What is briefly reviewed in this section are the philosophical or logical concerns that have the greatest relevance to the empirical data gathered in attempts to validate the cumulative hierarchy.

In his 1981 review of philosophical and educational issues related to the Taxonomy, Furst noted that the strictly linear assumption of the Taxonomy is "suspect on general philosophical grounds." (See p. 34 of this volume.) He cited Phillips and Kelly as theorists who would argue that any such straightforward, lockstep sequence based on a single attribute—in this case, complexity—is overly simplistic.

The cumulative hierarchy has also come under attack from philosophers and educators for more specific reasons. A recurring criticism of the structure is the distinction Bloom and his colleagues made between knowledge and the five higher levels of the taxonomy. In his discussion of the Knowledge level, Furst points out that some educators and theorists support the distinction between the narrow taxonomic conception of knowledge and the intellectual skills and abilities that are presumed to operate on that knowledge. (See pp. 35-36 in this volume.) Hill and McGaw note that the philosopher Gilbert Ryle also makes a distinction between "knowing that" (propositional knowledge) and "knowing how" (procedural knowledge).[3]

Yet another sort of criticism leveled at the taxonomic structure concerns distinctions among various categories. Indeed, for virtually any pair of taxonomic levels, a critic can be found who finds fault with the presumed order or even the separateness of those levels. For example, Calder asserted that "the Taxonomy's categories are extremely ill-defined, and processes of understanding and problem solving are misconstrued."[4] He then proceeded to explain how Knowledge is confused with Comprehension; likewise, Knowledge with Application, Comprehension with Application, Comprehension with Analysis, and Analysis with Evaluation. Furst summarizes other similar arguments that Evaluation is not, as the Taxonomy proposed, more complex than Synthesis, but that Synthesis involves Evaluation. (See chapter 3, this volume.)

Empirical Investigations of the Structure

Empirical studies related to the Taxonomy seem to be principally of two types. The more common type involves judges categorizing test items according to taxonomic levels; such studies typically report either the success with which the categorization was made or the relative taxonomic distribution of items on a given test. The success of categorization is often reported as the percentage of items on which judges agreed. Studies of this type include those by Stanley and Bolton, by Poole, and by Fairbrother.[5] The second type includes tests of the cumulative hierarchical structure of the Taxonomy. Kropp and Stoker provided the most extensive database related to this issue. Several reanalyses of their data have been conducted.[6]

CLASSIFICATION STUDIES

In his comprehensive review of empirical investigations of the Taxonomy, Seddon[7] considered such classification studies as speaking to Bloom's concern about the communicability of the Taxonomy: "A classification scheme may be validated with reference to the criteria of communicability, usefulness, and suggestiveness."[8] Seddon summarized the results of eight studies in which the number of judges classifying items varied from twenty-two to two and the degree of perfect agreement among the judges varied from 7 percent to 90 percent. Seddon considered Fairbrother's research the most relevant to Bloom's concern about communication, in that Fairbrother's twenty-two judges were schoolteachers—one of the presumed target audiences for the taxonomy. Fairbrother's teachers, however, largely failed to agree. Fairbrother compared their distribution of responses with chance distributions and found that the obtained response patterns were better than chance for only 33 out of 80 items, with the level of significance held at .10.

Much higher levels of agreement have been reported with different kinds of judges receiving different kinds of training in the rating task. The training Fairbrother provided his raters consisted of a scant paragraph about each of the taxonomic levels. He explained his results by noting that "it would have been better to gather the teachers together to discuss the interpretation of the instructions before asking them to analyze the questions."[9] In a discussion of the use of the Taxonomy in writing multiple-choice items, Wood noted that giving raters Bloom's definitions and some items to rate "is like asking people to sort fruit into apples, oranges, bananas, etc. without giving them more than the vaguest ideas of what an apple or banana looks like."[10] Studies in which raters were extensively trained prior to classifying items report much higher levels of interjudge agreement than did Fairbrother. For example, in their study of the Irish Leaving Certificate, Macnamara and Madaus reported perfect agreement between pairs of raters on at least 79 percent of the items classified.[11] Cox reported that "agreement on classification among the users of the taxonomy ranges from .63 to .85."[12]

This discussion of success in categorizing items is raised here for two reasons. First, these studies form the bulk of the empirical work using the Taxonomy and are cited as reflective of its validity or lack of validity.[13] Other critics, like Seddon, see them as helping to verify or debunk the claimed educational properties, specifically, the communicability, of the Taxonomy. The authors of this chapter see them as speaking more directly to the utility of the Taxonomy than to its structural validity. In short, if judges can reliably categorize items, then the Taxonomy is of greater use to educators and researchers.

The second reason these classificatory studies are discussed here is that they highlight one of the chief stumbling blocks to validating the Taxonomy's hierarchical structure: the reliability of the categorization of test items. Efforts to validate the structure can be no better than the precision of classification of the test items used to collect the data. As Wood pessimistically summarized, "attempts to verify . . . the hierarchical structure of the Taxonomy . . . are doomed in any case, for if the measures are 'dirty' to start with, nothing 'clean' is going to come out."[14]

Bloom and his coauthors acknowledged the inherent difficulty in classifying items:

Before the reader can classify a particular test exercise, he must know, or at least make some assumptions about, the learning situations which have preceded the test. He must also actually attempt to solve the test problem and note the mental processes he utilizes. The reader should also take into consideration the possibility that the processes used in selecting the correct answer in a recognition form of question may be somewhat different from those used in considering incorrect alternatives in the same question.[15]

While we are not as skeptical as Wood, neither are we as naive as Bloom et al. in thinking that assumptions about the preceding learning tasks or introspection about our own problem-solving processes can render classification invariably accurate. It is wise to keep in mind when reading the results of any validation study of the taxonomic structure that findings depend to some extent on the reliability of the initial item classifications. Results also depend on an even more slippery problem: the gap between items as written and items as experienced by the test taker. Even if one can secure high agreement among judges as to the taxonomic category, one can never know the mental processes of the test taker in encountering an item.

TESTS OF THE CUMULATIVE HIERARCHICAL STRUCTURE: KROPP AND STOKER

There have been numerous investigations of the cumulative hierarchical structure of the Taxonomy. One of the earliest, most ambitious, and certainly the most influential of these was undertaken by Kropp and Stoker in 1966.[16] Kropp and Stoker's efforts at test construction and data collection were so thorough that their study spawned another half dozen investigations reanalyzing their data with progressively more sophisticated techniques.

A great deal of the effort in Kropp and Stoker's study involved test construction and data collection.[17] Kropp and Stoker devised two science tests—"Atomic Structure" and "Glaciers"—and two social studies tests—"Lisbon Earthquake" and "Stages of Economic Growth." Each test consisted of a reading passage and 95 questions, divided among the six taxonomic levels as follows: 20 items each tapped Knowledge, Comprehension, Application, Analysis; 5 tapped the Synthesis level; and 10 tapped Evaluation. On every test, each set of items tapping a single taxonomic level was treated as a subtest. The tests were administered in ten Florida high schools to over one thousand students at each of four grade levels, 9 through 12. In addition, over one thousand of these students also took the Kit of Reference Tests (KIT) for Cognitive Factors, from which a general ability score could be derived.

Kropp and Stoker did not document exact levels of agreement among judges in assigning items to categories in the test development process. In an earlier paper, however, they reported the results of a classification study involving pilot versions of the tests.[18] For one of the pilot tests, there was perfect agreement among five judges for 56 percent of the items; for the other, there was perfect agreement among four judges for 31 percent of the items. They concluded optimistically that "interjudge agreement was found with respect to cognitive processes being sought in items,"[19] indicating that they were satisfied with perfect agreement on as few as a third of the items on a test. Additional light is shed on the tests from Kropp and Stoker's acknowledgment that construction of items for the Synthesis and Evaluation subtests proved most difficult.[20] Specifically, Kropp and Stoker surmised that there may have been a floor effect operating on these subtests. Kropp and Stoker did not mention a further problem with the data, namely the inherent uncertainty about the actual mental process used when the test takers answered the items.

Kropp and Stoker's voluminous report detailed the results of two investigations of the taxonomic structure. The first of these considered the mean performance of students on each of the six subtests. They assumed that decreasing mean performance on successive levels of the Taxonomy would support the claim of a cumulative hierarchy. Consistent with the findings from their pilot study,[21] Kropp and Stoker's findings generally supported the hypothesis of increasing difficulty. Specifically, the pattern of obtained means matched the predicted patterns for both social studies tests. The data from the science tests supported the hypothesis less strongly. For both science tests the Evaluation subtests were easier than the Synthesis tests, and for one of the science tests, Application proved easier than Comprehension.

In discussing the results of their mean performance analysis, however, Kropp and Stoker noted that the fundamental assumption behind analyses of mean performance is flawed. They cited Guttman, who contended in 1953 that item complexity and item difficulty are independent attributes.[22] Although this complexity/difficulty distinction violates intuition at some level, in his later review of attempts to validate the taxonomy Seddon also dismissed analyses of the relative difficulty of items at different taxonomic levels as irrelevant to the central validity question of increasing complexity. He noted that empirical studies have demonstrated that difficulty and complexity of examination subtests are not necessarily correlated.[23] As an example, one can easily imagine that the Knowledge-level task of reciting Dante's *Inferno* is far more difficult than an Analysis-level analogy question, such as appears on graduate school admissions tests. This evidence notwithstanding, some researchers, as is discussed below, persist in analyses of the relative difficulty of taxonomic subtests in attempting to validate the hierarchy. It should be remembered that the Taxonomy's authors themselves expected that difficulty would be related to taxonomic level.

The second of Kropp and Stoker's investigations was a simplex analysis. The cumulative hierarchy of the Taxonomy corresponds to what Guttman described mathematically in 1953 as a simplex structure. A simplex is made up of "a set of variables that differ only in terms of the degree of their complexity rather than in content."[24] Guttman portrayed the simplex graphically as a series of concentric circles, where the smallest and innermost circle represented the least complex class of behaviors (Knowledge in the Taxonomy) and the largest and outermost circle represented the most complex (Evaluation in the Taxonomy).

In Kropp and Stoker's analysis, correlation matrices of coefficients between subtests were examined to see whether they met the mathematical properties of a simplex. Of the sixteen correlation matrices examined (four tests at each of the four grade levels), those for only one test, "Lisbon Earthquake," conformed exactly to the hypothesized order of complexity. On the "Atomic Structure" test, only one discrepancy existed between the hypothesized and obtained correlations: Synthesis and Evaluation were placed between Knowledge and Comprehension. On the "Glaciers" test, Synthesis was located between Knowledge and Comprehension. This same discrepancy appeared on the "Stages of Economic Growth" test at one grade level; at another grade level on this same test Synthesis and Evaluation were reversed. Kropp and Stoker concluded with cautious optimism: "The hypothesis of simplicial structure appears not to be supported or rejected by the results. There is no statistical test of significance with which to reach a summary judgment. . . . The evidence is regarded in the main as more confirming than disconfirming of the hypothesis."[25]

REANALYSES OF KROPP AND STOKER DATA

Smith took a second look at the Kropp and Stoker data using hierarchical syndrome analysis.[26] In hierarchical syndrome analysis, progressive stages of analysis identify pairs of elements whose correlation coefficients indicate common characteristics. The analysis results in the classification of elements into a hierarchical system based on the degree of association between these elements.[27] After analyzing the sixteen correlation matrices, Smith concluded that the results in general supported the cumulative hierarchy of the Taxonomy. In particular, the three categories Comprehension, Application, and Analysis were consistently ordered as predicted, though "the 'Knowledge' and 'Evaluation' categories were generally found to behave in a manner inconsistent with the theoretical formulation."[28] Knowledge, in fact, did not appear from any of the matrices to be the first level of the hierarchy.

Seddon argued against the use of hierarchical syndrome analysis in investigating the hierarchical structure.[29] He noted that the results of hierarchical syndrome analysis can be inconsistent with those of simplex analysis even when applied to the same data. He asserted that since the imputed structure of the Taxonomy is unambiguously a simplex, any analysis that yielded results different from simplex analysis was not a defensible means of testing the cumulative hierarchy.

Madaus, Woods, and Nuttall reanalyzed the Kropp and Stoker data using a path analysis.[30] They posited that if the levels of the Taxonomy truly formed a cumulative hierarchy, then a path analysis fitted to the data would reveal significant direct relationships between adjacent levels of the Taxonomy and no significant indirect relationships between nonadjacent levels. They inferred the strength of the relationships from squared semipartial correlation coefficients. Analyses were conducted on data from a subsample of Kropp and Stoker's original subjects, specifically, 1,128 high school students who took the four subject area tests as well as the KIT tests.

The first analyses in the study were conducted on the four subject area tests only and resulted in eight strong indirect links between nonadjacent levels of the Taxonomy, and in very weak direct links between Analysis and Synthesis and between Synthesis and Evaluation. Clearly, these results did not support the cumulative hierarchy of the model. When a general ability factor from the KIT scores was introduced into the analysis, all but one of the indirect links disappeared from the path model. Addition of the general ability factor also removed the significant direct relationships between Analysis and Synthesis and between Synthesis and Evaluation. These findings led Madaus and his associates to concur with Ebel that test items at the most complex levels of the Taxonomy tap general ability more than specific content.[31] Further, they proposed that the Taxonomy was best represented by a Y-shaped structure, in which the stem of the Y originates at Knowledge and goes to Comprehension, one branch of the Y goes from Comprehension to Application to Synthesis, and the other branch goes from Comprehension to Analysis.

O'Hara, Snowman, and Miller also analyzed Kropp and Stoker data using a path analysis,[32] but they used both squared semipartial correlations to replicate the Madaus et al. analysis and standardized partial regression coefficients, which they considered more methodologically defensible. They reported that their use of the standardized regression coefficients resulted in an interpretation which reduced the importance of general ability relative to the Madaus et al. model. They also noted potentially important variation in grade-level patterns— variation that is masked when results are collapsed across grades. They concluded that their analyses generally supported a hierarchical structure, but found Evaluation to follow Comprehension rather than Synthesis.

In yet another study using Kropp and Stoker data, Miller, Snowman, and O'Hara employed multiple methods to investigate the structure of the Taxonomy. They used a subset of the data consisting of scores on the "Atomic Structure" test and general intelligence (KIT) scores of students from only one grade level, so as to avoid the potential problems associated with aggregating the data across grade levels. Miller and his associates employed path analysis, commonality analysis, factor analysis, and stepwise regression, and found that "all the techniques rejected a simple hierarchical interpretation."[33]

In their path analysis, path coefficients were inferred from standardized regression coefficients, rather than semipartial correlations as Madaus et al. had used. The path analysis resulted in large path coefficients between pairs of nonadjacent variables, and hence did not support a simple hierarchical taxonomic structure, though it suggested a Y-shaped structure similar to that of Madaus et al., where the stem began at general ability, through Knowledge and Comprehension, and ended at Application. At Application, one branch extended to Analysis, and the other to Synthesis and Evaluation. The commonality analysis also revealed patterns inconsistent with the hypothesized hierarchy, in particular with the Analysis, Synthesis, and Evaluation levels. The regression analysis failed to support the Madaus et al. model in which general ability preceded Knowledge. Finally, the factor analysis, which was undertaken on the assumption that hierarchically arranged subtests would result in a single factor and high communality estimates, suggested that, instead, two common factors reproduced the correlation matrix.

Hill and McGaw revisited the Kropp and Stoker data to engage in "rigorous testing of the theory expressed by the taxonomy"[34] through the preliminary use of the LISREL approach, a technique which integrates simplex analysis, causal analysis, and factor analysis. They fitted a six-factor quasi-simplex model to the data, and found it failed to explain the data. In particular, Knowledge did not appear to fit into the hierarchy. The model was thus altered by eliminating Knowledge in an analysis of the Atomic Structure test. The five-factor model seemed appropriate, and was applied to all four subject-area tests aggregated across grades as well as to grade-level data. In all cases, Hill and McGaw found their model, beginning at Comprehension and ending at Evaluation, to have "parsimony, theoretical validity, and good fit to the observed data."[35] The exclusion of Knowledge from the hierarchy was justified theoretically by the clear distinction Bloom et al. made between Knowledge and the higher classes, which involved skills and abilities.

Hill replicated the work of Hill and McGaw in a later and more extensive work. He reported on entering general ability as a variable into the model in a LISREL analysis, but found that it did not fit the data. He reached the same conclusions as had the preliminary LISREL analysis, namely, of a five-factor model from Comprehension to

Evaluation. He explained the conflicting findings of previous reanalyses of Kropp and Stoker data as

in part a reflection of the fact that, until recently, an entirely satisfactory method for the analysis of taxonomic data has not existed. The LISREL method represents a significant advance over methods used by previous investigators in that it incorporates these methods into a single analysis framework explicitly oriented towards theory-testing.[36]

Hill certainly evidenced the greatest satisfaction in his results among the many investigators who used Kropp and Stoker's data. Those data, despite their limitations as to reliability of classification and quality of the Synthesis and Evaluation subtests, remain, as far as we know, the most carefully and comprehensively collected with which to test the cumulative hierarchy assumption. These limitations, however, may have affected findings in some unknown way.

OTHER INVESTIGATIONS

As will be evident in reading the summaries below of studies that did not rely on Kropp and Stoker information, data collection problems are a leitmotif of most investigations of the hierarchy. Lipscomb did not use Kropp and Stoker's data; he did, however, use their items in a classification study.[37] Two different groups of raters each classified the same set of items using a different scheme. One used the Taxonomy; the other used a 6-point semantic differential scale, with the endpoints labeled "simple" and "complex." Lipscomb compared the two groups on the proportion of correct classifications, where the original categorical classifications of the Kropp and Stoker items were taken as correct. Using chi-square tests he found no significant difference in accuracy of ratings between the two classification systems. Lipscomb's claim that the similarity between the two classification schemes "lends informal support to a hierarchical structure"[38] is unsupported because he neglects to provide any information either about the distribution of responses across the six categories or about the reliability of the judgments.

Poole undertook two studies of the Taxonomy, the second of which was essentially a replication of the first. Poole's analysis relied on item characteristic curves from an eighth grade social studies test; he took the mean of those curves, conventionally considered as the item difficulty, as equivalent to the concept of "item complexity." In what is essentially yet another analysis of item difficulties by taxonomic level, he compared the item "complexity" of subtests defined by taxonomic level. In support of the taxonomic structure, he found in 1971 a "partial hierarchy" for Knowledge and Comprehension, in that the median "item complexity" value for Comprehension exceeded that of Knowledge. The order of the other levels was not supported. In the 1972 replication his data "suggested that if a hierarchy exists, it may be of a form opposite to that proposed by the Taxonomy."[39] Poole's data, however, appears by his own admission to be tainted by "item unrepresentativeness, item disproportionality, and item meagerness."[40] Specifically, Poole's 1971 test consisted of 32 items; 30 of these were judged by raters to tap the Knowledge and Comprehension levels. The 44-item 1972 test had only one item judged to be above the Comprehension level.

Stedman looked at the cumulative hierarchy of the Taxonomy by analyzing mean performance on 7-item subtests tapping the first four taxonomic levels.[41] He found no significant differences between scores on the Knowledge and Comprehension subtests, or between the Application and Analysis tests. Mean performance on Comprehension and Application subtests however, were found to differ significantly.

Fairbrother also considered mean performance vis-à-vis taxonomic level and found that physics questions at higher levels of the Taxonomy were more frequently missed than were questions at lower levels. He noted, however, as had Guttman much earlier, that at a conceptual level difficulty was not necessarily related to taxonomic task.[42]

Blumberg, Alschuler, and Rezmovic undertook another study relying on average performance as an indicator of complexity.[43] They used pairs of items judged subjectively to be of the same item difficulty, but deemed to cover the same content at different taxonomic levels. They expected support for the Taxonomy to be reflected by different obtained mean performance for the items making up the pairs. Instead, they found no significant differences in student performance on items at different taxonomic levels, where significance was tested by a z-test for the significance of difference between proportions.

Kunen, Cohen, and Solman employed a levels-of-processing analysis in investigating taxonomic structure. Their analysis started from the assumption that the amount of learning, operationalized as test scores, should increase as students engage in thinking at successively higher taxonomic levels, because memory is conceived of "as a by-product of encoding operations."[44] Their procedure was to give four groups of students the same stimulus material to read, consisting of thirty statements of basic principles from the sciences and social sciences. The subjects in each group were also given a different task to perform using the principles; tasks were written at the Knowledge, Application, Synthesis, and Evaluation levels. After subjects completed the tasks, they were unexpectedly presented with a recall test of the material. Kunen and his colleagues found, as they had hypothesized, that recall performance generally increased with the level of the taxonomic follow-up task, although subjects in the group performing Synthesis tasks outperformed those doing Evaluation.

Ekstrand examined data from over 1300 fifth-grade students from the National Longitudinal Study of Mathematical Abilities (NLSMA).[45] The mathematics tests from the NLSMA were constructed explicitly to tap the Taxonomy's first four levels. Ekstrand employed path analysis, factor analysis, and a LISREL analysis to verify the presumed taxonomic structure. Interpretation of the path analysis was muddied by very large error terms, but Ekstrand concluded that Bloom's taxonomical structure was nonetheless "weakly supported." The results of her factor analysis were judged to be inconclusive. The LISREL analysis, however, supported Bloom's taxonomic structure; specifically, the analysis revealed that a four-level hierarchical model fitted the data better than did a competing four-level nonhierarchical model. The author also noted parenthetically that replications of the LISREL analysis on three other grade-level NLSMA data sets (grades 8, 11, and 12) also supported the hierarchical structure.

Conclusion

In his 1978 review of empirical investigations of Bloom's Taxonomy, Seddon concluded:

As a final assessment of the validity of the claims concerning the psychological properties of the taxonomy, it is perhaps fairest to say that the picture is uncertain. No one has been able to demonstrate that these properties do not exist. Conversely, no one has been able to demonstrate that they do.[46]

The research record almost fifteen years later is not much more conclusive. The studies published since Seddon's review perhaps lean more toward support of the cumulative hierarchy than did the studies he considered. Certainly the use of more sophisticated statistical techniques, such as the LISREL analysis employed by Hill and by

Ekstrand, paint a portrait of the Taxonomy's structure not too far removed from the one Bloom et al. sketched; Hill's, of course, eliminated Knowledge from the hierarchy and Ekstrand's data set did not even include items at the Synthesis and Evaluation levels. Neither study quibbled with the order of the Comprehension, Application, and Analysis categories. Had Ekstrand included Synthesis and Evaluation items, however, the conclusions would still have to be tentative, because of the inevitable imprecision involved in knowing what tactics test takers employ in answering questions.

One could argue for the construction of purer test items (that is, items which could be reliably classified and about which something could be said of the test takers' actual problem-solving strategies) and for the use of ever fancier techniques with which to test the cumulative hierarchy. Instead, we suggest that the issue be allowed to simmer indefinitely on the back burner. As Gerard reminds us, "Making categories is man's great intellectual strength and weakness: strength, since only by dividing the world into categories can he reason with it; weakness, since he then takes the categories seriously."[47]

Bloom and his colleagues provided educators, and especially test constructors, with a schema that helped them make sense of a part of their world. As DeLandsheere summarized, "The enormous influences exercised by their imperfect tool proves that it answered a deep and urgently felt need."[48] Of course, it is also clear that the categories have been taken too seriously, as "eternal verities instead of . . . hypothetical constructs."[49] However, debunking or upholding the Taxonomy through empirical evidence is unlikely to change its status as truth in some educators' eyes or to alter its usefulness for others. Perhaps perseverating on the empirical truth also evidences an overly serious approach to Bloom's categories. The more interesting investigation to pursue would be the discovery of the kind of "evidence," intuitive or otherwise, that leads practitioners to use the Taxonomy.

NOTES

1. Benjamin S. Bloom et al., *Taxonomy of Educational Objectives: The Classification of Educational Goals. Handbook I: Cognitive Domain* (New York: David McKay, 1956). Unless otherwise noted, the page numbers given for quoted passages in the following pages are for this volume by Bloom et al.

2. For example, see Joseph Dunne, "Teaching and the Limits of Technique: An Analysis of the Behavioral Objectives Model," *Irish Journal of Education* 22, no. 2 (1988): 66-90; Francis Schrag, "Are There Levels of Thinking?" *Teachers College Record* 90, no. 4 (1989): 529-533.

3. Peter W. Hill and Barry McGaw, "Testing the Simplex Assumption Underlying Bloom's Taxonomy," *American Educational Research Journal* 18 (1981): 93-101; Gilbert Ryle, *The Concept of Mind* (London: Hutchinson, 1949).

4. J. R. Calder, "In the Cells of Bloom's Taxonomy," *Journal of Curriculum Studies* 15, no. 3 (1983): 291.

5. Julian C. Stanley and Dale Bolton, "A Review of 'Bloom's Taxonomy of Educational Objectives' and J. R. Gerberich's 'Specimen Objective Tests Items: A Guide to Achievement Test Construction'," *Educational and Psychological Measurement* 17, no. 4 (1957): 631-634; Richard L. Poole, "Characteristics of the Taxonomy of Educational Objectives, Cognitive Domain: A Replication," *Psychology in the Schools* 9, no. 1 (1972): 83-88; R. W. Fairbrother, "The Reliability of Teachers' Judgments of the Abilities Being Tested by Multiple-Choice Items," *Educational Research* 17, no. 3 (1975): 202-210.

6. Russell P. Kropp and Howard W. Stoker, *The Construction and Validation of Tests of the Cognitive Processes as Described in the Taxonomy of Educational Objectives* (Tallahassee, FL: Florida State University, Institute of Human Learning and Department of Educational Research and Testing, 1966), ERIC ED 010 044; Takeshi O'Hara, Jack Snowman, and William G. Miller, "Establishing a Causal Model for Bloom's Taxonomy through Path Analysis" (Paper presented at the Annual Meeting of the American Educational Research Association, Toronto, 1978), ERIC ED 166 202; Hill and McGaw, "Testing the Simplex Assumption Underlying Bloom's Taxonomy."

7. George M. Seddon, "The Properties of Bloom's Taxonomy of Educational Objectives for the Cognitive Domain," *Review of Educational Research* 48, no. 2 (1978): 303-323.

8. Bloom et al., *Taxonomy of Educational Objectives*, p. 17.

9. Fairbrother, "The Reliability of Teachers' Judgments of the Abilities Being Tested by Multiple-Choice Items," p. 205.

10. Robert Wood, "Multiple-Choice: A State of the Art Report," *Evaluation in Education* 1 (1977): 205.

11. John Macnamara and George F. Madaus, "The Quality of the Irish Leaving Certificate Examination," *Irish Journal of Education* 4, no. 1 (1970): 5-18.

12. As cited by Viviane DeLandsheere, "On Defining Educational Objectives," in *Evaluation in Education: International Progress* (Elmsford, NY: Pergamon Press, 1977), p. 106.

13. For example, Wood, "Multiple-Choice: A State of the Art Report."

14. Ibid., p. 205.

15. Bloom et al., *Taxonomy of Educational Objectives*, p. 51.

16. Kropp and Stoker, *The Construction and Validation of Tests of the Cognitive Processes*.

17. Russell P. Kropp, Howard W. Stoker, and W. Louis Bashaw, "The Validation of the Taxonomy of Educational Objectives," *Journal of Experimental Education* 34, no. 3 (1966): 69-76; Howard W. Stoker and Russell P. Kropp, "Measurement of Cognitive Processes," *Journal of Educational Measurement* 1, no. 1 (1964): 39-42.

18. Stoker and Kropp, "Measurement of Cognitive Processes."

19. Ibid., p. 42.

20. Kropp and Stoker, *The Construction and Validation of Tests of the Cognitive Processes*.

21. Stoker and Kropp, "Measurement of Cognitive Processes."

22. Louis Guttman, "Image Theory for the Structure of Quantitative Variables," *Psychometrics* 18, no. 4 (1953): 277-296.

23. See, for example, William R. Crawford, "Item Difficulty as Related to the Complexity of Intellectual Processes," *Journal of Educational Measurement* 5 (1968): 103-107.

24. Seddon, "The Properties of Bloom's Taxonomy of Educational Objectives for the Cognitive Domain," p. 307.

25. Kropp and Stoker, *The Construction and Validation of Tests of the Cognitive Processes*, p. 84.

26. Richard B. Smith, "An Empirical Examination of the Assumptions Underlying the 'Taxonomy of Educational Objectives for the Cognitive Domain'," *Journal of Educational Measurement* 5, no. 1 (1968): 125-127; idem, "An Empirical Investigation of Complexity and Process in Multiple-Choice Items," *Journal of Educational Measurement* 7 (1970): 33-41.

27. See Louis L. McQuitty, "Hierarchical Syndrome Analysis," *Educational and Psychological Measurement* 20 (1960): 293-304.

28. Smith, "An Empirical Examination of the Assumptions Underlying the 'Taxonomy of Educational Objectives for the Cognitive Domain'," p. 127.

29. Seddon, "The Properties of Bloom's Taxonomy of Educational Objectives for the Cognitive Domain."

30. George F. Madaus, Elinor M. Woods, and Ronald L. Nuttall, "A Causal Model Analysis of Bloom's Taxonomy," *American Educational Research Journal* 10, no. 4 (1973): 253-262.

31. Robert L. Ebel, "Some Measurement Problems in a National Assessment" (Paper presented at the Annual Meeting of the American Educational Research Association, Chicago, 1966).

32. O'Hara, Snowman, and Miller, "Establishing a Causal Model for Bloom's Taxonomy through Path Analysis."

33. William G. Miller, Jack Snowman, and Takeshi O'Hara, "Application of Alternative Statistical Techniques to Examine the Hierarchical Ordering in Bloom's Taxonomy," *American Educational Research Journal* 16, no. 3 (1979): 247.

34. Hill and McGaw, "Testing the Simplex Assumption Underlying Bloom's Taxonomy," p. 94.

35. Ibid., p. 97.

36. Peter W. Hill, "Testing Hierarchy in Educational Taxonomies: A Theoretical and Empirical Investigation," *Evaluation in Education* 8 (1984): 179-278.

37. John W. Lipscomb, "Is Bloom's Taxonomy Better than Intuitive Judgment for Classifying Test Questions?" *Education* 106, no. 1 (1985): 102-107.

38. Ibid., p. 106.

39. Richard L. Poole, "Characteristics of the Taxonomy of Educational Objectives: A Replication," p. 88.

40. Richard L. Poole, "Characteristics of the Taxonomy of Educational Objectives: Cognitive Domain," *Psychology in the Schools* 8 (1971): 384.

41. Carlton H. Stedman, "An Analysis of the Assumptions Underlying the Taxonomy of Educational Objectives: Cognitive Domain," *Journal of Research in Science Teaching* 10, no. 3 (1973): 235-241.

42. Fairbrother, "The Reliability of Teachers' Judgments of the Abilities Being Tested by Multiple-Choice Items."

43. Phyllis Blumberg, Marjorie D. Alschuler, and Victor Rezmovic, "Should Taxonomic Levels Be Considered in Developing Examinations?" *Educational and Psychological Measurement* 42 (1982): 1-7.

44. Seth Kunen, Ronald Cohen, and Robert Solman, "A Levels-of-Processing Analysis of Bloom's Taxonomy," *Journal of Educational Psychology* 73, no. 2 (1981): 208.

45. Judith M. Ekstrand, "Methods of Validating Learning Hierarchies with Applications to Mathematics Learning" (Paper presented at the Annual Meeting of the American Educational Research Association, New York City, 1982), ERIC ED 216 896.

46. Seddon, "The Properties of Bloom's Taxonomy of Educational Objectives for the Cognitive Domain," p. 321.

47. Ralph W. Gerard, "Hierarchy, Entitation, and Levels," in *Hierarchical Structures*, edited by Lancelot L. Whyte, Albert G. Wilson, and Donna Wilson (New York: American Elsevier, 1969), p. 216.

48. DeLandsheere, "On Defining Educational Objectives," p. 105.

49. Wood, "Multiple-Choice: A State of the Art Report," p. 204.

CHAPTER VI

The Impact of the Taxonomy on
Testing and Evaluation

PETER W. AIRASIAN

It was by no accident that the Taxonomy was dedicated to Ralph Tyler. His research, writing, and collegial interactions afforded the basic intellectual structure from which its authors proceeded. His work provided justification for its development and helped to fashion the educational context which made it relevant.[1] Thus, in considering the impact of the Taxonomy on testing and evaluation, it is both informative and necessary to understand Tyler's influence.

In fact, Tyler had four main influences on the development of the Taxonomy and its subsequent uses in testing and evaluation. First, he advocated and helped to persuade the educational world that a student's expected behavior after instruction was a crucial aspect of any statement of educational outcomes or objectives. Second, he explicitly linked the development of educational objectives to the process of evaluating instruction and learning. Third, he provided rich examples and applications of how evaluation could be carried out to determine student learning on a broad range of desired educational outcomes. Finally, he integrated evaluation into a general model of curriculum development and instructional planning. Each of these contributions presaged the development of the Taxonomy and the contexts within which it would be used.

Tyler and the Taxonomy

The use of the term "objective" did not originate with Tyler, nor did the idea of building achievement tests to measure students' learning of desired objectives.[2] Tyler contributed the idea that objectives should incorporate both a content referent and a clear

Peter Airasian is Professor of Education at Boston College and Chair of the program there in Research, Measurement, and Evaluation. Ann Jones and Stephen Court, graduate students at Boston College, contributed to the preparation of this chapter.

description of the behaviors students were expected to attain as a result of instruction on that content. Previously the term "objective" meant "a content topic." Achievement tests were constructed by selecting a sample of the content topics contained in a textbook or a course syllabus. Test items, usually written to tap factual learning, were used to measure students' acquisition of content. This approach to achievement testing derived from studies that showed high correlations between measurement of information in a content field and the ability to use that information in non-rote ways.[3] From these studies came the assumption that test items requiring recall of facts were valid surrogates for measuring more complex student behaviors such as reasoning with content or applying content in various ways.

Tyler reported on studies he conducted at Ohio State University that showed fairly low correlations between scores on memory tests and scores on tests of reasoning and application of principles.[4] On the basis of these studies he argued that there were many levels and distinct kinds of behavior a student could be expected to manifest for any given content topic. These behaviors ranged from rote memory to considerably more complex mental operations. He further argued that if teachers desired their students to master non-rote behaviors, then it was necessary for them to measure these behaviors specifically and separately from the measurement of information, because one could not rely upon tests of information to provide a valid indication of a student's ability to apply, analyze, or interpret. A logical consequence of this position is that a prerequisite to meaningful instructional planning and measurement is the need to identify and articulate the content and *all* the behaviors students were expected to perform with that content. Thus, achievement testing needed to be based upon more than a list of content topics; it also needed to incorporate the specific ways the students were to demonstrate their learning of that content. Three of Tyler's books, *Research Methods and Teachers' Problems: A Manual for Systematic Study of Classroom Procedures, Constructing Achievement Tests*, and *Basic Principles of Curriculum and Instruction* laid out procedures for evaluating students' achievement.[5]

By 1950, the concept of educational objectives as espoused by Tyler was well accepted in the testing and measurement community. But Tyler had left gaps in his legacy. In his 1950 book, *How to Make Achievement Tests*, Robert Travers prophetically lamented the omission of a means for improving the definition and articulation of educational goals:

The basic difficulty in defining educational goals is due to the fact that psychologists have not yet developed a classification of human behavior which is useful for this purpose. A comprehensive taxonomy of human behavior which had some numerical value assigned to each category of behavior would simplify the educator's task. It would also provide teachers with a common language for discussing educational goals and ensure that those who used the same terms referred to the same concepts.[6]

The Taxonomy and Educational Objectives

In assessing the impact of the Taxonomy on testing and evaluation, it is critical to recognize that the concept of an educational objective held by Tyler and the authors of the Taxonomy does not have the same meaning as it does for present-day curriculum builders and evaluators. Tyler, the Taxonomy's authors, and present-day curriculum builders and evaluators all share the understanding that educational objectives are statements of instructional intent that combine a content topic and the behavior a student is expected to perform with that topic. The main difference between objectives in the Tyler/Taxonomy sense and in the present-day sense is in their specificity: educational objectives as conceived by Tyler and presented in the Taxonomy are consciously and conspicuously more general. As Tyler remarked, "I tend to view objectives as general modes of reaction to be developed rather than highly specific habits to be acquired," and "Other things being equal, more general objectives are desirable rather than less general objectives."[7]

Krathwohl, one of the editors of the Taxonomy, distinguished among three levels of educational objectives: global objectives, behavioral objectives, and instructional guidance objectives.[8] Global objectives are what are commonly called "goals," that is, broad statements of outcomes that typically must be developed over many years of education and many educational experiences. An example of a global objective is "The student will develop the fundamental skills of reading and writing." More detailed analysis of this global objective would produce a set of behavioral objectives such as "The student can name and recognize the letters of the alphabet," "The student can write a coherent letter or paragraph," and "The student reads stories and books with understanding." Finally, for purposes of instruction, each of these behavioral objectives would need to be broken down further into very specific instructional guidance objectives such as "The student can identify four common punctuation marks," "The student can distinguish the letter O from the letter Q," and "The student can start each sentence with a capital letter." There can be literally hundreds of such instructional guidance objectives associated with a global objective.

Objectives as exemplified in the Taxonomy fit into the middle or behavioral objective level. The Taxonomy authors left the third level—instructional guidance objectives—for the classroom teacher to identify, preferring instead to focus on more generally stated objectives.

It is this focus which represents the major strength of the Taxonomy and, over time, its most lasting impact. The Taxonomy explicitly recognizes and gives names to classes of cognitive behaviors that extend well beyond rote memory. The Taxonomy exemplifies concern for transfer of learning, application as well as acquisition of information, and general modes of behavior which cannot be reduced to stimulus-response bonds. These emphases highlight the breadth and richness of potential learning outcomes. Whether one talks in terms of knowledge, comprehension, application, analysis, synthesis, and evaluation or in the simpler terminology of "lower" and "higher" level cognitive processes, the Taxonomy has been and continues to be at the root of these behavioral distinctions.

The Impact of the Taxonomy on Testing and Evaluation, 1956-1970

The Taxonomy was a potentially useful tool for helping practitioners state objectives, build curricula, and construct testing instruments and evaluation procedures. However, like all tools, its use was dependent upon the need for the services it could provide. The fact that the impact of any tool is mediated by prevailing contextual factors often makes it difficult to identify a direct, causal link between the tool and its influence on practice. It is, therefore, more reasonable to identify trends in testing and evaluation and to indicate how the Taxonomy might have influenced or enhanced them.

In the middle 1950s the focus in testing and evaluation was upon the two traditional approaches to gathering information: standardized norm-referenced tests and teacher-made classroom tests. Very few statewide testing or curriculum evaluation activities were occurring. While virtually all testing and measurement books of the period advocated the use of objectives in planning and evaluating instruction, objectives were not widely used at any level of schooling. Instruction focused on content topics; the distinction between higher- and lower-level student behaviors was not a matter of concern. The publication of the *Handbook* did not substantially alter the situation. Even the launch of Sputnik in 1957 and the resulting finger pointing at the educational establishment did not immediately provoke change.

Two movements that emerged in the 1960s—programmed instruction and federally mandated evaluations of compensatory education programs—did finally raise educational consciousness about the uses of behaviorally stated objectives. The rise of these movements, in turn, was predicated upon wider societal trends.[9] First, there was a growing criticism of standardized tests of achievement and ability. Critics like Hoffman, Holt, and Silberman questioned the relevancy of the tasks that were tested, the need to sort people on the basis of scores on norm-referenced tests, and the extent to which a multiple-choice item format captured the important outcomes of education.[10] For the most part, these critics concentrated their attacks on standardized testing, not on assessment or testing in general. Holt, for example, recognized the need for tests that permitted people to demonstrate their ability to meet professional standards in an occupation or profession (e.g., surgeon, teacher, architect) and tests that allowed people to check their progress toward mastery of a skill or topic. Neither of these comparatively benign testing purposes was well served by standardized, norm-referenced tests.

Second, there was a growing belief that all or at least most students could be helped to achieve competence in school subject areas. Educators and the public began to accept the notion that children's learning problems were not the result of native limitations, but instead of environmental factors that could be overcome with suitable instructional strategies.[11] Once the notion that most students could learn was accepted, the emphasis in testing shifted away from sorting individuals and toward finding ways to enhance and certify student learning. The critique of standardized tests and the growing belief in the power of environmental factors on learning led to new instructional approaches and educational programs which relied heavily upon educational objectives.

PROGRAMMED INSTRUCTION

The task of popularizing a technique for stating objectives within the programmed instruction framework fell to Robert Mager. His book, *Preparing Instructional Objectives*, was aimed at those interested in preparing materials for "auto-instructional presentation" (i.e., programmed instruction).[12] The book emphasized terminology appropriate to this purpose (e.g., "criterion performance," and "terminal behavior"). Furthermore, the book itself was written in the form of a programmed text. It enjoyed huge sales, far exceeding those of the *Handbook*.[13]

There is a natural affinity between the programmer and tester, since both find it difficult to work effectively if desired student behaviors are not clearly described. One might think, given this affinity, that the Taxonomy would have been an influential tool in the development of programmed instruction sequences. In one sense it was. Dale noted the value of the Taxonomy to programming, stating that "developments in educational testing and measurement are already moving toward a formulation of tests based on taxonomic analysis."[14] He meant that the Taxonomy's hierarchy of cognitive behaviors would be useful for identifying the cognitive levels in a programmed sequence and for developing appropriate testing procedures.

However, the Taxonomy was less useful in formulating programmed instruction objectives and in planning the sequence and conditions to implement these objectives. The lack of a clearly articulated relationship between stating and implementing objectives was a drawback of the Taxonomy. In response, Gagné postulated a different kind of taxonomy, one based upon conditions and strategies of learning.[15] Gagné identified eight types of learning: signal learning, stimulus-response learning, chaining, verbal association, multiple discrimination learning, concept learning, principle learning, and problem solving. He further described the conditions that produced these kinds of learning. By highlighting the conditions and prerequisite stages for various types of learning, Gagné provided programmers with a functional method for organizing and planning instructional sequences, whereas the Taxonomy did not.[16]

The programmed instruction movement contributed another important dimension to the relationship between educational objectives and testing and evaluation. In keeping with the view that all or at least most students could learn the objectives an instructional program set for them, authors of programmed instruction sequences faced the problem of measuring student learning. The more specific their objectives and the more successful pupils were in attaining them, the less useful were norm-referenced methods of testing and evaluation which sought to determine a student's relative standing among his or her peers.

Indeed, in the early 1960s, Glaser had raised questions about the suitability of relative, norm-referenced testing methods for judging the success of programmed instruction, since its aim was to help all students attain mastery of the program's objectives.[17] He proposed a "new" form of measurement which was criterion-referenced. A student's performance was not compared (or referenced) to the performance of other students; rather, it was compared to descriptions of what the student could and could not do with respect to a well-defined domain of behavior.

Not only did criterion-referenced measurement fit nicely with prevailing social views about equity and students' learning; it also established educational objectives as the criterion against which learning would be judged. This relationship prompted many new instructional approaches and uses for tests and evaluation. Criterion-referenced measurement allowed students to be rewarded on the basis of their attainment relative to the objectives of instruction, not their standing relative to their peers. It made the objectives the center of attention in planning and testing. Within the context of programmed instruction, it also permitted specific identification of a student's areas of nonmastery; that is, it provided formative evaluation. In sum, the programmed instruction movement had three main impacts: the popularization of behavioral objectives, the development of a practical, easy-to-follow guide to stating objectives, and the introduction of criterion-referenced measurement.

EVALUATIONS OF FEDERALLY MANDATED PROGRAMS

The early 1960s saw increasing federal attention directed toward the social and educational plight of the poor and the disadvantaged in American society.[18] Spurred by the decision of the U.S. Supreme Court in *Brown v. Board of Education of Topeka*, the growing civil rights movement, and consciousness raising books such as Michael Harrington's *The Other America*,[19] President Lyndon Johnson and the Congress declared a war on poverty. This war was manifested in a huge legislative program designed to "break the cycle of poverty." Educational reform was an important and prominent cornerstone of this program.

Although the Head Start Program for preschool enrichment activities was funded as part of the antipoverty program in 1964, the great educational breakthrough occurred in 1965 in the form of the Elementary and Secondary Education Act (ESEA). Title I of the act allocated funds to provide additional educational services to low-achieving students in schools with large concentrations of children in poverty. For the first time in history, substantial amounts of federal aid, more than a billion dollars a year at its inception, were funnelled into local school districts to meet the educational needs of disadvantaged children.

During debate on the ESEA, Senator Robert Kennedy became concerned that the Title I monies allocated to school districts would not be used for their intended remedial purpose. He argued for the insertion of a reporting requirement in the act which would make educators responsive to their constituencies and make educational achievement the main criterion in judging the success of local ESEA programs.[20]

The call for program accountability based upon educational achievement fit well with a new management orientation endorsed by the executive branch. Called the Planning, Programming, Budgeting System (PPBS) and initially utilized in the Pentagon, this management approach was predicated upon identifying the intended outcomes of a program and measuring the extent to which these outcomes had been achieved at the program's conclusion.

In its elemental form, PPBS was not altogether different from Tyler's model. For the federal government, however, it marked a distinct and abrupt change from prior accountability and oversight procedures, which had focused on fiscal appropriateness and legal correctness. The passage of ESEA, particularly the section of Title I relating to remediation and accountability, raised the prospect that thousands of local school districts would receive funds to develop and carry out educational programs for disadvantaged youth, with each program having to be evaluated in terms of students' achievement of the program's objectives.

Since most local educators had little experience in conducting such evaluations, the requirement to evaluate Title I programs and report the results to the federal government caused them concern. Fears of federal control of schools and the imposition of a national curriculum through the evaluation requirement were voiced in opposition to the requirement.[21] At the 1966 Annual Meeting of the American Educational Research Association, a group of its members suggested that the association's executive board go on record against the evaluation mandate because it was unrealistic and not practical given the state of the art.

In many ways they were correct. There were few available models on which to base evaluation studies. The notion of evaluating programs in terms of prespecified objectives was alien to most local practitioners and caught them unaware and unprepared. The nature of appropriate outcome measures was not clear. In the search for a viable model to guide program evaluation, Tyler's work came to be relied upon heavily, primarily because it was virtually the only available program evaluation model which provided a straightforward, easy-to-understand approach that linked objectives to evaluation.

Measurement, evaluation, and assessment textbooks from the 1960s to the present emphasize the distinction between lower- and higher-level objectives and test items. Furthermore, the Taxonomy is used as the exemplar through which teachers and evaluators are shown the possibilities of a wide range of objectives and items tapping varied pupil behaviors. Teachers are encouraged to examine the cognitive complexity of their intended outcomes and evaluation methods. Present-day emphasis on higher-order thinking skills and on alternatives to written responses in assessing performance produced a new wave of concern and a renewed use of the Taxonomy to classify objectives and assessment exercises.[22]

The Impact of the Taxonomy on Testing and Evaluation: the 1970s

By the start of the 1970s, the importance of clearly stated educational objectives, their relationship to appropriate achievement testing and evaluation, and the need to stress higher- and lower-order objectives in instruction were well established in the educational lore and, in many instances, in educational practice. In thinking about evaluating achievement, whether to judge the success of a program or to assess individual student learning, educational objectives were accepted as an indispensable consideration. The "ends-oriented," rational, simple-to-understand model presented by Tyler and the PPBS advocates was powerfully persuasive and widely accepted.[23]

At the same time, there were thoughtful critics of this approach and its heavy reliance upon behaviorally stated objectives.[24] In 1970, the National Council of Teachers of English at their annual convention passed a resolution rejecting behavioral objectives virtually *in toto*. Critics pointed out the frequent triviality of objectives stated in terms of student behavior, the restrictions such objectives placed on teachers' instruction and evaluation strategies, the behaviorist view of education implied in stating ahead of time how students were to be changed by instruction, the difficulty of stating many important student outcomes in behavioral terms, and the need to recognize that not all educational outcomes can be stated in advance nor expected to be uniform across a group of learners. While many of these objections were—and still are—valid, the voices of critics were drowned out by those advocating the benefits of objectives.

CURRICULUM EVALUATION

After 1970, curriculum evaluation expanded markedly. Through most of the 1960s, Tyler's model of curriculum development and evaluation was dominant.[25] Although Tyler combined behavioral objectives, curriculum planning, instruction, and evaluation into a logical and integrated system, it was essentially a closed one. That is, given a set of behavioral objectives, a teacher's instruction, learning experiences, and evaluation all flowed more or less directly from the objectives. One did not need to go outside the objectives-instruction-evaluation loop to implement Tyler's paradigm. There was no external review of the suitability of the objectives selected nor was there an emphasis on identifying or evaluating student outcomes that were not specified in the behavioral objectives. The paradigm put a great deal of responsibility on the individual teacher or school, without suggesting external checks and balances.

Stimulated by national curriculum projects in the sciences and by issues that arose in Title I evaluations, the late 1960s and early 1970s saw the production of a variety of new curriculum evaluation models.[26] Cronbach's seminal paper, "Course Improvement through Evaluation," urged the use of evaluation for course improvement and the need to broaden existing conceptions and applications of evaluation as a decision-making model.[27] Writing in 1967, Scriven outlined important distinctions in evaluation: roles versus goals, formative versus summative, intrinsic versus payoff. Subsequently, Scriven differentiated goal-directed from goal-free evaluation.[28]

Scriven's 1967 paper called for the evaluation of a program's objectives per se as a prerequisite to evaluation of a program's effects. Unlike Tyler, Scriven did not take as given the set of objectives stated for a program or curriculum. He argued that the objectives themselves should be evaluated to determine their appropriateness and goodness.

Other models, such as one proposed by Stufflebeam et al.—the CIPP (Context, Input, Process, Product) Model—emphasized evaluating to inform the various decisions needed in program planning, implementation, and evaluation.[29] These models extended the realm of curriculum evaluation well beyond that envisioned by Tyler and the authors of the Taxonomy. Program antecedents, transactions, inputs, and discrepancies became fair game for the evaluator and the array of data needed for evaluation and the number of relevant areas in which evaluation could inform decision making increased substantially. Yet the new models all relied, to some degree, upon educational objectives to help guide curriculum or program evaluation.[30] An interesting and rare retrospective on the heyday of model building for curriculum evaluation can be found in *Evaluation and Education*, the Ninetieth Yearbook, Part 2, of the National Society for the Study of Education.[31]

The curriculum evaluation movement had an impact on the use of objectives in testing and evaluation. Scriven's distinction between formative and summative evaluation (between evaluation while a process is underway and evaluation at the conclusion of a process) influenced the way objectives were stated, organized, and evaluated. Moreover, the idea that objectives themselves should be evaluated for their appropriateness made teachers look more critically at their objectives and the relationship of those objectives to their instructional intents and to their pupils' needs. In particular, as some of the model builders for curriculum evaluation suggested, objectives needed to be examined in terms of the levels of behavior they required of students, levels such as those outlined in the Taxonomy.[32]

STATEWIDE TESTING

An area of considerable growth in the 1970s was statewide assessment.[33] The advent of national evaluations such as those mandated by ESEA, the formation of the Exploratory Committee on the Assessment of Progress in Education (now the National Assessment of Educational Progress [NAEP]), and the publication of the Coleman report on *Equality of Educational Opportunity*,[34] were not lost on state governments. In the 1970s federal concern for measuring the performance of school children was mimicked at the state level. In 1960 there was one state-mandated assessment program in the United States; by 1985, there were thirty-two.[35]

The emphasis on evaluating pupil learning was a clear and sharp departure from previous assessment efforts, which had judged school quality in terms of indices such as per pupil expenditure, quality of the school plant, and teacher credentials. The new emphasis was on assessing pupil learning and was implemented under a variety of names: educational accountability, performance-based education, learner verification models, performance contracting, objectives-based education, and competency-based education. In spite of the differences in names, all these approaches were essentially variations on a common theme of assessing pupil mastery of statewide objectives by means of criterion-referenced measurement approaches.

The format of these assessments followed a fairly standard pattern. Legislatures would pass a bill, commonly referred to as an "accountability act," calling for an assessment of pupils' learning in the public schools of a state. The act would mandate the identification of appropriate educational objectives in given subject areas (usually "basic skills" subjects, but more recently "thinking" skills) and the construction of assessment instruments to measure pupils' attainment of the objectives.

The designers of these assessments relied on Glaser's criterion-referenced approach. As mentioned earlier in this chapter, Glaser had emphasized that criterion-referenced tests ought to provide information about how a student performed with respect to a well-defined domain of behavior. This level of information required that specifications for developing these tests be carefully and completely laid out in detail far exceeding that reflected in educational objectives.

The statewide assessments of the 1970s were not especially intrusive on the lives of school administrators, teachers, or pupils for a number of reasons.[36] First, their results were intended to monitor educational policy, not formulate or direct it. Second, statewide assessments generally were administered to samples of pupils and schools; it was not necessary to test every pupil or school in order to obtain useful statewide results. Third, there were no sanctions or threats that ensued from poor test performance, so the tests were not particularly threatening to pupils, teachers, or administrators. Fourth, rarely were decisions about individual teachers, pupils, or schools made on the basis of the assessment results.

In spite of the fact that statewide monitoring tests initially had few direct effects on schools and their inhabitants, they did have some indirect effects.[37] They forced legislators, educators, and the public in general to look beyond the bounds of their local school system in judging educational adequacy. They also conditioned policymakers to accept test scores as the primary indicator of educational success. Finally, when the results of the evaluations and assessments provided discouraging news about the status of American education and the literacy of its pupils and teachers, they set the stage for the next step in the evolution of testing and evaluation—competency or "high stakes" testing.

The Impact of the Taxonomy on Testing and Evaluation: 1980 to the Present

The trend towards routinization and standardization seen in the use of statewide assessments and in the continuing transformation of traditional textbooks into complete instructional packages continued into the 1980s, but with a new dimension to the relationship of objectives to testing and evaluation. That dimension was the association of "high stakes" with test performance.

In the late 1970s, new concern over the quality of American schools began to be expressed. There was a perception that standards and achievement in schools had declined and needed to be strengthened. The evidence that supported this perception was summarized by the National Commission on Excellence in Education in its report *A Nation at Risk*.[38] Scholastic Aptitude Test scores had declined yearly between 1963 and 1980. The National Assessment of Educational Progress indicated performance declines over time in most age levels and subject areas. On international achievement tests covering many subject areas, American pupils never ranked first or second, but ranked last seven times.

Standardized test performance was lower in the early 1980s than it was in the 1960s in spite of massive federal and state efforts to improve achievement. About one quarter of the courses taught in four-year public colleges were remedial ones. One quarter of recruits for the U.S. Navy could not read at a ninth grade level. This evidence conveyed a portrait of an educational system with falling standards and decreasing student achievement. The call was issued for "back to basics" and for more consequential forms of statewide testing to measure and certify pupils' and teachers' competence.[39]

Although many types of reform were initiated in response to the perceived need,[40] new state-mandated testing and accountability programs were the most influential and controversial. These programs became an important tool in the efforts of state governments to improve educational standards and to gain control over the educational process carried out in local school districts. The public acceptance of these new accountability approaches was very strong, due mainly to the symbolic function of testing and accountability in our society.[41]

The Florida Educational Accountability Act of 1976 was the first of the so-called "minimum competency testing programs." This act, implemented in the late 1970s, called for the definition and assessment of "functional literacy" skills in communication and mathematics for all eleventh graders in the state. A total of 24 functional literacy skills were identified: 11 communication skills (8 reading and 3 writing) and 13 mathematics skills. A 117-item test was constructed based upon objectives and corresponding domain specifications and a passing standard of 70 percent was set.[42] Students who failed to meet this standard over repeated trials were denied a high school diploma. The notion of associating high stakes (or consequential) decisions with test performance spread rapidly across the country in the late 1970s and early 1980s. In 1972 there was one state-level minimum competency testing program in existence; by 1985, there were thirty-four.

The state-mandated competency tests were different from traditional standardized educational tests and the statewide assessments of the 1970s in three key ways.[43] First, they were mandated for all schools and virtually all pupils within a state. Second, the mandate eliminated most of the local district or school discretion in test selection, administration, content coverage, scoring, and interpretation. Third, the tests had built-in sanctions associated with specific levels of performance. Each individual's test score was compared to a statewide standard of satisfactory performance and a pass/fail decision made about the individual.

The logic behind these testing programs was as follows. When an important consequence such as receiving a high school diploma or a teaching certificate is tied to test results, the test content will become incorporated into instruction. In current parlance, the tests will "drive" instruction.[44] Thus, high stakes testing programs sought to reverse the traditional relationship among classroom objectives, instruction, and evaluation. Since Tyler's earliest writings, evaluation of pupils' achievement had been viewed as an activity that flows and takes its direction from teachers' educational objectives and instruction. High stakes testing programs sought to establish a context in which instruction is essentially guided or directed by the measuring instrument and where *not* teaching to the test is a greater disservice to pupils than teaching to it.[45]

This orientation is far from the vision of the respective roles of objectives, instruction, and measurement as described by Tyler and the authors of the Taxonomy in the following ways. It is centralized at the state level, not school- or district-based. Objectives are not screened for local needs and appropriateness, but instead are common across a state. Achievement is measured almost exclusively by multiple-choice, paper-and-pencil tests, not the variety of procedures envisioned by the authors of the Taxonomy. Moreover, the onus for poor performance is placed solely on the test taker, not on other factors such as instruction or resources; sanctions are applied to test takers.

Most important for this discussion, the statewide mandated competency tests turn nearly a half century of curriculum and evaluation theory and practice on its head. Instead of testing and measurement being used in the service of educational objectives, curriculum, and instruction, the new tests put objectives, curriculum, and instruction in the service of measurement. One consequence of this approach is that educational objectives, regardless of the format or specificity with which they are stated, are less important than the actual test items used to assess them, because in the end it is the items that become the de facto educational objectives around which curriculum and instruction are developed. Testing has become both the new educational reform mechanism and the criterion used to judge the success of the reforms.[46] This is an unusual duality, and it marks a substantial transition from the concept of educational objectives as reflected in the Taxonomy and the concept as manifested in today's accountability-oriented educational culture.

The Future of Testing and Evaluation

In the early 1990s, the testing and evaluation landscape has changed again. Two issues related to policy on testing and evaluation bear discussing. The first is the recent effort to broaden testing from primary reliance on multiple-choice items to increased reliance on performance or authentic assessments. The second concerns the level (i.e., local, state, or national) at which the most influential testing and evaluation will be carried out in the future.

Performance assessments require students to demonstrate their knowledge in some way other than by selecting an answer from given options.[47] Dissatisfaction with the multiple-choice format and a desire to measure students' higher-level cognitive processes have prompted many states to move their assessment programs in the direction of performance exercises. Students are being asked to write, construct, explain, and demonstrate their achievement. Clearly, the potential for these "real" exercises to tap students' higher-level thinking is great, but their potential pitfalls and uncertainties are many, both in terms of implementation[48] and in terms of teachers' ability to teach higher-order thinking processes to all or most pupils.[49]

The content and behaviors tested in most performance assessments are similar to the general, transfer-oriented objectives advocated and modeled in the Taxonomy. Performance assessments, at their best, focus on general, non-rote intellectual processes and activities, and because of this emphasis have led to increased attention being focused on the Taxonomy.[50] We have, in a sense, come full circle. However, it is very important to recognize that if performance assessments become tied closely to high stakes decisions, they will quickly be subjected to pressures toward reductionism and corruption of their more general intents.

A second current issue in testing and evaluation relates to the level or levels from which future influential tests will be promulgated. The reforms of the 1970s and 1980s were primarily top-down efforts led and supported by state legislatures. In the late 1980s, additional but quite disparate testing and evaluation programs emerged coincidentally at the local school or district level and at the national level. At the local level the call was for a bottom-up approach centered on school-based management, local control, and teacher empowerment.[51] The local school or district would be the prime policymaking and implementing agency, setting achievement targets, managing instruction, and assessing outcomes. Curriculum and instructional differences among localities would be encouraged and supported.

However, at the same time that the bottom-up approach is being advocated, the specter of national testing has also emerged. The idea of the endeavor, unprecedented in U.S. history, to develop national tests and national achievement standards has received both wide public support and strong criticism. Nonetheless, it is proceeding in its development.[52] National tests and standards, especially if associated with high stakes consequences such as employment or entrance to higher education, will have the potential to impact on curriculum and instruction in more powerful ways than state-mandated policy assessments.

Conclusion

Since the publication of the *Handbook*, the role and use of educational objectives has changed. As exemplified in the *Handbook*, educational objectives were general statements of transfer-oriented student outcomes. They were aimed at the local school or district level and were intended to be tailored to local needs and realities. The classroom teacher had an important role and a great deal of discretion vis-à-vis educational objectives, since it was the teacher's responsibility to identify, elaborate, implement, and assess the objectives. Multiple testing and evaluation methods were encouraged to reflect the multitude of desired student outcomes that were associated with the six cognitive levels.

The intervening years have seen changes in the characteristics of and demands on education, with concomitant changes in the role and use of educational objectives. As noted, the Taxonomy is a tool and its use must fit the needs of the extant educational context. Since its publication, the educational context has moved away from the vision of general, locally focused objectives, instruction, and evaluation to a more centralized, standardized, and reductionist view. This view does not match the format of objectives presented in the *Handbook*.

In this chapter, the growth of mandated testing and evaluation has been charted and the increased implications, or high stakes, associated with these tests have been noted. The consequence of the growth in mandated tests is centralization and standardization, with loss of local discretion for many important decisions and policies.

Lord Kelvin's observation that "When you cannot measure it, and express it in numbers, your knowledge is of a meager and unsatisfactory kind" seemed to guide testing and evaluation policy through the 1980s. Lord Kelvin might also have noted, apropos education over the past thirty years, that if it can't be expressed in numbers, knowledge will be neither rhetorically powerful nor useful for achieving the general agreement needed to spur action. The price of this measurement-oriented view, especially when policies are centrally determined, is the often trivialization of general, more abstract educational objectives, since only those objectives which can be measured tend to be implemented.

In this context, educational objectives as conceptualized by the developers of the Taxonomy have had a diminishing impact on testing and evaluation practice. Objectives per se have been very influential in the testing and evaluation movement over the past quarter century, but not objectives stated in the form advocated in the Taxonomy. Rather, more narrow instructional guidance objectives and more detailed domain specifications have controlled important testing and evaluation programs.

The existence and importance of external testing programs has served to reduce the incentive for and reliance on locally stated educational objectives. This is one reason why the Taxonomy has not had a great impact on classroom teachers' planning, instruction, and evaluation. (See chapter 8 of this volume.) A second reason for the lack of classroom impact is the rise of instructional packages, which provide objectives, lesson plans, and evaluation devices for teachers, thereby making it unnecessary for them to generate their own. A third, and crucial, reason why the Taxonomy has failed to influence classroom practice was noted previously: it failed to provide explicit links relating objectives to the instructional process. Once teachers had stated objectives, the Taxonomy provided them little guidance regarding how to translate the objectives into an instructional program. Without this instructional piece, which occupies more of teachers' time and concern than do objectives or evaluation, there is little reason except external pressure for teachers to use educational objectives in a meaningful way.

Although frequently ignored, the major legacy of the Taxonomy has been in its definition of hierarchical levels of student learning. Since its publication, the Taxonomy has become the model and exemplar used to convey the notion of higher- and lower-level cognitive behaviors. It has become the glass through which educators view policies, objectives, instructional packages, and tests to determine the extent to which they emphasize both lower- and higher-level thinking behaviors. It has been the spur which provides the rationale and examples for recent calls to increase emphasis on student thinking. It has, in short, raised consciousness about the range and depth of valued educational objectives that can be pursued in schools and classrooms. Concomitantly, it has raised consciousness about the range of appropriate measurement techniques that can and should be used to capture the full breadth of students' cognitive learning. It is most unfortunate that the educational context and increased centralization have moved objectives, instruction, and evaluation toward a more narrow, rote orientation and away from the richness of outcomes the Taxonomy lays out for us.

100   IMPACT ON TESTING AND EVALUATION

NOTES

1. James P. Echols, "The Rise of the Evaluation Movement: 1920-1942" (Doctoral dissertation, Stanford University, 1973); George Madaus and Daniel L. Stufflebeam, *Educational Evaluation: The Classic Works of Ralph W. Tyler* (Boston: Kluwer Academic Publishers, 1989).

2. Philip W. Jackson, "Conceptions of Curriculum and Curriculum Specialists," in *Handbook of Research on Curriculum*, edited by Philip W. Jackson (New York: Macmillan, 1992), pp. 3-40.

3. J. W. Tilton, *The Relationship between Association and Higher Mental Processes*, Teachers College Contributions to Education, No. 218 (New York: Bureau of Publications, Teachers College, 1926); Ben D. Wood, *Measurement in Higher Education* (Yonkers-on-Hudson: World Book Co., 1923).

4. Ralph W. Tyler, *Constructing Achievement Tests* (Columbus, OH: Bureau of Educational Research, Ohio State University, 1934).

5. Douglas Waples and Ralph W. Tyler, *Research Methods and Teachers' Problems: A Manual for Systematic Study of Classroom Procedures* (New York: Macmillan, 1930); Tyler, *Constructing Achievement Tests*; Ralph W. Tyler, *Basic Principles of Curriculum and Instruction* (Chicago: University of Chicago Press, 1949).

6. Robert M. W. Travers, *How to Make Achievement Tests* (New York: Odyssey Press, 1950), p. 10.

7. Tyler, *Basic Principles of Curriculum and Instruction*, pp. 28, 37.

8. David R. Krathwohl and David A. Payne. "Defining and Assessing Educational Objectives," in *Educational Measurement*, edited by Robert L. Thorndike (Washington, DC: American Council on Education, 1971), pp. 17-45.

9. Peter W. Airasian and George F. Madaus, "Criterion-referenced Testing in the Classroom," *NCME Measurement in Education* 3, no. 4 (1972): 1-7.

10. Banesh Hoffman, *The Tyranny of Testing* (New York: Collier Books, 1962); John W. Holt, *On Testing* (Cambridge, MA: Pinck Leodas Associates, 1968); Charles E. Silberman, *Crisis in the Classroom* (New York: Vintage Books, 1970).

11. Jerome S. Bruner, *The Process of Education* (Cambridge, MA: Harvard University Press, 1959); J. McVicker Hunt, *Intelligence and Experience* (New York: Ronald Press, 1961); Benjamin S. Bloom, *Stability and Change in Human Characteristics* (New York: Wiley, 1964).

12. Robert F. Mager, *Preparing Instructional Objectives* (Palo Alto, CA: Fearon Press, 1962).

13. W. James Popham, *The Uses of Instructional Objectives* (Belmont, CA: Fearon Publishers, 1973).

14. Edgar Dale, "Historical Setting of Programmed Instruction," in *Programmed Instruction*, edited by Phil C. Lange, Sixty-sixth Yearbook of the National Society for the Study of Education, Part 2 (Chicago: University of Chicago Press, 1967), p. 37.

15. Robert W. Gagné, *The Conditions of Learning* (New York: Holt, Rinehart and Winston, 1975).

16. Peter W. Airasian, "Formative Evaluation Instruments: A Construction and Validation of Tests to Evaluate Learning over Short Time Periods" (Doctoral dissertation, University of Chicago, 1969).

17. Robert Glaser, "Instructional Technology and the Measurement of Learning Outcomes: Some Questions," *American Psychologist* 18 (1963): 519-521.

18. David K. Cohen, "Politics and Research: Evaluation of Social Action Programs in Education," *Review of Educational Research* 40, no. 2 (1970): 213-238; George F. Madaus, Peter W. Airasian, and Thomas Kellaghan, *School Effectiveness: A Reassessment of the Evidence* (New York: McGraw-Hill, 1980).

19. Michael Harrington, *The Other America* (New York: Penguin Books, 1969).

20. Milbrey W. McLaughlin, *Evaluation and Reform* (Cambridge, MA: Ballinger, 1975).

21. Ibid.

22. H. Jerome Freiberg and Amy Driscoll, *Universal Teaching Strategies* (Boston: Allyn and Bacon, 1992); Norah Morgan and Juliana Saxton, *Teaching, Questioning, and Learning* (London: Routledge, 1991).

23. Jackson, "Conceptions of Curriculum and Curriculum Specialists."

24. Elliot W. Eisner, "Educational Objectives: Help or Hindrance?" *School Review* 75, no. 3 (1967): 250-260; J. Myron Atkin, "Behavioral Objectives in Curriculum Design: A Cautionary Note," *Science Teacher* 35, no. 5 (1968): 27-30.

25. Harold Berlak, "Values, Goals, Public Policy, and Educational Evaluation," *Review of Educational Research* 40, no. 2 (1970): 261-278.

26. Blaine R. Worthen and James R. Sanders, *Educational Evaluation: Theory and Practice* (Worthington, OH: Charles A. Jones, 1973); George F. Madaus, Michael Scriven, and Daniel L. Stufflebeam, editors, *Evaluation Models: Viewpoints on Educational and Human Services Evaluation* (Boston: Kluwer-Nijhoff, 1983).

27. Lee J. Cronbach, "Course Improvement through Evaluation," *Teachers College Record* 64, no. 8 (1963): 672-683.

28. Michael Scriven, "The Methodology of Evaluation," in *Curriculum Evaluation*, edited by Robert F. Stake, American Educational Research Association Monograph Series on Evaluation, no. 1 (Chicago: Rand McNally, 1967), pp. 39-83; idem, "Pros and Cons about Goal-free Evaluation," *Evaluation Comment* 3, no. 4 (1972): 1-7.

29. Daniel L. Stufflebeam, W. J. Foley, William J. Gephart, Egon G. Guba, L. R. Hammond, H. O. Merriman, and Malcolm M. Provus, *Educational Evaluation and Decision Making in Education* (Itasca, IL: Peacock, 1971).

30. Worthen and Sanders, *Educational Evaluation*.

31. Milbrey W. McLaughlin and D. C. Phillips, editors, *Evaluation and Education: At Quarter Century*, Ninetieth Yearbook of the National Society for the Study of Education, Part 2 (Chicago: University of Chicago Press, 1991).

32. Cronbach, "Course Improvement through Evaluation"; Robert E. Stake, "Retrospective on 'The Countenance of Evaluation,'" in *Evaluation and Education: At Quarter Century*, edited by Milbrey W. McLaughlin and D. C. Phillips, Ninetieth Yearbook of the National Society for the Study of Education, Part 2 (Chicago: University of Chicago Press, 1991), pp. 67-88.

33. Popham, *The Uses of Instructional Objectives*; Arthur E. Wise, *Legislated Learning: The Bureaucratization of the American Classroom* (Berkeley, CA: University of California Press, 1979).

34. James S. Coleman, Ernest Q. Campbell, Carol J. Hobson, James McPartland, Alexander M. Mood, Frederick D. Weinfeld, and Robert L. York, *Equality of Educational Opportunity* (Washington, DC: Office of Education, U.S. Department of Health, Education, and Welfare, 1966).

35. U.S. Congress, Office of Technology Assessment, "Performance Asessments: Models and Practices," in *Testing in American Schools: Asking the Right Questions* (Washington, DC: U.S. Government Printing Office, 1991), pp. 201-249.

36. Peter W. Airasian, "State-mandated Testing and Educational Reform: Context and Consequences," *American Journal of Education* 95, no. 3 (1987): 392-412; Beverly Anderson, "Test Use Today in Elementary and Secondary Schools," in *Ability Testing: Uses, Consequences, and Controversies, Part II*, edited by Alexandria K. Wigdon and Wendell R. Garner (Washington, DC: National Academy Press, 1982), pp. 232-285.

37. Airasian, "State-mandated Testing and Educational Reform."

38. National Commission on Excellence in Education, *A Nation at Risk* (Washington, DC: U.S. Government Printing Office, 1983).

39. Airasian, "State-mandated Testing and Educational Reform"; Wise, *Legislated Learning*.

40. Joseph Murphy, "The Educational Reform Movement of the 1980s: A Comprehensive Analysis," in *The Educational Reform Movement of the 1980s: Perspectives and Cases*, edited by Joseph Murphy (Berkeley, CA: McCutchan, 1990), pp. 3-55.

41. Peter W. Airasian, "Symbolic Validation: The Case of State-mandated, High Stakes Testing," *Educational Evaluation and Policy Analysis* 10, no. 4 (1988): 301-313.

42. Walter Haney, "Validity and Competency Tests: The Debra P. Case, Conceptions of Validity, and Strategies for the Future," in *The Courts, Validity, and Minimum Competency Testing*, edited by George F. Madaus (Boston: Kluwer-Nijhoff, 1983), pp. 63-93.

43. Airasian, "State-mandated Testing and Educational Reform."

44. W. James Popham, "The Merits of Measurement-driven Instruction," *Phi Delta Kappan* 68, no. 9 (1987): 679-682.

45. Airasian, "State-mandated Testing and Educational Reform."

46. Airasian, "Policy-driven Assessment or Assessment-driven Policy?" *Measurement and Evaluation in Counseling and Development*, in press.

47. Grant Wiggins, "A True Test: Toward More Authentic and Equitable Assessment," *Phi Delta Kappan* 71, no. 9 (1989): 703-713.

48. Gene I. Maeroff, "Assessing Alternative Assessment," *Phi Delta Kappan* 73, no. 4 (1991): 274-281; Robert L. Linn, Eva L. Baker, and S. B. Dunbar, "Complex Performance-based Assessment: Expectations and Validation Criteria," *Educational Researcher* 20, no. 8 (1991): 15-21.

49. Peter W. Airasian, "Measurement-driven Instruction: A Closer Look," *Educational Measurement Issues and Practices* 7, no. 4 (1988): 6-11.

50. Freiberg and Driscoll, *Universal Teaching Strategies*.

51. Marshall S. Smith and Jennifer O'Day, "Systemic School Reform," in *The Politics of Curriculum and Testing*, edited by Susan H. Fuhrman and Betty Malen, 1990 Yearbook of the Politics of Education Association (New York: Falmer Press, 1991), pp. 233-267.

52. National Education Goals Panel, *Measuring Progress toward the National Education Goals: Potential Indicators and Measurement Strategies* (Washington, DC: U.S. Government Printing Office, 1991).

CHAPTER VII

The Taxonomy, Curriculum, and Their Relations

LAUREN A. SOSNIAK

In September of 1989 the St. Louis Public School system published and distributed to its teachers a new curriculum guide for the language arts, Kindergarten through Grade 5. The appendix included a section titled "A Brief Summary of the Taxonomy of Educational Objectives, Cognitive Domain." The two-page summary describes "major categories" of cognitive objectives, and, for each category, offers examples of objectives and "some good verbs for stating expected learning outcomes." A footnote indicates that the "basic structure" for the "major categories" comes from Bloom et al., *Taxonomy of Educational Objectives, Handbook 1: Cognitive Domain;*[1] the correspondence would be immediately obvious to persons at all familiar with that classic text.

The appendix to the St. Louis Public School curriculum guide is intended to help teachers as they work with the guide and their students. While I have made no effort to survey curriculum guides for different school districts small and large across the country, or curriculum guides for different subject matters, I have no doubt that many of them refer explicitly or implicitly to the *Handbook*. The Taxonomy has become part of the language of curriculum theory and practice. It is referenced in virtually every textbook on curriculum. On the surface, at least, the Taxonomy has realized the hopes and expectations its authors expressed in the opening pages of the volume. (See chapter 2 in this volume.)

Over time, and as measured by the frequency with which it is cited, the Taxonomy clearly has been accepted by people who work in the field of curriculum. However, acceptance as measured by frequent reference to the work is hardly sufficient for judging or even understanding how the Taxonomy might be or might have been a useful and effective tool for curriculum theory and practice. In fact,

---

Lauren A. Sosniak is Associate Professor of Education at Washington University, St. Louis, MO.

although the opening paragraph of the *Handbook* indicates a desire to be of help to persons who work on curricular problems, there is ample evidence that the volume was not intended to serve curriculum work. And there are good reasons to question how well served curriculum work has been by the undeniably popular text.

The place of the Taxonomy in curriculum theory and practice, and the place of curriculum thought and action in the Taxonomy, are the subjects of this chapter. I begin with the latter concern, examining curriculum considerations in the *Handbook*, and then turn to the place of the Taxonomy in the field of curriculum. Finally, I discuss tensions apparent in the relations between the Taxonomy and curriculum work. For the most part I exclude from this chapter issues associated with curriculum evaluation or with the translation of curriculum into classroom instruction, as these matters are discussed elsewhere in this volume.

The Taxonomy: Curriculum Considerations as an Afterthought?

The expectation that appears on the first page of the *Handbook*— that the work will "be of general help . . . with curricular and evaluation problems"—suggests that curriculum and evaluation were considered equally, or almost so, in the construction of the Taxonomy. How odd that seems given that the task of developing the Taxonomy was undertaken by a group of college examiners. In fact, there is considerable evidence that concern with curriculum may have been an afterthought, and certainly was of only minor importance to the authors of the volume.

The 1956 edition of the *Handbook* uses the word "curriculum" liberally. An earlier Preliminary Edition of the volume, published in 1954, includes the term far less frequently. The changes from the Preliminary Edition to the final version are instructive with regard to the place of curriculum in the development of the Taxonomy and its supporting material.

One thousand copies of the Preliminary Edition were printed by Longmans, Green, and Company at the request of the authors of the *Handbook*, and were sent to a large group of college and secondary school teachers, administrators, curriculum directors, and educational research specialists. The intent, according to the authors, was to solicit "comments, suggestions, and criticisms of a larger and more representative group of educators, teachers, and educational research workers."[2]

When the *Handbook* was published in the well-known 1956 edition, the changes in the text from the 1954 edition were few, but they are particularly noticeable in the use of the word "curriculum." Apparently the "larger and more representative group of educators" saw curricular implications that the group of college examiners either had not seen at the start or had chosen to ignore.

Let me provide a few examples of the small but hardly innocuous changes readers of the two versions would encounter. Beginning with the introduction to the development of the Taxonomy, both editions indicate that at an informal meeting of college examiners there was an expressed interest in "a theoretical framework which could be used to facilitate communication among examiners." "After considerable discussion," the working group agreed that such a framework might be obtained through some system of classifying "educational objectives" (in the Preliminary Edition) or "the goals of the educational process" (in 1956). The explanation for the reasonableness of this strategy signals the place of curriculum thought in the development of the Taxonomy. In the Preliminary Edition the authors wrote: "Objectives provide the criteria for validating testing procedures, and, in large measure, dictate the kind of educational research in which testing is involved" (p. 1). Two years later, in the 1956 edition of the *Handbook*, the authors wrote: "Objectives provide the basis for building curricula and tests and represent the starting point for much of our educational research" (p. 4). In 1954, the focus is consistent around matters of testing and educational research; in 1956, curriculum (at least the term) is woven into the discussion.

Similarly, in discussions of principles by which the Taxonomy might be developed, both editions indicate that "first importance should be given to educational considerations." The Preliminary Edition continues: "Distinctions should be made with regard to those objectives and behaviors which teachers regard as distinct in their teaching and planning" (p. 3). The final edition phrases the idea differently, including now the word "curricula": "Insofar as possible, the boundaries between categories should be closely related to the distinctions teachers make in planning curricula or in choosing learning situations" (p. 6).

Changes in wording of the sorts noted here may be small, but they are not trivial. They suggest that the Taxonomy was developed first; attention to curriculum was inserted later. Nowhere is this more evident than in chapter 2 of the 1956 edition of the *Handbook*. That chapter, entitled "Educational Objectives and Curriculum Development," was not in the Preliminary Edition. Its opening paragraph seems especially instructive regarding the place of curriculum considerations in the development and use of the Taxonomy:

We have had some question about the relevance of this section in a handbook devoted to the details of a classification system. We have finally included it because we believe the classification and evaluation of educational objectives must be considered as a part of the total process of curriculum development. Some of these considerations help to clarify the distinctions made in the taxonomy. It is hoped that many teachers will find this chapter useful as a summary of some of the arguments for inclusion of a greater range of educational objectives than is typical at the secondary school or college level.[3]

Thus, after distributing 1000 copies of a Preliminary Edition for informal review, the authors found themselves prodded into paying some attention to curriculum. They did so reluctantly, for purposes of speaking to a larger audience and helping the larger educational community understand and appreciate the significance of their work.

The reluctance to speak about curriculum in the *Handbook* is further evident in the fact that the "new" Chapter 2 is new mostly in title. The bulk of the content of the chapter was taken from various places in the Preliminary Edition, especially from the section previously headed "Educational Significance of the Major Classes of Cognitive Behaviors." When examined carefully, only two sections of this chapter are truly new.

First, there is a new three-page opening, the first paragraph of which is reproduced above. The discussion, following notice of the authors' uneasiness about including the section, consists of a brief outline of curricular thinking of the day. Mention is made of Tyler's now famous four questions. There is some elaboration on Tyler's discussion of the first of these questions, "What educational purposes or objectives should the school or course seek to attain?" Interestingly, the reference supporting these questions as central to curriculum work is *not* to the classic source, *Basic Principles of Curriculum and Instruction,*[4] but rather to a chapter elsewhere by Tyler titled "Achievement Testing and Curriculum Construction."[5] Thus, even the source used for a discussion of curriculum theory is one that puts achievement testing first.

The second part of the chapter that is new also is an addition principally in title. The subsection that in the Preliminary Edition had been labeled "some special problems" (associated with knowledge objectives) in the 1956 edition is labeled "curricular decisions to be made about knowledge objectives." While the content of this section changes little substantively, it has been reorganized.

Thus we see the authors of the *Handbook* integrating the term *curriculum* into the existing text without considerable rethinking or rewriting of the volume. Something prompted a serious effort to use the term in the 1956 edition, but nothing prompted a reconsideration of the basic ideas presented in the text. The absence of any serious rethinking in relation to the sudden inclusion of the term *curriculum* is particularly evident in the fact that the bulk of the book, the full description of the Taxonomy itself with "illustrative materials," is the same in both editions.

We might ask whether the initial draft of the *Handbook* was sufficiently attentive to curriculum considerations, even though it had not used the term *curriculum*. In other words, perhaps the only addition necessary was a change in language, because the curricular thought was already embedded in the text. In part, the test of this hypothesis is found in a later section of this chapter, when the voices of curriculum scholars are brought to bear on the Taxonomy. In part, however, the authors of the Taxonomy themselves indicate a variety of curricular considerations that they believe lie outside the boundaries of their work.

PUTTING A DISTANCE BETWEEN CURRICULUM AND TESTING

In the Preliminary Edition of the *Handbook* the authors expressed discomfort with possible relations between their handbook and curriculum work. In a section about "problems" raised in the working-group discussions, they wrote:

There was some concern expressed in the early meetings that the availability of the taxonomy might tend to abort the thinking and planning of teachers with regard to curriculum, particularly if teachers merely selected what they believed to be desirable objectives from the list provided in the taxonomy. The process of thinking about educational objectives, defining them, and relating them to teaching and testing procedures was regarded as a very important step on the part of teachers. It was suggested that the taxonomy could be most useful to teachers who have already gone through some of the steps in thinking about educational objectives and curriculum.[6]

This paragraph remains in the 1956 edition. Nowhere is there any discussion of the work teachers ought to "have already gone through" before turning to the Taxonomy.

Perhaps the most obvious distancing of the *Handbook* and the Taxonomy from curriculum work is the choice made by the authors to exclude from consideration any attention to subject-matter content in their schema. Instead, for purposes of developing their classification scheme, the authors argue that "classes of behavior" for students across grades and subject matters are relatively small in number and "should be applicable in all these instances [across subject matters, from elementary school through college]."[7]

The authors of the *Handbook* are well aware of, but apparently uninterested in, the fact that fundamental curriculum decisions associated with educational objectives have to do with choices that must be made from a too large body of possibly desirable *content*. With respect to "knowledge" objectives, for example, the authors write: "[T]here is a tremendous wealth of these specifics and there must always be some selection for educational purposes, since it is almost inconceivable that a student can learn all of the specifics relevant to a particular field."[8] However, the authors assign such decisions to others: "The teacher or curriculum specialist must make choices as to what is basic and what is only of secondary importance or of importance primarily to the specialist."[9] The *Handbook* provides no guidance for such choices, except the implicit guidance that the manner of student work with chosen content should balance attention across the psychological processes represented by the taxonomic categories.

That said, it is important to acknowledge that the Taxonomy is not content-free. There are countless examples of curricular content embedded in discussion of the taxonomic categories. Each category and subcategory is richly illustrated, typically with multiple-choice test items. These test items were

selected from published examinations as well as from examinations available in the files of the cooperating examiners. While some effort has been made to draw these examples from the different subject fields and from secondary as well as college courses, it is likely that particular areas and particular levels are not as fully illustrated as desirable.[10]

There is no further mention made about the content of the illustrations. Nowhere is there any discussion of the criteria for judging the worth of a test item in relation to its content. Nowhere is there any discussion of the nature of what students might be studying when they encounter such an item, and of the relation of the item to students' learning opportunities at the moment, in their recent past, and in their near future. These, of course, are issues critical to curriculum deliberations.

Another obvious distancing of the Taxonomy from matters of curriculum comes in the authors' remarks about the starting point for their work:

[W]e began work by gathering a large list of educational objectives from our own institutions and the literature. We determined which part of the objective stated the behavior intended. . . . We then attempted to find divisions or groups into which the behaviors could be placed.[11]

In this passage, and throughout the book, it is clear that the authors have chosen to ignore questions about what educational objectives schools or courses *should* work toward. Instead, they limit their concern to ways of classifying objectives that are readily available, without pausing to reflect on the worth of those objectives for particular students studying a particular subject matter in a specific educational setting.

The authors of the Taxonomy also are explicit about limits to the objectives that can be included in their scheme. Although their intention was to create a "purely descriptive scheme in which every type of educational goal can be represented in a relatively neutral fashion,"[12] they acknowledge that they were not able to do so entirely. They settle for a system that

cannot be used to classify educational plans which are made in such a way that either the student behaviors cannot be specified or only a single (unanalyz-able) term or phrase such as "understanding," or "desirable citizen," is used to describe the outcomes.[13]

Thus, for the authors of the Taxonomy, questions about the appropriate rhetorical level for objectives for different curricula were pushed aside in favor of appropriate wording of objectives for purposes of testing and educational research.

Finally, the authors of the Taxonomy are explicit that "[i]t is outside the scope of the task we set ourselves to properly treat the matter of determining the appropriate value to be placed on the different degrees of achievement of the objectives of instruction."[14] Once again, matters of value, whether associated with what should be learned, who should learn it, or to what degree something should be learned—considerations fundamental to curriculum work—are clearly separated from the concerns of the authors of the Taxonomy. The authors provide a direct summary statement to that effect: "A comprehensive taxonomy of educational objectives must, in our opinion, include all the educational objectives represented in American education without making judgments about their value, meaningfulness, or appropriateness."[15]

In summary, the place of curriculum theory and practice in the *Handbook* seems to be minor at best. The authors of the Taxonomy acknowledge curriculum work as related to their efforts. That is, the classification and evaluation of educational objectives, the subject of the *Handbook*, is said to be a piece of a process that includes curriculum development (which the authors concede directly) and curriculum enactment (which they address indirectly). At the same time, however, the nature of the relationships between curriculum work and the classification and evaluation of educational objectives is something the authors choose not to examine. Instead, they define their role and speak generally about how the work of examiners *may* fit with other arenas of educational thought and action.

We are told that careful attention to matters of testing, with emphasis on "greater precision" in the classification of learner outcomes, is influenced by curriculum and in turn should influence curriculum. Objectives come from the work of curriculum developers, and the contributions of examiners in elaborating a scheme for more carefully describing and classifying objectives should inform subsequent efforts by curriculum developers. It is suggested that the Taxonomy can, as a collateral benefit, promote attention in different curricula to the inclusion of a greater range of educational objectives than is typical at the secondary school or college level. We are told little more than that about relationships between the Taxonomy and curriculum.

Curriculum Theory and Practice:
The Taxonomy as an Afterthought?

In a tit-for-tat arrangement, the Taxonomy has also typically been something of an afterthought for curriculum authors. While it is frequently included by name in literature on the curriculum, it is seldom included as close to the heart of the matter. The Taxonomy is mentioned in widely used textbooks on curriculum published as early as 1957 and as recently as 1992.[16] For all the mentioning, however, there is little significant use made of the Taxonomy in the curriculum literature, either as an organizing scheme for thinking about curriculum or as a framework for structuring the work of curriculum making.

In their *Fundamentals of Curriculum Development*, Smith, Stanley, and Shores merely mention the *Handbook* as the last of their "suggested readings" for their chapter on the validation of educational objectives.[17] The *Handbook* is given somewhat more attention by Taba in her chapters on the objectives of education and on types of behavioral objectives.[18] Thirty years later, Posner gives the *Handbook* essentially the same place, embedding it in a much larger discussion of educational purposes.[19]

In the nearly half century since the appearance of the *Handbook*, its mention in curriculum textbooks has settled into a predictable pattern. Along with its companion piece, *Handbook II: Affective Domain*,[20] the Taxonomy typically is included as a metaphorical appendix to a discussion of "aims, goals, and objectives," a perennial topic in curriculum conversation. The Taxonomy is presented as a "tool"[21] available to make curriculum work easier or as "a procedure for defining goals in a systematic, comprehensive manner."[22] That is, curriculum textbooks take their description of the Taxonomy almost directly from the *Handbook*. Some brief mention usually is made of both possibilities and limitations associated with various uses of the "tool."

Reference to the Taxonomy in other writing about curriculum is more difficult to discuss because of the breadth of curriculum literature generally. Still, there seems to be something of a pattern here as well. The most typical reference seems to depict the Taxonomy as a tool useful for *analyzing* a curriculum. A common sentence in reports of studies of enacted or intended curricula typically reads something like this: "We used a modified version of Bloom's taxonomy to examine the cognitive demands of X," where X is the specific curriculum being investigated. This particular use of the Taxonomy undoubtedly accounts for a goodly number of citations to the work.

Journal articles that describe the use of the Taxonomy for purposes of curricular *planning* rather than curricular *analysis* are interesting principally for the diversity of educational settings included. The Taxonomy has been mentioned as useful for curricular planning by educators in the United States and abroad, and by educators working at all levels of schooling from elementary school through graduate school. Sometimes the Taxonomy is so taken for granted that a traditional reference seems quite unnecessary. For example, in describing a national precollegiate curriculum development project in history, geography, and social science, Blyth writes about the early stage of the project as follows: "A tentative list of pupil objectives was drawn up, with a fairly liberal interpretation of the Bloom paradigm in mind, and this list was discussed at . . ."[23] At the other extreme, even several decades after its publication, there is an apparent need to introduce the *Handbook* and the taxonomic categories to specialized audiences not already acquainted with them and their usefulness.[24]

How or even how often the Taxonomy is used in actual curriculum practice seems impossible to determine from the literature. The assumption many curriculum writers make is that it is used frequently, almost automatically and largely unreflectively, at the start of a curriculum development project, in the manner represented by Blyth's remark noted above. The appendix to the St. Louis language arts curriculum guide (mentioned at the beginning of this chapter) suggests that the Taxonomy may often be included in curriculum work, but without serious thought about why or how it is to be used. Although apparently there is no literature to support empirically the assumption of widespread use, that assumption is so strongly held that some scholars have speculated about the reasons for it.

A common explanation for the (assumed) persistent presence of the Taxonomy in curriculum projects is a result of pressures brought to bear by government or foundation support for curriculum projects. Stenhouse, for example, argues that dogmatic insistence on the use of an "objectives model" for curriculum work is a result of "pressure . . . from funding agencies, which are able by the use of the objectives model to operate an over-simplified but comforting pay-ment-by-results system in making curriculum research and develop-ment allocations."[25] Yet despite considerable mentioning of persistent use of the Taxonomy, and of pressures for its use, there is very little elaboration of these assumptions, either theoretically or empirically.

The frequent mentioning of the *Handbook* in the literature about curriculum tells only that the volume has attracted attention; it says nothing at all about its usefulness (or lack thereof) for curriculum work. Claims have been made for both the potential of the Taxonomy for curriculum development and for the harm the Taxonomy could do and has done to curriculum theory and practice. Each will be discussed briefly here.

THE MERITS OF THE TAXONOMY FOR CURRICULUM THEORY AND PRACTICE

Favorable discussion of the *Handbook* centers most frequently on a single feature: the attention it calls to the fact that good education necessarily aims at more than mere recall of factual information. The *Handbook* might be said to have raised our sights educationally, by directing our attention to "intellectual abilities and skills." As Posner puts it, "the taxonomy has served as a vocabulary for the criticism of fact-oriented curricula."[26]

There were prior criticisms of the fact-oriented curricula, of course. The authors of the *Handbook* themselves remind us of the history of concern for "intellectual abilities and skills," which they note as having been "labeled 'critical thinking' by some, 'reflective thinking' by Dewey and others, and 'problem solving' by still others."[27] None of these prior criticisms of the fact-oriented curricula seems to have attracted the attention of the educational community as fully as has the Taxonomy.

The emphasis in schooling on factual recall and a general lack of attention to intelligent use of acquired knowledge were not trivial concerns in the early 1950s as evidenced by the length to which the authors of the *Handbook* went to explain and defend this aspect of their work. They remain major concerns today. In her presidential address to the American Educational Research Association, Nancy Cole spoke about the current dominant conceptions of educational achievement, which divide into what we now think of as "lower-level" and "higher-order" conceptions of knowledge and skill. She said: "In terms of public understanding of the integration of the two, it appears that we have come little further than Bloom and [his] colleagues took us over three decades ago. At that stage in our history, we recognized the two conceptions as different levels of a hierarchy of achievement."[28]

If all the *Handbook* had done was to serve as an inspirational tract, as a document to remind us of curricular possibilities, it would have served an important function in the development of ideas about schooling. But there are other claims for the Taxonomy beyond its power to inspire. At the least, as the authors of the *Handbook* themselves claim and as has been demonstrated richly over the years, a central use of the conceptual scheme for curriculum research has been and continues to be its value in allowing us to examine systematically the extent to which programs attend to "lower-level" and "higher-order" concerns.

Other potential benefits of the Taxonomy for curriculum development tend to be more speculative. For example, in claim at least, the Taxonomy has potential for helping curriculum developers specify and classify their educational intentions systematically and in a manner that would support sharing of curriculum work across contexts and over time.[29] The Taxonomy also has been said to be useful as a model for the variety of ways language can be used to communicate different curricular intentions, and to suggest to curriculum developers classes of objectives they may not have considered previously. Zumwalt proposes that the Taxonomy may be especially useful for new teachers, in the ways listed above and in helping new teachers focus their work, set their priorities, and appreciate their considerable role in defining the curriculum for the students in their classes.[30] Similarly, in principle the Taxonomy is said to be useful in planning for a desired balance or range of cognitive demands on students through the learning opportunities provided for them.

As a tool the Taxonomy could logically be useful in all of these ways. The evidence is not strong that it has been useful in any of those ways, except for describing and analyzing the cognitive demands of intended and implemented curricula. The absence of evidence for the usefulness of the taxonomy for curriculum theory and practice is hardly the fault of the authors of the *Handbook*. Instead, it reflects the fact that curriculum scholars have tended not to concern themselves with questions about how curricula actually are developed. They do not appear to have intentionally ignored the Taxonomy per se; rather, the very idea of examining the processes of developing and enacting curricula has gotten short shrift.[31]

THE LIMITATIONS OF THE TAXONOMY FOR CURRICULUM THEORY AND PRACTICE

Criticism of the Taxonomy and its influence on curriculum theory and practice shares common features with accolades bestowed on the work. It tends to be speculative rather than theoretically or empirically developed, and it tends to be somewhat distant from the *Handbook* itself, focusing instead on a general "objectives model" or "means-ends model" for curriculum work.

When the focus is on the *Handbook*, criticism tends to point to the very curricular issues that the authors of that volume set as outside the boundaries of their work. That is, questions are raised about the absence of consideration about content, the inattention to educational aims other than those that can be phrased in behavioral form, and the place of values in the conceptual scheme. Of course, the same issues arise when the Taxonomy is used principally as an example of a larger problem in the field of curriculum, a problem associated with a means-ends model of thinking that developed long before the Taxonomy,[32] and for which the Taxonomy was merely a specific technical advance. In this instance, however, when the discussion is more generally about the means-ends model for curriculum work, questions about values frequently take center stage.

The central theme of the various criticisms of the Taxonomy and the means-ends model for curriculum work has to do with the question of whether the Taxonomy is useful for clarifying goals, as it claims, or whether it has obscured the normative foundation of curriculum deliberation and substituted technical expertise for serious and substantive discussion. The authors of the Taxonomy claim that it is value-free. Critics note, however, that "the taxonomy itself, as with any type of classification system, is suited to the expression of certain values and unsuited to the expression of others. . . . [It] throws emphasis onto certain qualities and tends to diminish the apparent significance of others."[33] Given that the starting point for curriculum development or analysis rests with a commitment to values, the values implicit in the Taxonomy as well as the lack of explicit attention to them in the Handbook, would both seem to be particularly problematic.

Speaking generally about objectives rather than specifically about the Taxonomy, Stenhouse argues that

objectives are inadequate as definitions of value positions. Their analytic nature, far from clarifying and defining value divergence, appears to make it possible to mask such divergence. . . . Groups of teachers who claim to have agreed on their objectives often demonstrate in the classroom that their agreement was illusory.[34]

Macdonald and Clark claim that the problem is worse than merely allowing for an illusion of agreement. In their words, "What in effect takes place is that a personal bias or preference is in operation under the guise of an objective and scientific determination."[35] For Furst, there is the related problem with the Taxonomy of confusing an objective with its indicator.[36]

Critics have claimed that several specific values having potentially serious negative consequences for curriculum work are hidden in the Taxonomy. Both Eisner and Weiss suggest that the Taxonomy advocates the synthetic breakdown of human characteristics into cognitive, affective, and psychomotor domains.[37] Putnam, Lampert, and Peterson as well as Eisner question the assumption that knowledge is decomposable; they also question the necessity for being as specific as possible in setting objectives for instruction.[38] Shaw points out that the *Handbook* ignores questions about who has the power to declare and prioritize objectives.[39] Indeed, the authors of the *Handbook* seem to assume a set of definable aims inherent in the idea of education. Of course, as Dewey reminds us, "Education as such has no aims; only persons, parents, teachers, etc., have aims."[40]

Macdonald summarizes the strongest critical position arising from questions of value: "The production of the taxonomies is significant evidence of an academic mentality which utilizes technical rationality divorced from consideration of ends. Thus, what can be done and measured becomes what ought to be done."[41]

Tensions in the Relations between the Taxonomy and Curriculum Work

In curriculum theory and practice there is a history of trying to identify a rational system for coping with the complex problem of defining the curriculum. This history emphasizes focusing intently on objectives of education, trying to become more "scientific" in defining and describing our intentions, and assuming all else follows naturally and obviously from careful specification of objectives. Franklin Bobbitt ranks among the early influential educators in this arena; Ralph Tyler is among the best known to contemporary educators.

There is also a history in the field of curriculum of trying to be "helpful" to educational practitioners—trying to provide "advice" that will serve teachers and school administrators who may be too busy in the action arena to think in a sustained way about selected problems.[42] Again, Bobbitt and Tyler figure prominently in this history.

The *Handbook* clearly fits within and extends this curricular history. It is consistent with these central curriculum themes. It was developed by students of Tyler, who was influenced in no small measure by Bobbitt. To the extent that the directions Bobbitt and Tyler were promoting *for* the field of curriculum were the directions *of* the field (and these were very influential men, not only in the field of curriculum but also in education much more broadly), the *Handbook* and the Taxonomy more specifically were almost certain to become integrated in some fashion *with* the field.

The *Handbook* promoted an educational philosophy consistent with the curriculum theory of its time. This theory emphasized educational objectives as an organizing theme around which curricula should be developed, a language of objectives attuned to student behavior, and the segmenting of educational objectives into discrete and measurable units. The *Handbook* thus appears to be something of a guidebook for translating theory into practice. Whether as a "tool" or "technique," the Taxonomy would seem to make the work of identifying and stating objectives easier than heretofore had been the case.

In addition, and likely of major importance, the *Handbook* was written in a style well known to and historically well-received by people seeking curricular advice.[43] The main ideas were small in number, painted in broad strokes, presented in a chatty style, with repeated appeals to common sense, and with multiple examples demonstrating a fundamental connection with and respect for the persons who might find the advice helpful. The *Handbook* is easy reading, although perhaps it is easier reading for persons looking for practical help than it is for persons looking for theoretical discussion and development.

The Taxonomy thus could be said to have had every advantage in capturing the hearts and minds of persons engaged in curriculum theory and practice. And so it did, for a time, at least at the level of widespread and sustained "mentioning." Curriculum scholars such as Goodlad promoted the Taxonomy as particularly useful in efforts to become more rational about curriculum work.[44] Bloom himself participated in national and international curriculum conferences, using the *Handbook* as a centerpiece for his involvement in such efforts. Yet despite the momentum surrounding the Taxonomy, it is merely mentioned in the literature about curriculum and seems to have become only a footnote to curriculum practice.

How might we account for such a phenomenon? My explanation, purely speculative, is informed by the changing nature of curriculum literature subsequent to the publication of Tyler's classic volume, *Basic Principles of Curriculum and Instruction*, and of the *Handbook* itself.

The Taxonomy was a conceptual and technical advance in thinking about and working with educational objectives. The direction of work following from the Taxonomy involved increasing specificity in the language of objectives, and in turn became increasingly more problematic for curriculum theory and practice. Educational objectives were replaced by "instructional" objectives;[45] these were transformed later into "behavioral" or "performance" objectives. Each shift in terminology was associated with more precise details regarding how objectives should be written and why they should be written as described. The shift in terminology also typically signaled the need for increasing numbers of carefully worded objectives to specify the goals that had been indicated earlier by a smaller number of more loosely worded intentions. In this regard, the behavioral objectives movement is said to have collapsed under its own weight.

Not only did it become a practical burden to work with the increasing specificity demanded for the language of objectives, but, just as importantly, the technical advances ran headlong into a debate about the nature of objectives most helpful for promoting the most important intentions associated with schooling as an educational institution, and even about the very place of objectives in curriculum theory and practice. Ralph Tyler himself was one of the critics of the use of the taxonomies *for curriculum work*. At a conference on educational objectives, Tyler pointed out that if the intent was to guide the selection of learning experiences and the appraisal of results, then specifying the kinds of *behavior* to be developed without also specifying the kinds of *content* involved was inadequate. Further, Tyler argued that the specificity aimed for by the authors of the *Handbook* was not always necessary or desirable; rather, objectives "should be stated at the level of generality of behavior that you are seeking to help the student acquire."[46] Finally, Tyler pointed to the need for discussion, missing in the *Handbook*, of considerations involved in selecting objectives, a task which should be done *before* working on the defining of objectives in terms of behavior and content.

Other educators, also still assuming a central place for objectives in curriculum work, have challenged the assumptions embedded in behavioral objectives of the sort promoted by the *Handbook*. Eisner, for example, argues consistently that there is no single legitimate way to formulate educational aims, and to pretend otherwise is to limit the possibilities that might arise if teachers and other curriculum workers felt free to apply their conceptual ability and creativity to this important aspect of curriculum work.[47] As alternatives to traditional behavioral objectives he proposes "expressive objectives" and "problem-solving objectives," both of which are intended to be evocative rather than prescriptive and to promote diversity of student responses rather than homogeneity in student learning.

Expressive objectives describe an encounter that a student is to have rather than a behavior a student is supposed to be able to demonstrate after an educational activity. Curriculum activities are "intentionally planned to provide a fertile field for personal purposing and experience." Problem-solving objectives are described this way: "The problem is posed and the criteria that need to be achieved to resolve the problem are fairly clear. But the forms of its solution are virtually infinite."[48] Eisner claims that problem-solving objectives especially tend toward the creation of curriculum activities which are likely to be taken seriously by students and which place a premium on higher mental processes.

Eisner's alternative forms of objectives are a response to what he believes are questionable assumptions embedded in traditional discussions of objectives. He challenges the assumptions that all important educational intentions are or should be specifiable in advance, and that success in teaching consists of bringing about predictable outcomes. And he challenges the assumptions that knowledge is external to a student and that it can be segmented easily for purposes of instruction and evaluation. Stenhouse similarly raises questions about "action disciplined by preconceived goals," and suggests "action disciplined by form or by principles of procedure" as an alternative for curriculum research and planning.[49]

Hirst is not as agreeable as Eisner to merely adding alternative forms of objectives that still emphasize student behavior. He argues:

Most of the central objectives we are interested in in education are not themselves reducible to observable states, and to imagine they are, whatever the basis of that claim, is to lose the heart of the business. What is certainly true is that the observable correlates are the only evidence we have that objectives which label states of mind have been achieved, but states of mind should never be confused with the evidence for them. . . . Assessment and evaluation rely on observable evidence, but these evidences are not the objective of the teaching enterprise.[50]

Scholars have challenged not only the assumptions embedded in objectives as the *Handbook* describes them, but also the very idea of objectives as a starting point or a centerpiece for more rational curricular work. Perhaps the most generous position has been taken by Schwab, who attempts to promote the relation between means and ends in education as "mutually determining."[51]

Peters is less enthusiastic about a focus of attention on objectives, even if the attention is shared equally with the means of education. In an essay entitled "Must an Educator Have an Aim?" Peters contends that "we have got the wrong picture of the way in which values must enter into education."

In my view, disputes between educationists, which take the form of disputes about aims, have largely been disputes about the desirability of a variety of principles involved in such procedures. Values are involved in education not so much as goals or end-products, but as principles implicit in different manners of proceeding or producing.[52]

Blyth separates values from both the means and ends of education. He argues: "In practice, any table of objectives must be derived from a value-position, though this is not always clearly stated. What is not so readily indicated is that a value-position is something more basic and stable than a list of objectives."[53] This argument is consistent with the "naturalistic model" for curriculum development described by Walker, in which the foundation of a curriculum is a "platform" (including the beliefs and values curriculum developers bring to their task) rather than a set of agreed upon objectives.[54] In Walker's model, objectives are a "late development" following from the platform, rather than a starting point.

Walker subsequently argued not only that curriculum development does not typically begin with careful attention to objectives, but also that it *should not*. His preference is that a curriculum development group begin with rough statements of general aims, postpone concern for precision, and allow the development of aims to take place alongside the development of other aspects of the curriculum. He argues that selecting or defining ends as a starting point in curriculum development is counterproductive.

Devoting much time early to reaching agreement among the developers on statements of precise objectives can be distracting and divisive. Often there is little basis for a decision yet, since the consequences for the project of choosing one objective over another can seldom be anticipated. . . . Even when they go as well as possible, early discussions of precise objectives are generally frustrating and unsatisfying for team members eager to grapple with materials design issues.[55]

In sum, the technical advance of the Taxonomy promoted serious discussion *about* curriculum work, discussion which did not always support the use of the Taxonomy *for* curriculum work. This discussion reminded us of the centrality of values in curriculum conversation. It reminded us that curriculum involves thinking about both intentions and activities (which include content, materials, and instructional strategies) and, especially, their relationships. It reminded us that curriculum work is a deliberative undertaking, a search for defensible decisions for particular students and particular contexts. Or, as Macdonald and Clark put it: "The plain fact of the matter is that curriculum development is a continuous process of making human value judgments about what to include and exclude, what to aim for and avoid, and how to go about it—difficult judgments even when aided by technical and scientific data and processes."[56]

Conclusion

In recent years, long lists of precisely worded objectives created in the spirit of and perhaps with the help of the Taxonomy seem to have gone out of favor. In their place are objectives that resemble more closely Tyler's view that objectives should be small in number, consistent in philosophy, and focus on those general goals believed to be most important. Further, it appears that more attention is being given to words other than objectives for representing educational intentions. "Goals" and "purposes" are being used increasingly in both school-based statements and statements intended for larger audiences. Meeting "standards," which the National Council of Teachers of Mathematics explains "are statements about what is valued," has become another popular way of speaking about what one hopes for as a result of educational activity.[57] Finally, and perhaps most interestingly, statements of "principles," rather than objectives, seem to be increasing in popularity.[58]

Statements of principles are not new to curriculum development or curriculum theory. Writing on curriculum reveals a commingling of "principles" and "objectives."[59] Sometimes this commingling demonstrates confusion of one with the other; sometimes it demonstrates deliberate distinctions and purposeful relations. Granheim and Lundgren assert that principles should be decided first and should be the foundation for the development of teaching goals.[60] In this light, principles might be seen to be serving as a "platform," as proposed by Walker, or as a value-position, as suggested by Blyth.

Statements of principles may serve educators generally and curriculum workers more particularly in several important ways. First, it seems possible that attention to principles will serve as a powerful reminder of the value positions embedded in all decisions about both objectives and activities. This could be an important correction in curriculum work following from the lengthy technical emphasis of the Taxonomy and similar classification schemes. Second, statements of principles may provide some intermediary vantage point from which curriculum developers are helped to think about the objectives they truly want to aim toward, the activities that might serve well in support of those objectives, and, then, the relationships between objectives and activities. It remains to be seen whether principles are useful or whether they become another form of the language of intentions that restricts or obscures as much as it clarifies and provides guidance.

What has not changed in recent years is the quick leap typically made between objectives and evaluation, with limited attention to the curricular concerns of student activities in support of particular intentions however these are labeled. Sometimes the leaps are made from intentions to evaluation, or, as Abramson described the situation with respect to curriculum research, "a vaulting from the framing of objectives directly to the construction of measures of assessment, passing over the intermediate stages of the representation of the objectives within curriculum content, within the instructional situation, and within the teaching process."[61] Sometimes, perhaps more unfortunately, the leaps are made in the opposite direction: from what is testable to what is worth aiming for. Either way, such talk and action also are legacies of the *Handbook*.

For all of the emphasis on student behavior in the *Handbook*, the volume nevertheless was based on and promoted discourse about teaching and learning distant from teachers and learners living and working in classrooms. Defining intentions and determining whether or not they were realized could be done (perhaps by administrators) without attention to the classroom activities and student experiences that help define the curriculum and shape education. In theory, classroom activity would follow from intentions; however, the authors of the *Handbook* and many other writers on curriculum never make explicit how that might happen or if it does. Many educators and educational policymakers apparently continue to believe that relationships between intentions and classroom activities are, or should be, nonproblematic.

Thus the influence of the Taxonomy on the field of curriculum continues to be strong in some respects and has waned considerably in others. It has been positive in its influence in significant ways, and perhaps unhelpful in others. However, no one can doubt that the *Handbook* spurred important conversation about curriculum and its development. For this alone, it has been of great service to the field of curriculum.

NOTES

1. Benjamin S. Bloom et al., *Taxonomy of Educational Objectives, The Classification of Educational Goals, Handbook I: Cognitive Domain* (New York: David McKay, 1956).

2. Bloom et al., *Taxonomy of Educational Objectives*, Preliminary edition (New York: Longmans, Green, and Co., 1954), p. 5.

3. Bloom et al., *Taxonomy of Educational Objectives*, 1956 ed., p. 25.

4. Ralph W. Tyler, *Basic Principles of Curriculum and Instruction* (Chicago: University of Chicago Press, 1949).

5. Ralph W. Tyler, "Achievement Testing and Curriculum Construction," in *Trends in Student Personnel Work*, edited by E. G. Williamson (Minneapolis: University of Minnesota Press, 1949), pp. 391-407.

6. Bloom et al., *Taxonomy of Educational Objectives*, Preliminary ed., p. 2.

7. Bloom et al., *Taxonomy of Educational Objectives*, 1956 ed., p. 12.

8. Ibid., p. 63.

9. Ibid., p. 66.

10. Ibid., p. 45.

11. Ibid., p. 15.

12. Ibid., p. 14.

13. Ibid., p. 15.

14. Ibid., p. 13.

15. Ibid., p. 30.

16. For example, B. Othanel Smith, William O. Stanley, and J. Harlan Shores, *Fundamentals of Curriculum Development*, rev. ed. (New York: Harcourt, Brace and World, 1956); George J. Posner, *Analyzing the Curriculum* (New York: McGraw-Hill, 1992).

17. Smith, Stanley, and Shores, *Fundamentals of Curriculum Development*, p. 125.

18. Hilda Taba, *Curriculum Development: Theory and Practice* (New York: Harcourt, Brace and World, 1962), chapters 13 and 14.

19. Posner, *Analyzing the Curriculum*, chapter 4.

20. David R. Krathwohl, Benjamin S. Bloom, and Bertram B. Masia, *Taxonomy of Educational Objectives, The Classification of Educational Goals, Handbook II: Affective Domain* (New York: David McKay, 1964).

21. See, for example, M. Frances Klein, "Instructional Decisions in Curriculum," in John I. Goodlad and Associates, *Curriculum Inquiry: The Study of Curriculum Practice* (New York: McGraw-Hill, 1979), and Decker Walker, *Fundamentals of Curriculum* (San Diego, CA: Harcourt Brace Jovanovich, 1990).

22. J. Galen Saylor and William M. Alexander, *Planning Curriculum for Schools* (New York: Holt, Rinehart and Winston, 1974), p. 180.

23. William A. L. Blyth, "One Development Project's Awkward Thinking about Objectives," *Journal of Curriculum Studies* 6, no. 2 (1975): 99-111.

24. See, for example, Charlotte A. Vaughan, "Identifying Course Goals: Domains and Levels of Learning," *Teaching Sociology* 7, no. 3 (1980): 265-279, and Jay Feinman and Marc Feldman, "Pedagogy and Politics," *Georgetown Law Journal* 73 (1985): 875-930.

25. Lawrence Stenhouse, "Some Limitations of the Use of Objectives in Curriculum Research and Planning," *Paedagogica Europaea* 6 (1970): 73-83.

26. Posner, *Analyzing the Curriculum*, p. 82.

27. Bloom et al., *Taxonomy of Educational Objectives*, 1956 ed., p. 38.

28. Nancy S. Cole, "Conceptions of Educational Achievement," *Educational Researcher* 19, no. 3 (1990): 5.

29. David R. Krathwohl, "The Taxonomy of Educational Objectives: Its Use in Curriculum Building," in *Defining Educational Objectives*, edited by C. M. Lindvall (Pittsburgh: University of Pittsburgh Press, 1964), pp. 19-36.

30. Karen K. Zumwalt, "Beginning Professional Teachers: The Need for a Curricular Vision of Teaching," in *Knowledge Base for the Beginning Teacher*, edited by Maynard C. Reynolds (Oxford: Pergamon Press, 1989), pp. 173-184.

31. Decker Walker, "A Naturalistic Model for Curriculum Development," *School Review* 80 (1971): 51-65; Jon Snyder, Francis Bolin, and Karen Zumwalt, "Curriculum Implementation," in *Handbook of Research on Curriculum*, edited by Philip W. Jackson (New York: Macmillan, 1992), pp. 402-435.

32. See, for example, Franklin Bobbitt, *The Curriculum* (New York: Arno Press, 1918), and idem, *How To Make a Curriculum* (Boston: Houghton Mifflin, 1924).

33. Christopher P. Ormell, "Bloom's Taxonomy and the Objectives of Education," *Educational Research* 17, no. 1 (1974): 3-4.

34. Stenhouse, "Some Limitations of the Use of Objectives in Curriculum Research and Practice," pp. 78-79.

35. James B. Macdonald and Dwight Clark, "Critical Value Questions and the Analysis of Objectives and Curricula," in *Second Handbook of Research on Teaching*, edited by Robert M. W. Travers (Chicago: Rand McNally, 1973), pp. 405-412.

36. See chapter 3 of this volume.

37. Elliot W. Eisner, *The Educational Imagination: On the Design and Evaluation of School Programs*, 2d ed. (New York: Macmillan, 1985); Joel Weiss, "Assessing Nonconventional Outcomes of Schooling," in *Review of Research in Education*, vol. 8, edited by David C. Berliner (Washington, DC: American Educational Research Association, 1980).

38. Ralph T. Putnam, Magdalene Lampert, and Penelope L. Peterson, "Alternative Perspectives on Knowing Mathematics in Elementary Schools," in *Review of Research in Education*, vol. 16, edited by Courtney B. Cazden (Washington, DC: American Educational Research Association, 1990), pp. 57-150.

39. Ken Shaw, "Curriculum, Management, and the Improvement of Education: Forging a Practical Alliance," *Journal of Curriculum Studies* 19, no. 3 (1987): 203-217.

40. John Dewey, *Democracy and Education* (New York: Free Press, 1916), p. 107.

41. James B. Macdonald, "Responsible Curriculum Development," in *Confronting Curriculum Reform*, edited by Elliot W. Eisner (Boston: Little, Brown, 1971), p. 124.

42. See Philip W. Jackson, "Conceptions of Curriculum and Curriculum Specialists," in *Handbook of Research on Curriculum*, edited by Philip W. Jackson (New York: Macmillan, 1992), pp. 3-40.

43. Ibid.

44. Elizabeth C. Wilson, "Designing Institutional Curricula: A Case Study of Curriculum Practice," in John I. Goodlad and Associates, *Curriculum Inquiry: The Study of Curriculum Practice* (New York: McGraw-Hill, 1979), pp. 405-454.

45. Robert F. Mager, *Preparing Instructional Objectives* (Palo Alto, CA: Fearon, 1962).

46. Ralph W. Tyler, "Some Persisting Questions on the Defining of Objectives," in *Defining Educational Objectives*, edited by C. M. Lindvall (Pittsburgh: University of Pittsburgh Press, 1964), p. 79.

47. Elliott W. Eisner, "Instructional and Expressive Objectives: Their Formulation and Use in Curriculum," in *Curriculum Evaluation: Instructional Objectives*, edited by W. James Popham (Chicago: Rand McNally, 1969); Eisner, *The Educational Imagination*.

48. Eisner, *The Educational Imagination*, pp. 120, 118.

49. Stenhouse, "Some Limitations of the Use of Objectives in Curriculum Research and Planning," p. 76.

50. Paul H. Hirst, "The Nature and Structure of Curriculum Objectives," in Paul H. Hirst, *Knowledge and the Curriculum: A Collection of Philosophical Papers* (London: Routledge and Kegan Paul, 1974).

51. Joseph J. Schwab, "The Practical: A Language for Curriculum," *School Review* 78 (1969): 1-23.

52. Richard S. Peters, "Must an Educator Have an Aim?" in Richard S. Peters, *Authority, Responsibility, and Education* (London: George Allen and Unwin, 1959).

53. Blyth, "One Development Project's Awkward Thinking about Objectives," p. 102.

54. Walker, "A Naturalistic Model for Curriculum Development."

55. Walker, *Fundamentals of Curriculum*, p. 489.

56. Macdonald and Clark, "Critical Value Questions and the Analysis of Objectives and Curricula," p. 408.

57. National Council of Teachers of Mathematics, *Curriculum and Evaluation Standards for School Mathematics* (Reston, VA: National Council of Teachers of Mathematics, 1989), p. 2.

58. See, for example, Theodore R. Sizer, *Horace's Compromise: The Dilemma of the American High School* (Boston: Houghton Mifflin, 1985).

59. See, for example, Blyth, "One Development Project's Awkward Thinking about Objectives"; Marit K. Granheim and Ulf P. Lundgren, "Steering by Goals and Evaluation in the Norwegian Education System: A Report from the EMIL Project," *Journal of Curriculum Studies* 23, no. 6 (1991): 481-505.

60. Granheim and Lundgren, "Steering by Goals and Evaluation in the Norwegian Education System."

61. David A. Abramson, "Curriculum Research and Evaluation," *Review of Educational Research* 36, no. 3 (1966): 391.

CHAPTER VIII

Research on Teaching and Teacher Education

LORIN W. ANDERSON

The purpose of this chapter is to explore the extent to which the Bloom *Taxonomy of Educational Objectives* has had an impact on educational researchers, teacher educators, and teachers. As we shall see, the Taxonomy has had a strong impact on researchers who study classroom instruction and teaching. It appears to have had less of an impact on teacher educators and very little lasting impact on teachers themselves, particularly those in the United States.[1]

The Impact of the Taxonomy on Researchers

Classroom researchers have used the Taxonomy to examine a variety of topics: teaching methods, instructional strategies, teacher questioning, and the tasks teachers assign to students. In their studies, these researchers rarely have employed all six major categories of the Taxonomy. Rather, they have tended to focus on two generic categories, labeled "lower-order" and "higher-order" objectives.

DISTINGUISHING BETWEEN HIGHER-ORDER AND LOWER-ORDER OBJECTIVES

There is considerable disagreement among researchers as to the point on the continuum which separates lower-order and higher-order objectives. As Crooks has pointed out, the "lower level has been defined to include the bottom one, two, or three categories" (Knowledge, Comprehension, Application).[2] Consistent with the authors of the Taxonomy, Andre asserted that knowledge objectives have traditionally been referred to as lower order, while the other five taxonomic levels have been considered higher order.[3] However, in 1963 Bloom himself referred to the Analysis, Synthesis, and Evaluation

Lorin W. Anderson is a Professor in the Department of Educational Leadership and Policies, University of South Carolina—Columbia.

levels of the Taxonomy as involving "higher mental processes." According to Bloom, these higher mental processes were to be differentiated from knowledge and problem solving (which was some combination of comprehension and application).[4]

Between these two extremes are other varied interpretations. For example, Winne regarded objectives in the "knowledge" and "comprehension" categories as lower-order objectives and those in all other categories as higher-order objectives.[5] Hegarty suggested that the differentiation between lower- and higher-order objectives occurred *within the comprehension category*.[6] For her, objectives in the "translation" subcategory under comprehension were lower-order while those in the "interpretation" and "extrapolation" subcategories under comprehension (and in all subsequent categories) were considered higher-order objectives. Mevarech and Werner differentiated between lower- and higher-order objectives *within the application category*. For them, objectives in the knowledge and comprehension categories and in the "routine application" subcategory (under application) were labeled lower-order objectives, while those in the "nonroutine application" subcategory and in the analysis, synthesis, and evaluation categories were referred to as higher-order objectives.[7]

In light of the above discussion, it should come as no surprise that some educators, confused as to the proper placement of the comprehension and application categories, suggested the formation of three broad categories: knowledge; comprehension and routine, well-practiced application; and nonroutine application, analysis, synthesis, and evaluation.[8] These categories are quite similar to those described by Bloom in 1963 to which I have already referred.

RESEARCH ON TEACHING METHODS

Historically, there has been a consensus that different teaching methods are needed to teach different types or levels of objectives. In various studies based partially or totally on the Taxonomy, this consensus takes the form of several different propositions.

Perhaps the most prevalent proposition is that teaching methods which emphasize efficient one-way communication (e.g., lectures) are more useful in helping students acquire lower-order objectives, while those which emphasize two-way communication either among students themselves (e.g., cooperative learning) or between students and teachers (e.g., discussion) are more useful in helping students achieve higher-order objectives.[9] This proposition has received substantial empirical support.[10]

A second proposition is that teaching methods which include "real world" experiences are more appropriate for facilitating the acquisition of higher-order objectives, while those which rely on classroom experiences *only* are more likely to result in the learning of lower-order objectives. The assumption here is that students are more actively involved in and see the importance of "real world" experiences, while classroom experiences are primarily passive and of questionable relevance.

In this regard Mevarech and Werner randomly assigned 58 college sophomores enrolled in a course entitled "Introduction to Gerontology" to one of three instructional treatments.[11] Students in the first two treatments either received lectures (Treatment A) or read articles and answered questions (Treatment B). Students in Treatment C, on the other hand, engaged in activities such as interviewing old people, visiting special facilities for the aged, and participating in simulations. As predicted, Treatment A produced students with the highest mean score on a test of lower-order objectives. In contrast, Treatment C produced students with the highest mean score on a test of higher-order objectives as well as students with the highest mean ratings of their ability to analyze case study reports.

A third proposition is that lecture methods are more appropriate in those subject areas in which the knowledge base is generally agreed upon (e.g., mathematics, physical sciences, and engineering), while discussion methods are more useful in subject areas in which there is some disagreement as to what constitutes the body of knowledge (e.g., social sciences, humanities). If one can reasonably assume that the first set of subject areas contains large numbers of objectives which emphasize knowledge and comprehension of well-specified facts and principles, while the second set, by virtue of its ambiguity, includes objectives primarily at the higher taxonomic levels, the relationship between this hypothesis and the initial one is quite clear. Gage and Berliner summarize a set of research studies which support this proposition.[12]

A fourth proposition is that teacher-directed methods are more appropriate when subject matters are defined in terms of the facts and principles to be memorized than when these same subject matters are defined in terms of the basic concepts and their interrelationships. While the third proposition concerns the way in which subject areas may appear "in nature," this fourth one addresses the way in which they are presented to students. However, the prediction implied by the proposition is the same. If one can reasonably assume that facts and principles are typically taught at the "knowledge" level and possibly at the "application" level of the Taxonomy, while concepts are taught at the "comprehension" level and often at the "analysis" level, this proposition is congruent with the previous one. Kazanas and Chawhan provide data in support of this proposition.[13]

RESEARCH ON MASTERY LEARNING

The most obvious application of the Taxonomy to research on instructional strategies is in the area of mastery learning.[14] Since Bloom developed the concept of mastery learning, this application should come as no surprise. What is surprising is the longevity of mastery learning in educational theory and practice. In fact, over the past two decades several volumes have been devoted to the application of mastery learning principles.[15] For the purpose of this discussion, the basic principles of mastery learning and procedures for implementing these principles in schools and classrooms will be summarized briefly.

Mastery learning is an instructional strategy based on the premise that virtually all students *can* and *will learn* what schools have to teach. Mastery learning relies heavily on total class instruction, providing individualized or small-group attention and assistance to students only as necessary. Several components of the mastery learning strategy appear to be central to its success. (See table 1.)

The Taxonomy has impacted on research on mastery learning in two primary ways. First, researchers on mastery learning have used the Taxonomy to develop highly valid unit and course assessments.[16] Test blueprints (also known as "tables of specifications") are developed in accordance with the Taxonomy to ensure a clear match between the content to be taught and the content to be tested. When such a correspondence between curriculum and assessment has been established, the likelihood of detecting instructional effects is increased substantially.

Second, and consistent with the concerns of researchers on teaching methods, the Taxonomy has enabled researchers to examine the impact of mastery learning on the acquisition of higher-order as well as lower-order objectives.[17] In this case, researchers have used the Taxonomy to ensure that items related to both lower- and higher-order objectives are included on the criterion test. Separate scores are computed for the two sets of objectives and the performance of students taught using mastery learning methods is compared with those taught by more conventional methods on both sets of scores.

TABLE 1

KEY COMPONENTS OF SUCCESSFUL MASTERY LEARNING PROGRAMS

Course Planning

1. Essential objectives are identified and organized into instructional units which are sequenced.
2. Appropriate assessment instruments and/or procedures are developed to chart student progress in terms of the objectives within each unit and across units.
3. Standards of mastery are set for each assessment instrument and/or procedure.

Instructional Delivery

4. Learning expectations (e.g., objectives, standards) are communicated to students at the beginning of each unit.
5. In each unit, instruction which focuses on the learning expectations is provided to an entire class of students.
6. Following a period of initial instruction, student learning of the unit objectives is assessed and judged in terms of the preset mastery standards.
7. Based on this evaluation of student learning, students are divided into two groups: (1) those who have mastered the unit, and (2) those who need more time and assistance to master the unit.
8. Group 1 students are given enrichment activities (to extend and enhance their learning relative to the unit) or asked to tutor those students in Group 2.
9. Group 2 students are given extra time and assistance to master the unit objectives. They subsequently are reassessed on the unit objectives.

Evaluation

10. Periodically, students are administered cumulative, comprehensive assessments for the purpose of examining their retention of previously taught objectives and assigning grades.

Studies by Mevarech and by Mevarech and Werner are exemplary investigations of this use of the Taxonomy.[18]

RESEARCH ON TEACHER QUESTIONING AND STUDENT TASKS

Research on teacher questioning is perhaps the most visible application of the Taxonomy to the study of teaching. While there are other systems that have been used to classify classroom questions,[19] Taxonomy-based analytic systems are by far the most frequently used.[20] Within this context, researchers have asked two fundamental questions about teacher questions. First, how many and what kinds of questions do teachers ask? Second, what is the relationship between the questions teachers ask and what their students learn?

Descriptive studies. Teachers' questions consume no more than one-sixth of all classroom time.[21] With respect to frequency, teachers

on the average ask about two questions during each minute they are in
the classroom.[22] When these two findings are combined we see that
teachers ask large numbers of very short questions. In contrast,
students' questions of teachers are rare.[23] Berliner has estimated that on
average an individual student asks a question of a teacher about once
per month.[24]

The vast majority of questions asked of students focus on lower-
order objectives. Gall estimated that approximately 20 percent of
teachers' questions required students to think (rather than recall or
routinely apply what they had been taught).[25] Dunkin and Biddle
estimated that between one-quarter and one-third of all questions
focus on higher-order objectives.[26] In a cross-national observational
study of 429 classrooms in 275 schools in eight countries, Anderson,
Ryan, and Shapiro found that higher-order questions accounted for
less than 10 percent of the questions in four countries (Australia,
Canada, Nigeria, and Thailand) and represented less than 25 percent
of the questions in three countries (Israel, the Republic of Korea, and
the Netherlands).[27] In Hungary over one-half of the questions were
classified as higher-order.

Somewhat surprisingly, lower-order questions predominate even
in classrooms occupied by high ability students. Gallagher observed
ten junior and senior high school classes for academically gifted
students.[28] In these classes, approximately 54 percent of the questions
required simple recall of memorized information. Less than 20 percent
required higher-order thinking on the part of students.

In summary, then, researchers have discovered that teachers ask
large numbers of questions, the vast majority of which require
students to remember what they were taught. Furthermore, these
findings appear to be consistent across subject matters, age levels,
ability levels, and countries. (As a historical note, Stevens found in
1912 that most questions asked by teachers emphasized memory and
"smothered" pupils' expression.)[29]

Correlational and experimental studies. Do students learn more or
better if they are asked more questions that focus on higher-order
objectives? Unfortunately, the answer to this rather simple question is
quite complex. Four major reviews related to this question are cited
here.

Gall concluded that teachers' use of higher-order questions was
positively associated with student achievement.[30] However, most of
the studies reviewed by Gall were naturalistic and correlational in
nature.

In contrast, Winne limited his review to experimental studies. Two types of experimental studies were differentiated: training studies (in which teachers were trained in the use of questions but were free to use them as they wished in their classrooms) and skills studies (in which the frequency and manner of teacher questioning were prescribed by the experimenter). Winne concluded his review by stating that "whether teachers use predominantly higher cognitive questions or predominantly fact questions makes little difference in student achievement."[31]

Redfield and Rousseau in essence reanalyzed the studies reviewed by Winne (adding two studies to the eighteen Winne had reviewed). Rather than tallying the results in terms of whether or not higher-order questioning produced greater student achievement as Winne had done, Redfield and Rousseau calculated the magnitude of the effect of the questioning treatment. Based on their analysis, Redfield and Rousseau concluded that "teachers' predominant use of higher cognitive questions has a positive effect on student achievement."[32]

Samson et al. updated Redfield and Rousseau's review and used effect sizes as well.[33] They concluded that higher-order questions did influence student achievement, but the effect in general was not as great as that estimated by Redfield and Rousseau. However, the effect was greater in better designed studies and in studies which lasted for longer periods of time (e.g., twenty days or more). In these studies, the effect size was very close to that estimated by Redfield and Rousseau.

In recent years, attention has shifted to explanations for the varied results found in these reviews. One possible explanation is that different definitions of lower-order and higher-order questions are being used.

Another possible explanation is the ambiguity of the criterion measure (i.e., the achievement test). Unlike research on teaching methods and strategies, where the achievement test has been purposefully designed to reflect different levels of objectives, research on teacher questioning has relied extensively on generic achievement tests.[34] It seems reasonable to assume that simply asking higher-order questions will not have much effect on student achievement if the achievement test is composed of items testing lower-level objectives.

A third possible explanation is that the level at which a question actually functions in the classroom (in contrast to the level at which it was intended to function) depends on the instruction provided or on the students' prior knowledge related to the question being asked. Carlsen nicely illustrates this point:

The question, "What are the functions of the human skeleton?" would be considered a high-level question . . . if asked to a group of biology students just beginning their study of the skeletal system. If, on the other hand, the teacher had spent the previous lesson listing functions on the chalkboard and warning students there would be a quiz on the topic, the question would become a low-level, recall question.[35]

It must be pointed out, however, that the developers of the Taxonomy were well aware of this potential problem. Consider the following quotation from the *Handbook*: "Before the reader can classify a particular test exercise he must know, or at least make some assumptions about, the learning situations which have preceded the test. He must also actually attempt to solve the test problem and note the mental process he utilizes."[36] In this regard, there is evidence that older students, who have more knowledge and experience, benefit more from higher-order questions than do younger students[37] and that economically disadvantaged students benefit more from lower-order questions than do economically advantaged students.[38]

Andre has provided a useful summary of what is known about the relationship between the asking of questions and students' learning.[39] Higher-order questions are likely to be appropriate and useful when the objective is higher-order learning. Higher-order questions do not hinder lower-order learning. Lower-order questions do not facilitate the acquisition of higher-order objectives. It can also be said that lower-order questions are, in fact, the most effective way of producing lower-order learning.[40]

Tasks assigned to students. In addition to being asked questions, students are assigned activities to perform or tasks to be completed. In the past two decades the Taxonomy has been used in research studies to describe and classify these activities and tasks.

Like classroom questions, the tasks assigned to students tend to be at the lowest level of the Taxonomy. In her observational study of fifth grade students Stodolsky found that 97 percent of the mathematics activities in which students were engaged in the classroom focused either on the knowledge or comprehension level. In social studies, this figure was approximately 75 percent.[41]

Calfee and Calfee conducted observations in a number of second and fifth grade classrooms.[42] In the second grade, the percentage of tasks at the application level or above was approximately 6 percent in reading/language arts and 3 percent in mathematics. In the fifth grade, these figures were 12 percent and 5 percent, respectively.

Similarly, Kerry analyzed 1638 transactions between teachers and students in secondary classrooms.[43] One of the most intriguing findings was that 54 percent of those transactions involved behavior or classroom management. Of the 46 percent of the interactions that pertained to instruction, however, slightly less than 10 percent required some type of thinking by students, rather than recall of what had previously been taught.

In comparison with data on classroom questions, then, the data collected on activities and tasks suggests an even greater emphasis on lower-order objectives. Goodlad, Klein, and their associates summarize these findings:

Rather than probing, seeking, inquiring, children were predominantly responding and covering. Even when using materials of curriculum projects presumably emphasizing "discovery" methods, pupils appeared bent on covering the content of textbooks, workbooks, and supplementary reading material.[44]

It is important to note that this preponderance of lower-order tasks can be reduced. Fisher and Hiebert compared a skills-oriented approach to literacy instruction of second and sixth grade students with a literature-based approach. In the skills-oriented approach, following a period of whole-class instruction students "completed teacher-assigned work sheets and other assignments that provided practice on particular skills or read assigned textbook passages."[45] In contrast, in the literature-based approach, following a brief teacher-led lesson on reading strategies, students "selected trade books to read or wrote on topics of their choosing" for about forty-five minutes. During this time period, the teacher also read or wrote.

The results indicated that the tasks assigned to and completed by the students in the two approaches differed substantially in their taxonomic level. In the skills-oriented approach, 93 percent of the tasks for the second grade students and 80 percent of the tasks for the sixth grade students emphasized knowledge or comprehension. In the literature-based approach only 38 percent of the tasks in the second grade and 32 percent of the tasks in the sixth grade emphasized these two lowest levels of the Taxonomy.

In summary, researchers who used the Taxonomy in their studies of classroom instruction have learned that helping students master different types or levels of objectives requires quite different teaching methods and instructional strategies. Second, the Taxonomy has helped many researchers realize the need for highly valid forms of assessment in order to be able to detect differences in the effectiveness of various teaching methods or instructional strategies. Third, fewer than one third of the questions asked or the tasks assigned by teachers require students to engage in higher-order thinking. Fourth, when teachers use higher-order questions or assign higher-order tasks their students generally are able to engage in higher levels of thinking. Furthermore, when this relationship between higher-order tasks or questions and complex student learning does not exist, there are quite reasonable explanations for its absence.

The Impact of the Taxonomy on Teacher Educators

With the amount of knowledge gained from classroom research involving the Taxonomy, one might expect that teacher educators would incorporate the Taxonomy in their own curriculum and instruction. To a certain extent, this has been done. Within a decade after its publication, the Taxonomy was used to analyze the curriculum and objectives of teacher education programs in the United States[46] and throughout the world (see chapter 9 in this volume). Furthermore, during the past several decades, teacher educators have used the Taxonomy to help teachers in four general areas: (1) specifying lesson objectives, (2) preparing tests, (3) asking questions at different taxonomic levels, and (4) increasing the cognitive levels of activities and tasks they assign to students.

Specifying lesson objectives. While course and even unit objectives often are developed by textbook publishers, state departments of education, curriculum specialists, and school administrators, lesson objectives tend to be specified by classroom teachers. In fact, lesson planning is the most frequent type of planning performed by teachers and, as a result, teacher educators have made several attempts to help teachers use the Taxonomy to plan their lessons and formulate their lesson objectives.[47] Unfortunately, the effectiveness of most of these efforts has not been evaluated systematically.

Teacher-made tests. Teacher-made tests are of critical importance to classroom teachers, particularly those at the upper elementary, middle school, and senior high school levels. Herman and Door-Bremme reported that approximately three-fourths of the tests used by over 350 high school teachers in making decisions about students (e.g., determining students' need for additional assistance, deciding on the grades to be assigned to students) were developed by teachers.[48]

Teacher educators have helped teachers to analyze their own tests in terms of the Taxonomy.[49] Teachers also have been helped to write items at various levels of the Taxonomy. In one high school district in the early 1960s, the Taxonomy was used to develop banks of test items in English, mathematics, foreign languages, geography, and social studies.[50]

Asking questions. Sanders was one of the first teacher educators to incorporate the Taxonomy in an effort to improve the quality of the questions teachers asked in their classrooms. Sanders believed that asking questions at a variety of taxonomic levels was more important than asking questions at any single level. In fact, he clearly stated that the objective of his book is to "describe a practical plan to ensure a *varied* intellectual atmosphere in a classroom."[51] Moreover, he believed that an increase in "higher-order" questions was necessary to achieve this objective: "The approach [used in this book] is through a systematic consideration of questions that require students to *use* ideas, rather than simply to *remember* them."[52] Sanders' volume, *Classroom Questions*, has been used as the basis for teacher training programs developed by Ghee and by Lucking among others.[53] Other programs derived directly from the Taxonomy have also been developed.[54]

In addition to being trained in highly prescriptive programs, teachers have been taught to improve their classroom questioning by observing other teachers or reflecting on their own questioning. For example, Olmo describes one such approach in which preservice teachers were encouraged to

record and identify the questions from lessons they observed and designed in terms of the various classifications of cognition. . . . Later, in methods class, the questions were evaluated in terms of the level of thinking required. Striving for higher levels of thinking beyond recall and interpretation to analysis, synthesis, and evaluation, the prospective teachers began formulating their own questions.[55]

Videotaped lessons have also been used to train teachers to ask analytic questions.[56] And, instruments designed to help teachers examine the types of questions they ask have been developed within the framework of the Taxonomy.[57]

During the past two decades, concerns for helping teachers learn to ask different types of questions have been incorporated into

comprehensive staff development efforts.[58] International examples
include programs developed in Indonesia and in Thailand.[59]

Assigning activities and tasks to students. Teacher educators have also
attempted to teach teachers about the activities and tasks they assign to
their students. Teachers have been told that simply assigning tasks
with instructions to focus on higher-order learning does not guarantee
that higher-order learning will occur.[60] Rather, teachers must establish
the context for and conditions within which the desired learning is to
occur.

In order to facilitate higher-order learning, teachers have been
taught two separate strategies. The first relies on advance organizers
prior to the assignment of tasks and activities. Advance organizers are
"appropriately relevant and inclusive introductory materials [which
are] presented at a higher level of abstraction, generality, and
inclusiveness than the content to be learned."[61] If, for example,
students are expected to learn a simple computer programming
language, an advance organizer might present a model of the computer
and include the relationship of each program statement to the model.
Snapp and Glover provided evidence that advance organizers written
at the analysis level facilitate students' ability to analyze written
material.[62] Additional evidence related to the effect of advance
organizers on transfer of learning (also a higher-order operation) is
provided by Mayer.[63]

A second strategy for enhancing the learning of higher-order
objectives is for the teacher to assign tasks that are likely to foster such
learning and to work with the students as they proceed through these
tasks. An excellent example of this approach is provided in materials
recently prepared and used by the Mississippi Department of
Education in working with primary school teachers.[64] First, teachers
are introduced to the Taxonomy. Next, they are given a variety of
classroom projects that exemplify the various levels of the Taxonomy.
The following example is intended to help students learn to evaluate
what they have learned:

Cut out several pictures of food products from a magazine [and place them on
the bulletin board]. Be sure you have a variety from each food group. Let
your students establish a criterion for what constitutes a balanced diet using
the pictures you have cut out. Then, let each child come to the board and
evaluate whether or not he or she had a balanced diet the day before.[65]

Teachers are then asked to design their own activities which
emphasize different levels of the Taxonomy. For example,

Plan a science experience where children will predict something, observe or test it, then draw conclusions. Use at least three of Bloom's levels. Make notes of the children's reactions.[66]

Finally, teachers are helped to understand the importance of higher-order thinking in their classrooms and provided with additional classroom applications.

Impact of the Taxonomy on Teachers

In the previous section we have seen that teacher educators have used the Taxonomy to help teachers plan their lessons, prepare their tests, ask questions, and assign tasks. What has been the overall effect of these efforts on the practice of teaching? Unfortunately, the effect has been quite minimal.

With respect to lesson planning, a great deal of evidence leads to the conclusion that teachers begin their lesson planning with classroom activities (i.e., what they want their students to do), rather than with learning objectives (i.e., what they want their students to learn).[67] From a teacher's perspective, classroom activities may be more important than objectives. They are concrete, under teacher control, and keep students busy (therefore serving a classroom management function). In contrast, learning objectives are abstract and under student control. In addition, the implementation of objectives-based planning may result in problems of classroom management because some students achieve objectives faster than others.

Despite substantial evidence that teachers can be taught to increase their use of higher-order questions in their classrooms,[68] there is equally compelling evidence that teachers continue to rely on lower-order questions.[69] Elementary students in particular are not being taught to think, reason, and defend their points of view.

The vast majority of the items which appear on teacher-made tests continue to be written at the lowest levels of the Taxonomy. Fleming and Chambers, for example, analyzed almost 9000 test items prepared by teachers at all grade levels and in a variety of subject areas.[70] They concluded that about 80 percent of all the items were written at the knowledge level, and of the items written by high school teachers, about 66 percent were at that level. These findings were supported by research conducted by Kirby and Oescher.[71] Furthermore, Carter reported that high school teachers have great difficulty matching test items with the corresponding taxonomic level, and that this difficulty increased at the higher taxonomic levels. Even at the end of training in writing test items these teachers felt insecure about their testmaking skills, particularly in writing items at the higher taxonomic levels.[72] In her analysis of teacher-made tests prepared by high school English teachers, Pfeiffer noted a tendency for the teachers to write test items at taxonomic levels that are lower than those embedded in the objectives they have established for their students.[73] More recently, Haertel concluded that classroom tests "often failed to reflect teachers' stated instructional objectives, frequently requiring little more than repetition of material presented in the textbook or in class, or the solution of problems much like those encountered during instruction."[74]

Thus, forty years after the development of the Taxonomy, teachers plan classroom activities, not objectives, construct tests that include a preponderance of knowledge-level items, and ask questions of their students that in the main require them to recall or recognize what they have been taught. These findings hold true despite the knowledge gained from research concerning the benefits of objective-based planning, the usefulness of tests for assessing higher-order thinking, and the value of classroom questions that require students to do more than merely recall information. Furthermore, these findings hold true despite teacher educators' attempts to change the way in which teachers approach their planning, testing, and classroom interactions.

Why Do Teachers Make Such Little Use of the Taxonomy?

There are several plausible explanations for the findings that teachers, while clearly cognizant of the Taxonomy, tend not to use it widely in their planning, teaching, or testing. First, using the Taxonomy takes far more time than teachers typically have at their disposal. Teachers, particularly elementary school teachers, have little if any scheduled planning time. Secondary school teachers may indeed have scheduled planning time, but they typically teach more than one course each day. In both cases, then, it is small wonder that teachers rely on the content, objectives, and activities contained in commercially produced materials. If these materials have been developed with the Taxonomy in mind, then one can argue that the Taxonomy is being used *indirectly* by the teachers. Unless this relationship between the materials and the Taxonomy is made explicit to teachers, the teachers themselves would likely not report using the Taxonomy.

Second, teachers may have beliefs about teaching and learning that are inconsistent with using the Taxonomy. Some teachers may believe that many students, particularly those from economically disadvantaged homes, are unable to master objectives much above the lowest level of the Taxonomy—knowledge. These teachers would consider an emphasis on higher-order objectives a waste of time. Other teachers may believe that they are under great external pressure to cover as much content as they can in a very short time period. The easiest way to conform to this pressure is to focus almost exclusively on lower-level objectives. For these teachers, while addressing higher-level objectives would be "nice," it would not be "practical." Still other teachers, confronted with the need not only to assign marks or grades to students but also to justify the marks or grades assigned, may shy away from assessing higher-order objectives. Assignments and test items derived from knowledge objectives typically have right or wrong answers that can readily be confirmed by "looking in the book." Assignments and test items requiring analysis, synthesis, or evaluation may have multiple answers. Which answer is more plausible, more defensible, more accurate, or more reasonable, and why? In addition, when skills of analysis, synthesis, and evaluation are assessed, the reasoning behind the answer is often more important than the answer itself. Defending one explanation as more appropriate, complete, or compelling than another is a task that some teachers would prefer to avoid.

Third, the Taxonomy may be too rational or too complex for some teachers. Teachers tend to prefer personal knowledge (that is, knowledge gained from personal experience) over propositional knowledge (that is, knowledge represented in propositional form derived from rational argument and/or evidence). The continuing use of common practices, therefore, is likely to take precedence over any type of change derived from a formal conceptual framework. Furthermore, consistent with Carter's findings, conceptualizing and applying higher-order objectives in planning, teaching, and/or testing may be very difficult for many teachers.[75] And, if, as Carter concluded, those teachers who are unable to do so lack confidence in their ability, it seems unreasonable to expect they will conceptualize and apply higher-order objectives on their own.

The first three explanations attribute the lack of use of the Taxonomy either to teachers or to the conditions of teaching. A fourth explanation is inherent in the Taxonomy itself, for it was not intended to change teaching practice. Rather, the authors of the

Taxonomy were more interested in classifying existing objectives than in suggesting what objectives might be established. In fact, they refrained from making such suggestions, retreating instead behind their argument that the Taxonomy was "value free" or "value neutral." Furthermore, even when possible changes were considered the wording related to these changes was quite cautious:

A teacher, in classifying the goals of a teaching unit, *may find* they all fall within the taxonomic category of recalling or remembering knowledge. Looking at the taxonomic categories *may suggest* to him that, for example, he *could include* some goals dealing with the application of knowledge and with the analysis of the situations in which the knowledge is used.[76]

Relative to teaching and teacher education, then, the Taxonomy remains something of an enigma. Like the weather, everyone talks about it but no one does much about it. But before one bemoans this state of affairs, it should be remembered that the primary purpose of the Taxonomy was to facilitate communication. As the authors themselves wrote:

The major purpose in constructing a taxonomy of educational objectives is to facilitate communication. In our original consideration of the project we conceived it as a method of improving the exchange of ideas and materials among test workers, as well as other persons concerned with educational research and curriculum development.[77]

There is a good possibility that the Taxonomy will stimulate conversation among teachers and teacher educators for some time to come, perhaps another forty years.

Notes

1. This generalization apparently applies only to literature published in the United States. See chapter 9 for a discussion of the impact of the Taxonomy elsewhere.

2. Terence J. Crooks, "The Impact of Classroom Evaluation Practices on Students," *Review of Educational Research* 58 (1988): 454.

3. Thomas Andre, "Does Answering Higher Level Questions While Reading Facilitate Productive Learning?" *Review of Educational Research* 49 (1979): 280-318.

4. Benjamin S. Bloom, "Testing Cognitive Ability and Achievement," in *Handbook of Research on Teaching*, edited by Nathaniel L. Gage (Chicago: Rand McNally, 1963).

5. Philip H. Winne, "Experiments Relating Teachers' Use of Higher Cognitive Questions to Student Achievement," *Review of Educational Research* 49 (1979): 13-50.

6. Elizabeth H. Hegarty, "Levels of Scientific Enquiry in University Science Laboratory Classes: Implications of Curriculum Deliberations," *Research in Science Education* 8 (1978): 45-57.

142   TEACHING AND TEACHER EDUCATION

7. Zemira R. Mevarech and Shulamit Werner, "Are Mastery Learning Strategies Beneficial for Developing Problem Solving Skills?" *Higher Education* 14 (1985): 425-432.

8. Crooks, "The Impact of Classroom Evaluation Practices on Students."

9. Wilbert J. McKeachie, "Research on Teaching at the College and University Level," in *Handbook of Research on Teaching*, edited by Nathaniel L. Gage (Chicago: Rand McNally, 1963); Shlomo Sharan, "Cooperative Learning in Small Groups: Recent Methods and Effects on Achievement, Attitudes, and Ethnic Relations," *Review of Educational Research* 50 (1980): 241-273.

10. Wilbert J. McKeachie and James A. Kulik, "Effective College Teaching," in *Review of Research in Education*, vol. 3, edited by Fred N. Kerlinger (Itasca, IL: Peacock, 1975); David W. Johnson and Roger T. Johnson, "Classroom Instruction and Cooperative Learning," in *Effective Teaching: Current Research*, edited by Hersholt C. Waxman and Herbert J. Walberg (Berkeley, CA: McCutchan, 1991).

11. Mevarech and Werner, "Are Mastery Learning Strategies Beneficial for Developing Problem Solving Skills?"

12. Nathaniel L. Gage and David C. Berliner, *Educational Psychology*, 2d ed. (Boston: Houghton Mifflin, 1979).

13. H. C. Kazanas and A. R. Chawhan, "Effects of Two Treatments on Cognitive Achievement of Students Varying in Problem Solving Ability," *Journal of Educational Research* 75 (1975): 269-273.

14. Benjamin S. Bloom, "Learning for Mastery," *UCLA Evaluation Comment* 1, no. 2 (1968): 1-12.

15. James H. Block, editor, *Mastery Learning: Theory and Practice* (New York: Holt, Rinehart and Winston, 1971); James H. Block and Lorin W. Anderson, *Mastery Learning in Classroom Instruction* (New York: Macmillan, 1975); Kay P. Torshen, *The Mastery Approach to Competency-Based Education* (Orlando, FL: Academic Press, 1977); Jeffrey F. Lee and Kenneth W. Pruitt, *Providing for Individual Differences in Student Learning: A Mastery Learning Approach* (Springfield, IL: Thomas Publishers, 1984); Thomas R. Guskey, *Implementing Mastery Learning* (Belmont, CA: Wadsworth, 1985); Daniel U. Levine, editor, *Improving Student Achievement through Mastery Learning Programs* (San Francisco: Jossey-Bass, 1985); James H. Block, Helen E. Efthim, and Robert B. Burns, *Building Effective Mastery Learning Schools* (New York: Longman, 1989).

16. Block and Anderson, *Mastery Learning in Classroom Instruction.*

17. James H. Block and Robert B. Burns, "Mastery Learning," in *Review of Research in Education*, vol. 4, edited by Lee S. Shulman (Itasca, IL: Peacock, 1976).

18. Zemira R. Mevarech, "The Effects of Cooperative Mastery Learning Strategies on Mathematics Achievement," *Journal of Educational Research* 78 (1985): 372-377. Mevarech and Werner, "Are Mastery Learning Strategies Beneficial for Developing Problem Solving Skills?"

19. Robert T. Pate and Neville H. Bremer, "Guiding Learning through Skillful Questioning," *Elementary School Journal* 67 (1967): 417-422.

20. Stanley Doenau, "Soliciting," in *International Encyclopedia of Teaching and Teacher Education*, edited by Michael J. Dunkin (Oxford: Pergamon Press, 1987).

21. Michael J. Dunkin and Bruce J. Biddle, *The Study of Teaching* (New York: Holt, Rinehart and Winston, 1974); Peter Mortimore, Pamela Sammons, Louise Stoll, David Lewis, and Russell Ecob, *School Matters* (Berkeley, CA: University of California Press, 1988).

22. Meredith D. Gall, "The Use of Questions in Teaching," *Review of Educational Research* 40 (1970): 707-721.

23. Donald M. Medley, "Research in Teacher Effectiveness: Where It Is and How It Got There," *Journal of Classroom Interaction* 13, no. 2 (1978): 16-21; Lorin W. Anderson, Doris W. Ryan, and Bernard J. Shapiro, editors, *The IEA Classroom Environment Study* (Oxford: Pergamon Press, 1989).

24. David C. Berliner, "Asking Questions," in *The Effective Teacher, Lesson 18*, edited by Lorin W. Anderson (videotape), Columbia, SC: South Carolina Educational Television and the University of South Carolina, 1988.

25. Gall, "The Use of Questions in Teaching."

26. Dunkin and Biddle, *The Study of Teaching*.

27. Anderson, Ryan, and Shapiro, *The IEA Classroom Environment Study*.

28. James J. Gallagher, "Expressive Thought by Gifted Children in the Classroom," *Elementary English* 45 (1965): 559-568.

29. Romiett Stevens, *The Question as a Measure of Efficiency in Instruction: A Cultural Study of Classroom Practice* (New York: Teachers College Press, 1912).

30. Gall, "The Use of Questions in Teaching."

31. Winne, "Experiments Relating Teachers' Use of Higher Cognitive Questions to Student Achievement," p. 43.

32. Doris L. Redfield and Elaine W. Rousseau, "A Meta-analysis of Experimental Research on Teacher Questioning Behavior," *Review of Educational Research* 51 (1981): 244.

33. Gordon E. Samson, Bernadette Strykowski, Thomas Weinstein, and Herbert J. Walberg, "The Effects of Teacher Questioning Levels on Student Achievement: A Quantitative Synthesis," *Journal of Educational Research* 80 (1987): 290-295.

34. Crooks, "The Impact of Classroom Evaluation Practices on Students."

35. William S. Carlsen, "Questioning in Classrooms: A Sociolinguistic Perspective," *Review of Educational Research* 61 (1991): 166.

36. Benjamin S. Bloom et al., *Taxonomy of Educational Objectives: The Classification of Educational Goals, Handbook I: Cognitive Domain* (New York: David McKay, 1956), p. 51.

37. Robert S. Soar and Ruth M. Soar, "Emotional Climate and Management," in *Research on Teaching: Concepts, Findings, and Implications*, edited by Penelope L. Peterson and Herbert J. Walberg (Berkeley, CA: McCutchan, 1979).

38. Medley, "Research in Teacher Effectiveness."

39. Andre, "Does Answering Higher Level Questions While Reading Facilitate Productive Learning?"

40. Barak V. Rosenshine, "Content, Time, and Direct Instruction," in *Research on Teaching*, edited by Penelope L. Peterson and Herbert J. Walberg (Berkeley, CA: McCutchan, 1979); Crooks, "The Impact of Classroom Evaluation Practices on Students."

41. Susan S. Stodolsky, *The Subject Matters* (Chicago: University of Chicago Press, 1988).

42. Robert Calfee and Kathryn Calfee, *Beginning Teacher Evaluation Study: Phase II, 1973-74, Final Report* (Princeton, NJ: Educational Testing Service, 1976).

43. Trevor Kerry, "Analyzing the Cognitive Demand Made by Classroom Tasks in Mixed-Ability Classes," in *Classroom Teaching Skills*, edited by E. C. Wragg (London: Croom Helm, 1984).

44. John I. Goodlad, M. Frances Klein, and Associates, *Looking Behind the Classroom Door* (Belmont, CA: Wadsworth, 1974), p. 79.

45. Charles W. Fisher and Elfrieda H. Hiebert, "Characteristics of Tasks in Two Approaches to Literacy Instruction," *Elementary School Journal* 91 (1990): 4.

46. Jean M. Wood, *A Survey of Objectives for Teacher Education* (San Bernardino, CA: San Bernardino City School System, 1960); Louise L. Tyler and Laura J. Okumu, "A Beginning Step: A System for Analyzing Courses in Teacher Education," *Journal of Teacher Education* 16 (1965): 438-444.

47. Clifford B. Elliott, Philip R. Merrifield, and O. L. Davis, Jr., "Cognitive Dimensions of Lesson Objectives Set by Secondary Student Teachers" (Paper presented at the Annual Meeting of the American Educational Research Association, Chicago, 1966); Madeline Hunter, *Mastery Teaching* (El Segundo, CA: TIP Publications, 1984).

48. Joan L. Herman and Donald W. Door-Bremme, "Assessing Students: Teachers' Routine Practices and Reasoning" (Paper presented at the Annual Meeting of the American Educational Research Association, Los Angeles, 1982).

49. Isobel L. Pfeiffer and O. L. Davis, Jr., "Teacher-made Examinations: What Kinds of Thinking Do They Demand?" *NASSP Bulletin* 49 (1966): 1-10; Kathy Carter, "Do Teachers Understand the Principles for Writing Tests?" *Journal of Teacher Education* 35 (1984): 57-60.

50. Leon Lessinger, "Test Building and Test Banks through the Use of the 'Taxonomy of Educational Objectives'," *California Journal of Educational Research* 14 (1963): 195-201.

51. Norris M. Sanders, *Classroom Questions: What Kinds?* (New York: Harper and Row, 1966), p. 2 (emphasis added).

52. Ibid.

53. Harry J. Ghee, "A Study of the Effects of High Level Cognitive Questions on the Levels of Responses and Critical Thinking Abilities in Students of Two Social Problems Classes" (Doct. diss., University of Virginia, 1975); Robert A. Lucking, "A Study of the Effects of a Hierarchically-ordered Questioning Technique on Adolescents' Responses to Short Stories" (Doct. diss., University of Nebraska, 1975).

54. Susan W. Coolidge, *Using Higher Order Questions in the Primary Classroom to Improve Comprehension* (Fort Lauderdale, FL: Nova University Center for the Advancement of Education, 1989).

55. Barbara M. Olmo, "Questioning: Heart of Social Studies," *Social Education* 69 (1969): 949.

56. John J. Koran, "Supervision: An Attempt to Modify Behavior," *Educational Leadership* 69 (1969): 754-757.

57. O. L. Davis, Jr., Kevin Morse, Virginia M. Rogers, and Drew Tinsley, "Studying the Cognitive Emphases of Teachers' Classroom Questions," *Educational Leadership* 26 (1969): 711-719.

58. Linda M. Anderson, Carolyn Evertson, and Jere Brophy, "An Experimental Study of Effective Teaching in First-grade Reading Groups," *Elementary School Journal* 79 (1979): 193-223; Thomas Good and Douglas Grouws, "The Missouri Mathematics Effectiveness Project: An Experimental Study in Fourth-grade Classrooms," *Journal of Educational Psychology* 71 (1979): 335-362.

59. Aria Djalil and Lorin W. Anderson, "The Impact of a Research-based Teacher Training Program on Indonesian Teachers, Classrooms, and Students," *Teaching and Teacher Education* 5 (1989): 165-178; Malee Nitsaisook and Lorin W. Anderson, "An Experimental Investigation of the Effectiveness of In-service Teacher Education in Thailand," *Teaching and Teacher Education* 5 (1989): 287-302.

60. Andre, "Does Answering Higher Level Questions While Reading Facilitate Productive Learning?"; Douglas Barker and Walter G. Hapkiewicz, "The Effects of Behavioral Objectives on Relevant and Incidental Learning at Two Levels of Bloom's Taxonomy," *Journal of Educational Research* 72 (1979): 334-338; Orpha K. Duell,

"Effect of Type of Objective, Level of Test Question, and the Judged Importance of Test Materials upon Posttest Performance," *Journal of Educational Psychology* 66 (1974): 225-232.

61. David P. Ausubel, *Educational Psychology: A Cognitive View* (New York: Holt, Rinehart and Winston, 1968), p. 148.

62. Jim C. Snapp and John A. Glover, "Advance Organizers and Study Questions," *Journal of Educational Research* 20 (1990): 266-271.

63. Richard E. Mayer, "Can Advance Organizers Influence Meaningful Learning?" *Review of Educational Research* 49 (1979): 371-383.

64. Mississippi Department of Education, *Developing Thinking Skills in Young Children* (Jackson, MS: Mississippi Department of Education, 1990). ERIC ED 281 655.

65. Ibid., p. 65.

66. Ibid., p. 70.

67. Penelope L. Peterson and Christopher Clark, "Teachers' Thought Processes," in *Handbook of Research on Teaching*, 3rd ed., edited by Merlin C. Wittrock (New York: Macmillan, 1986).

68. Winne, "Experiments Relating Teachers' Use of Higher Cognitive Questions to Student Achievement"; Doenau, "Soliciting."

69. Anderson et al., *The IEA Classroom Environment Study*; Mortimore et al., *School Matters*.

70. Margaret Fleming and Barbara Chambers, "Teacher-made Tests: Windows on the Classroom," in *Testing in the Schools: New Directions for Testing and Measurement*, edited by W. E. Hathaway (San Francisco: Jossey-Bass, 1983).

71. Peggy C. Kirby and Jeffrey Oescher, "Assessing Teacher-made Math and Science Tests," *American Secondary Education* 18 (1989): 6-12.

72. Carter, "Do Teachers Understand the Principles for Writing Tests?"

73. Isobel L. Pfeiffer, "Teaching in Ability-grouped English Classes: A Study of Verbal Interaction and Cognitive Goals" (Doct. diss., Kent State University, 1966).

74. Edward Haertel, "Choosing and Using Classroom Tests: Teachers' Perspectives on Assessment" (Paper presented at the Annual Meeting of the American Educational Research Association, San Francisco, 1986).

75. Carter, "Do Teachers Understand the Principles for Writing Tests?"

76. Bloom et al., *Taxonomy of Educational Objectives*, p. 76 (emphasis added).

77. Ibid., p. 10.

CHAPTER IX

The Taxonomy of Educational Objectives in Continental Europe, the Mediterranean, and the Middle East

ARIEH LEWY AND ZOLTÁN BÁTHORY

Though philosophical empiricism and empirical research have their roots in Europe, empirical research as a systematic approach to studying education began in the United States. Even today, North American scholars strongly influence, and in some cases dominate, empirical research in education throughout the world. Their concerns set the educational research agenda for the globe. In some highly prestigious universities on the European continent, mainly in France and Germany, empirical research in education must be highly theory-oriented or it will have a status inferior to that of analytical and philosophical studies. In these institutions empirical studies in education are tied more strongly to trends in the United States than to analytical studies on the campus.

The Taxonomy is one American idea that was welcomed and used intensively by educators and educational researchers in continental Europe, the Mediterranean, and the Middle East for test construction, curriculum development, lesson planning, and teacher training. In most of these countries, the Taxonomy became part of the curriculum of teacher training programs, and most teachers trained in the last twenty years in these regions should have at least a rudimentary knowledge of it. Its popularity is quite likely due to its appealing simplicity, apparent usefulness, and convenient teachability; however, one should by no means underestimate the role of the strategies used in its dissemination.

Without deliberate planning the Taxonomy spread in a highly effective manner which was consistent with what Katz described as

Arieh Lewy is Professor of Education at Tel Aviv University, Tel Aviv, Israel. Zoltán Báthory is Professor of Education, University of Miskolo, Budapest, Hungary, and Director of the Center for Evaluation Studies at the National Institute of Education in Budapest.

the two-step flow model.[1] The model combines person-to-person persuasion with a support campaign provided by mass communication. Direct personal persuasion took place through three channels. First, courses in the Department of Education at the University of Chicago dealt with the Taxonomy and attracted a large number of students from abroad. In many countries these students later disseminated it and translated it into local languages. Second, the authors of the Taxonomy, including Bloom, delivered lectures around the world explaining their views on the topic. They spoke at a series of seminars initiated by international organizations such as UNESCO and the Organization for Economic Cooperation and Development (OECD), at national institutions and universities (such as the Max Planck Institute in Germany, the National Institute of Pedagogy in Hungary, and the National Conference of Educators and Educational Researchers in the then Soviet Union). The international seminar for curriculum development and evaluation, held in Gränna, Sweden, in 1971 facilitated the spread of the Taxonomy considerably. Third, the comparative studies of the International Association for the Evaluation of Educational Achievement (IEA), in which scholars from more than forty countries have participated, used the Taxonomy for curriculum analysis, test construction, and data summary, and thereby gave scholars from many countries opportunities to study and use it.

Mass communication took place through empirical and analytical studies published in leading journals and in a variety of handbooks. These publications indicated the support of and the legitimation by the professional community.

To grasp the impact of the Taxonomy in the non-English-speaking countries of Europe, the Mediterranean, and the Middle East, one has to be aware of two factors: the major concerns of the educational systems when the Taxonomy reached them, and the linguistic grouping of the countries. The concerns of the educational systems provided the context for the reception of the Taxonomy. The Taxonomy was published in the United States at a time when multiple-choice tests had gradually reduced the use of open-ended type questions in school examinations. Some observers worried that this test format would shift the emphasis in student learning towards rote memorization of facts, thereby reducing classroom attention to higher-order mental operations, such as problem solving and independent thinking.

The *Handbook* responded to this concern. Its authors clearly showed that multiple-choice items could be used to test the mastery of higher-order cognitive skills. Indeed, most illustrative items in the *Handbook* are multiple-choice questions, despite the indisputable fact that in the natural processes of teaching and learning, higher-order mental operations are triggered mainly by open-ended questions. The authors of the *Handbook* wanted to demonstrate the power of multiple-choice items to assess the mastery of mental processes of different types.

In contrast, teachers on the European continent generally prepared open-ended questions. Thus, the message of the *Handbook* did not reach European educators until the mid-1960s when the major concern of educational systems across the world was curriculum reform. In Europe as well as countries on neighboring continents the Taxonomy was used first in curriculum development and teaching, and only later came to the attention of experts in educational evaluation and measurement.

As to the linguistic grouping of the countries in this geographic area, two facts stand out. First, the languages of wider communication are English, French, German, and to a lesser degree Russian. Second, there are tremendous differences across the countries in the proportion of people who can easily communicate in non-native tongues. For example, in Sweden most educated people speak English, and in Rumania a high percentage of intellectuals speak French. In several other countries, however, most teachers can communicate only in the official language of the country and therefore learn about professional innovations beyond their country's borders through reports in translations.

In French-speaking areas (e.g., France, western Belgium, the eastern cantons of Switzerland, and the countries of Northern Africa) as well as in Romance language countries where French is the language of wider communication (e.g., Rumania, Italy, and Spain), a high proportion of educators became acquainted with the *Handbook* through its French translation. This translation, prepared in Canada, aroused less interest in France itself than in the other French-speaking areas. In regions where before the World War II German was the *lingua franca*, only a small proportion of the population now speaks a foreign language. Therefore, acquaintance with the *Handbook* was through its translation into national languages (e.g., Hungarian, Turkish, and Greek).

In countries where English was widely spoken among teachers (e.g., Sweden), the English version of the *Handbook* helped stimulate its use, and in these countries the publication of the *Handbook* in the national language provides no valid measure of the interest in it. An extensive literature about the Taxonomy appeared in Latin American countries, but it hardly reached Spain. Finally, some countries with different traditions of education but with common languages have struck up special alliances in dealing with the Taxonomy (e.g., Greece and Cyprus; the Netherlands and Flemish Belgium).

This chapter contains only partial information on the impact of the Taxonomy in the geographic region of our interest. The authors were highly dependent on the information they were able to collect, and by no means do the references in this article represent the full scope of the publications.

Manifestations of the Impact of the Taxonomy

After reviewing reports by national experts on the use of the Taxonomy in their countries and examining a sample of publications on this topic, we recognized that the impact was manifested in a broad variety of phenomena which can be grouped into several categories. To describe them, a scheme derived from the combination of the categories of the Affective Taxonomy[2] and of the Development Model of Levels of Use (LoU) constructed by Hall and Loucks[3] was used. Accordingly, distinctions were made among the following manifestations:

1. becoming aware of the existence of the Taxonomy and using it in a routine way;

2. adapting the Taxonomy to the unique needs of an educational system;

3. using the Taxonomy to deal with issues of concern in an educational system (studies in this category constitute a lateral extension of research on the Taxonomy);

4. dealing with conceptual issues related to the use of the Taxonomy; and

5. contributing to the integrated body of knowledge about the Taxonomy which has accumulated across the world.

While these categories resemble the definitions used in the schemes mentioned above, we make no claim that they represent a hierarchically ordered sequence. Unlike the Affective Taxonomy, which provides a scheme for classifying affective behaviors of an individual, and unlike the Developmental Model of Levels of Use, which measures the implementation of a particular innovation, the categories above refer to a variety of uncoordinated activities carried out by groups within an educational system. In principle, it may happen that in a certain country a small group of researchers in education makes a significant contribution to the body of knowledge, but little use is made of the Taxonomy in the educational system. Hence, most teachers are unfamiliar with it or are even ignorant of its existence. Therefore, one should view the scope of publication of the *Handbook* in a country as an index of its impact on educational research, rather than on practice.

BECOMING AWARE OF THE EXISTENCE OF THE TAXONOMY AND USING IT IN A ROUTINE WAY

Long before the publication of the *Handbook* in 1956, some of its ideas had been acknowledged and used by educators in various countries, at least in some rudimentary form. For example, adopting the view that learning entails more than remembering what the teacher says, the Jewish community of Bordeaux (France) issued "Regulations" in the tenth century that divided the weekly study schedule into two parts. The first consisted of a few lectures delivered by the teacher, and the second of independent studies by the students themselves, without teacher intervention. At the end of the week, the teacher had to conduct two examinations: one on what he himself taught, and the other on what the students learned on their own.[4] This bifurcation of study very much resembles the twofold division of the objectives included in the Taxonomy into the lower and higher mental functions.

Another example of the early use of ideas reflected in the Taxonomy appears in a 1720 Swedish document describing a reading lesson in the town of Norrbotten, which refers to the distinction between memorizing a text and comprehending it:

From the very beginning, children shall have become accustomed to reading clearly and diligently and to making firm observance of each sentence to its very end. Furthermore, they shall have become fully aware of the text they are reading and heed its utterance as if they heard it spoken by another [(!)]. In this manner, the children should gradually acquire a firm grasp of the textual meaning and content, and be able to articulate such in words other than those given in the text. In like measure, they shall answer with their own words to the questions posed them in the test.[5]

Swedish scholars view the Swedish Church Law from 1686, which contains the regulations for assessing the ability to read religious texts and know and interpret concepts from the Lutheran Catechisms, as a forerunner of a formal taxonomy.[6]

The German scholar Jegensdorf views Aristotle's distinction among three major categories of human action—thinking, feeling, and handling objects—as a precursor of the threefold division of the educational objectives suggested by the authors of the *Handbook* (i.e., cognitive, affective, and psychomotor domains).[7] Similarly, Lemke likens these three domains to Pestalozzi's relation of educational activities to three organs of the human body, "the three Hs: head, heart, and hand."[8]

Such scattered allusions suggest that the ideas contained in the *Handbook* have deep roots in the commonsense pedagogy of the enlightened tradition of European education. It is, therefore, no wonder that as soon as it appeared as a fully articulated, comprehensive model, it had a strong appeal to European scholars. Aided by the powerful dissemination strategy described above, it became well known in most countries of Europe. The fact that its ideas were not entirely new to its European readers helped raise interest in it. As Lindblom and Cohen convincingly argue, discipline-oriented scientific inquiry in the social sciences frequently does not generate new knowledge; rather it refines ideas derived from ordinary knowledge.[9]

The translation of the *Handbook* into European languages helped spread awareness of it significantly. (The translations are listed following the Notes at the end of this chapter.) However, the number of translations does not fully convey the extent to which educational professionals are familiar with the Taxonomy. In those countries in which educators and researchers can read only the local language, introductory books in curriculum, teaching practice, and educational evaluation contain a concise version of the Taxonomy. Thus, readers of Arabic, Czech, Croatian, Dutch, French, Finnish, German, Greek, Hungarian, Hebrew, Italian, Portuguese, Polish, Rumanian, Serbian, Slovene, Spanish, Turkish, and other languages spoken in Europe are able to become acquainted with the Taxonomy by reading publications in their mother tongues.[10]

ADAPTING TO UNIQUE SITUATIONS

Adaptation, in this context, refers to the flexible use of the Taxonomy and entails both cognitive and affective reaction to it. Cognitively, adaptation is the capacity to examine each element of an idea separately and judge its relevance to the issue of concern.

Affectively, adaptation is not only awareness of the innovation, but also the user's personal recognition of the importance of the innovation and its potential contribution to carrying out a task successfully.

Indeed, critics of the Taxonomy have pointed out that the verbatim reference to the taxonomic categories exactly as they appear in the original version of the *Handbook* frequently reflects a lack of complete understanding and an inability to adapt or redefine the categories to deal with the topic at hand. Birzea expressed concern about the perfunctory use of the Taxonomy by teachers and curriculum developers who do not fully comprehend its message.[11] Leimu reported complaints about the simplistic or erroneous use of the Taxonomy in Finland.[12] Teachers frequently misinterpret the meaning of the taxonomic categories and unjustifiably use the Taxonomy to determine the sequence of tasks and learning assignments.

In the literature relevant to the issue of adaptation, two means of adapting the Taxonomy to local needs stand out. The first is the development of taxonomies geared to specific subjects for the purpose of facilitating curriculum development and test construction. The second is the analysis of curricula and textbooks. Instances of these two types of adaptation have appeared in numerous countries.

Subject-specific taxonomies. In Germany, Fuller published a taxonomy of learning objectives in music.[13] In Rumania, a taxonomy of objectives in teaching foreign languages was prepared by Noveanu and Pana.[14] In Sweden, a taxonomy of mathematics instruction was constructed by Magne and Thorn.[15] In Hungary, Szebenyi developed a scheme for classifying educational objectives in civic education,[16] and in Israel, Eden produced a framework for classifying the objectives of a seventh grade civics course.[17]

Curriculum analysis. Curriculum analysis studies entail the classification of subject-specific curricular artifacts, such as educational objectives listed in a course syllabus, study assignments, test items, and textbook learning units. To carry out this task, the researchers first have to identify the subject-specific equivalents of the categories in the generalized taxonomic scheme. An interesting study of this type was carried out in the Netherlands.[18] The author used both the cognitive and affective taxonomies to examine the geography curricula in the Dutch educational system. Comparison was made of educational goals specified in geographic curricula of various school types, grade levels, and topics, as well as study units dealing with geographic regions taught in school.

EXTENDING THE TAXONOMY

Lateral extension here denotes studies which do not examine issues related to the use of the Taxonomy. Rather, those conducting these studies refer to the Taxonomy in the course of addressing some other concern. Studies in this category provide evidence about the internalization of the Taxonomy by educational researchers. Two studies of this type will be described here. One, published in Germany, deals with the legitimization of educational objectives and the other, conducted by two Israeli researchers, examines teachers' attitudes.

Schaefer examined the legitimization process of deriving operationally defined educational objectives from the goal of a biology course.[19] In the German literature on the curriculum, the legitimization process of educational goals and objectives is intensively studied. The process typically proceeds in a cascade-like sequence of steps beginning with a general goal statement, such as "the knowledge of biological structures and methods." (See fig. 1.) Intermediate statements and, later, operationally defined objectives are derived from this general statement. Their legitimization is based on the logical adequacy of the stepwise derivation process.

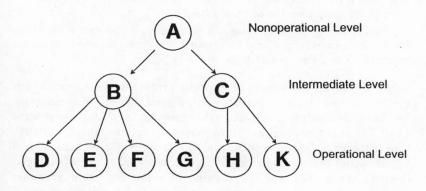

Fig. 1. Cascade diagram representing the process
of operationalizing educational goals

Schaefer questions the validity of this approach and claims that it cannot sufficiently guide curriculum developers in selecting course objectives, since the time allocated for courses usually precludes dealing with all potential objectives that are identified at the last step of the process. Decision makers may be better informed by moving in the opposite direction, that is, moving from the lowest operationally defined objectives toward the more abstract ones, and employing both a minimal criterion (do the operational objectives pertain to intermediate objectives?) and a maximal one (are the operational objectives necessary to attain the intermediate objectives?). The indirect bearing of this study on the Taxonomy lies in Schaefer's use (as statements of general goals) of statements borrowed from a variety of internationally reputed classification schemes (like the stages of Piaget and Gagné), from categories of subject taxonomies (like those in the Biological Sciences Curriculum Study [BSCS] and Nuffield study guides), from Robinson's areas of life, and from the Taxonomy.

The second study deals with a new technique of scalogram analysis called Partial Order Scalogram Analysis (POSA), a two-dimensional extension of the widely used Guttman Scale. Lewy and Shye used POSA in a summative evaluation of an innovative science curriculum in Israel.[20] In this study a six-item questionnaire examined teachers' attitudes toward teaching Higher Mental Function Curricular Objectives (HMCO), such as comprehension and analysis, to disadvantaged learners. Illustrative items from the questionnaire are:

It is enough if the disadvantaged learner masters basic facts. One should not demand full comprehension of what is taught.

Too much time spent on carrying out experiments in the class (of students from disadvantaged educational backgrounds) may miss the point, because it reduces time available for systematic studies.

POSA identified subsets of response profiles to scale items which can be ordered in a way that reveals a second dimension of the trait. In the scale analyzed, the second dimension of "attitude toward HMCO" was identified as "complacency-instrumentality" polarity. The negative or "complacency" end of this dimension is characterized by the belief that rote learning is a sufficient goal for disadvantaged learners, since they are not capable of mastering comprehension objectives. The positive or "instrumentality" end of this dimension is characterized by the belief that rote learning is a useful stage toward further learning, and eventually will also help in mastering comprehension objectives. Although this study aimed to explore the applicability of a new scalogram analysis technique and attitude scales used in curriculum evaluation, its relevance to the Taxonomy is quite obvious.

EXPLORING CONCEPTUAL ISSUES RELATED TO THE TAXONOMY

Parallel with growing interest in and increased use of the Taxonomy in Europe, one may observe attempts to clarify conceptual issues related to the Taxonomy and to describe pedagogical gains and losses from its use.[21] In more colloquial terms, scholars ask where and how the Taxonomy could best be used. Isenegger addressed the question of "where," and suggested the following answers.[22] The Taxonomy can be used for:

a) Measuring how much knowledge transfers from lower taxonomic levels to higher ones;

b) Evaluating the coverage of educational objectives of taxonomic categories of various types;

c) Measuring the level of fidelity of curriculum implementation (Do curriculum planners, textbook writers, and teachers pay sufficient attention to objectives representing various categories of the Taxonomy?);

d) Adding a new set of criteria for designing learning activities to the criteria borrowed from job, task, and content analysis;

e) Determining the sequence of learning activities;

f) Planning the conditions of delivering the curriculum;

g) Selecting adequate teaching methods;

h) Selecting adequate instructional materials and media; and,

i) Building hypotheses related to curriculum studies and to other courses in foundations of education.

These functions fall into three clusters: measurement, planning, and theory development.

The question of "how" has triggered suggestions about modifying the taxonomic structure and combining its categories with dimensions of learning tasks. Roth reduced the Taxonomy to four levels and used terms which can be more easily related to observable behaviors.[23] The lowest level of his scheme is Reproduction, or reproducing content elements as they were taught in the class. The second level is Reorganization, the ordered and meaningful presentation of separately acquired pieces of knowledge. This ordering may be done with standard methods. The third level is Transfer, and has the same definition that "application" has in the Taxonomy. The highest level is Problem-Solving Oriented Thinking. While these terms seem to approximate task definitions used in teaching practice, no empirical studies have been identified which used these terms in dealing with school-related issues.

Koystakos conceptualized the "how" differently.[24] He proposed a two-dimensional scheme to improve the selection of educational objectives. One dimension contains the six major categories of the Taxonomy, and the other rates the objectives according to the following attributes: basic or complementary; potential contribution to attaining a broad array of worthwhile goals; typicality of the concept being dealt with; adequacy to the target group; usefulness outside the school; and novelty of the approach to learning.

Báthory also suggested a two-dimensional framework to help curriculum developers and teachers determine at which cognitive level they should teach particular content.[25] (See fig. 2.) The dimensions are the level of the behavior and the nature of the content. "Knowledge" refers to simple mental activities using memory for reciting or recognizing a particular bit of information. Nevertheless, it not only deals with facts, but also touches upon issues expressed in terms of concepts. "Comprehension" has a broader scope, dealing mostly with concepts, but also touching on facts and relationships. "Application" may refer to a spectrum of operations, from the simple use of a rule, to the employment of a complex theory in an entirely new context. Finally, the term "higher mental operation" refers to analysis, synthesis, and evaluation in the Taxonomy, and these categories contain some elements of creativity. The two-dimensional scheme, representing a

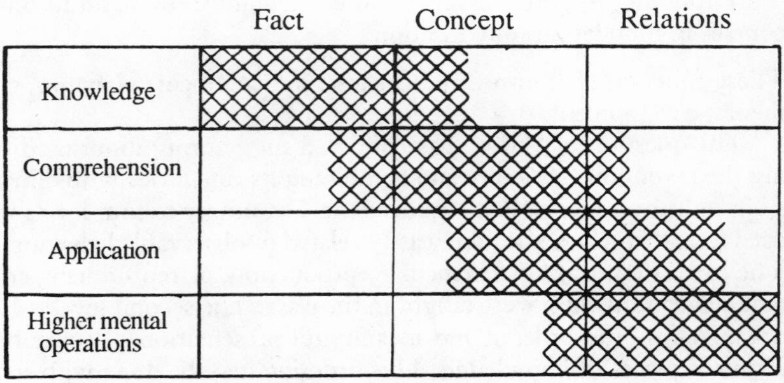

	Fact	Concept	Relations
Knowledge	▨	▨	
Comprehension		▨	▨
Application		▨	▨
Higher mental operations			▨

Fig. 2. Diagonal relationship between mental operations and content types

somewhat diagonal relationship between mental operations and content types, reflects a potentially desirable pedagogical logic which differentiates between assignments relying mostly on memory and those which emphasize the process of thinking.

Báthory also used the taxonomic categories in dealing with the dilemma of determining Minimum Competency Requirements (MCR) in various subjects. He presented two sets of histograms to describe alternative distribution patterns of assignments in a particular subject area, and posed the question: Which of the two patterns should be used for setting MCRs? Should one prefer a pattern which involves a balance among assignments of lower- and higher-order mental operations, or a pattern which emphasizes lower-order operations at the expense of higher-order ones?

The merits and demerits of the Taxonomy also have been critically examined by educational experts in the former Soviet Union. In general, there has been considerably less interest in the behavioral dimension of the Taxonomy than in the scientific basis for selecting teaching/learning *content* and structuring content into a learning program. Thus, the scientific basis for theories of specific subject domains has been of foremost interest.

Kraevskii and Lerner, for example, dealt with the Taxonomy in their chapter on "bourgeois pedagogics."[26] They recognized Bloom's positive influence on developing a hierarchical structure for learning goals as well as his attempt to account for individual differences in learning. Most of their comments, however, are devoted to a critique of the Taxonomy. The main points of this critique are as follows.

1. The principle of value neutrality is not acceptable, as this is both futile and undesirable. One must have ideals and value preferences, as these are the most important goals.

2. The influence of behaviorism (with all its faults) is evident in the conceptual approach to the Taxonomy.

3. The conception of knowledge is problematic. The Taxonomy is built rather "analytically" and "piecemeal" from small elements which are used as building blocks to form complex conceptual entities. This view of knowledge does not necessarily represent reality.

4. There is a good deal of individualism and personal choice built into the use of the Taxonomy. Its implications have not, however, been fully (or sufficiently) developed, and as a consequence, it remains ostensibly an empty shell.

5. Similarly, while the inclusion of the cognitive, affective, and psychomotor domains are commended (although better established grounds are desired for these distinctions), the synthesis of the three has not been very successful. The cognitive domain receives the most weight.

MAKING CONTRIBUTIONS TO THE WORLDWIDE ACCUMULATED KNOWLEDGE ABOUT THE TAXONOMY

The studies reported herein originated in continental Europe, the Mediterranean, and the Middle East. Most were inspired by the concerns of American researchers; yet since they were written in languages other than English, their ideas are seldom known to those American scholars, let alone to the community of researchers and educators interested in the Taxonomy. The communication about taxonomy-related research has had a one-way flow, almost entirely from American and other English-writing authors to the worldwide community of researchers. Thus, the ideas of non-English-writing authors have usually inspired little reaction from English-language researchers, and have not entered into the cumulative body of knowledge about the Taxonomy.

Exceptions do exist, however, most of Belgian origin. Because of the two different language zones in Belgium, Flemish and French, Belgium has become a clearinghouse for research published in these languages, not only from Belgium, but also from neighboring countries, notably France, Luxembourg, Switzerland, and the Netherlands. Moreover, Belgium has served as a link between educational researchers who published in Western European languages and those who published in English. Since Flemish and French language scholars shared keen interest in the Taxonomy and generated original ideas, some of their taxonomy-related ideas became part and parcel of Taxonomy lore across the world. Indeed, the most comprehensive study of the Taxonomy was prepared by Belgian researchers and published first in French.[27] It served as a basis for an essay in English about defining educational objectives.[28] D'Hainaut produced a highly comprehensive classification system of educational objectives, meant as an alternative to the Taxonomy.[29] DeLandsheere claimed that the work of Bloom, Guilford, Gagné, and Mager inspired this taxonomy, and that it attempts to suggest a general synthesis of the methodology for defining objectives. She presented a concise description of the scheme in a form which can be viewed as a basis of a mapping sentence derived from Guttman's theory on scalogram analysis.

DeCorte developed a four-dimensional model for dealing with educational objectives.[30] One dimension described varieties of cognitive operations. Distinguishing between receiving and producing operations, DeCorte lists cognitive operations such as perception of information, recall of information, reproduction of information, and productive and evaluative operations.

Finally, DeBlock developed a three-dimensional model describing teaching objectives.[31] (See fig. 3.) One dimension is the method continuum, in which four categories are distinguished (know, understand, apply, integrate). The first three of these are borrowed from the Taxonomy and the fourth one fuses the remaining three categories. The second dimension is the content and includes six categories: facts, concepts, relations, structures, methods, and attitudes. Finally, the third dimension represents the level of generalization of the content learned, and it distinguishes among three categories: limited transfer, more general transfer, and general transfer. In combination, the three dimensions yield 72 classes, far more than can be conveniently used in the practice of teaching.

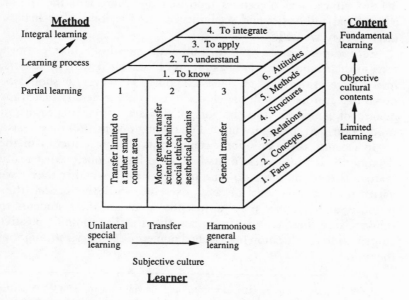

Fig. 3. De Block's model of instruction

Concluding Remarks

The message of the Taxonomy reached Europe, the Mediterranean, and the Middle East a short time after its publication in the United States. The Taxonomy has been translated into several European languages, and in most countries surveyed, concise versions of the Taxonomy have been included in teachers' guides, curriculum guides, and textbooks on didactics, measurement, and evaluation. In addition, it became a topic of discussion in joint seminars attended by American and Russian educators. Although not translated into Russian, it nevertheless helped to pave the way for international cooperation in education.

Educational researchers in these regions have used the Taxonomy, tried to persuade teachers to use it, and sought to modify it so that it responded better to local needs. At the same time, however, educators recognized its shortcomings and warned against its simplistic or even "false" use by people who failed to understand it fully. They criticized not only the consequences of its misinterpretation, but also the planned and unplanned consequences of its proper use. For example, Finnish educators complained that specifying behaviorally defined educational objectives increased the control of the central educational authorities and set limits on the freedom of teachers to teach as they wanted.[32]

European educators have attributed the spread of multiple-choice tests in their schools to the Taxonomy. Dissatisfied with these tests, many were also averse to the Taxonomy. However, it should be noted that European multiple-choice tests do not generally match the quality of American tests, because of the lack of experience in test production, and the highly limited marketing potential of these tests.

In closing, then, one point stands out. Despite criticism of the Taxonomy and awareness of its limits and limitations,[33] what really matters is that educators do raise questions as to whether they have varied the cognitive level of tasks, exercises, and examinations they propose, and whether they sufficiently stimulate their students to think. Using these criteria, it is plain that the Taxonomy's positive contribution to education has reached numerous countries throughout the world.

We wish to acknowledge assistance from the following experts from the countries surveyed: Brazil, Telma Bender (previously at University of Pernambuco, presently at Tel-Aviv University); Croatia, Maria Bratanic (University of Zagreb); Cyprus, N. Matsankou (Institute of Pedagogy); Finland, Kimmo Leimu (University of Jyvaskyla);

France, Ta Ngoc Chau (UNESCO and IIEP); Germany, Rolf Langeheine (University of Kiel); Greece, Alexandra Lamprake-Paganou (University of Athens), I. Kanakis (University of Crete), Marie Elious (University of Athens): Guatemala, Mario Leyton Soto (Ministry of Education); Israel, Y. Brosch (Tel-Aviv University); Italy, Anna Salerini (University of Roma, "La Sapienza"); The Netherlands, Nico Verloop (CITO); Slovenia, Barica Pozarnik-Marentic (University of Ljubljana); Sweden, Sexten Marklund (University of Stockholm); Rumania, Ena Elena (Institute of Educational Research); Turkey, Giray Berberoglu (Middle East Technical University).

NOTES

1. Elihu Katz, "The Two-step Flow of Communication: An Up-to-date Report on a Hypothesis," *Public Opinion Quarterly* 21 (1957): 61-78.

2. David R. Krathwohl, Benjamin S. Bloom, and Bertram Masia, *Taxonomy of Educational Objectives, Handbook II: Affective Domain* (New York: David McKay, 1964).

3. Gene E. Hall and Susan F. Loucks, "A Developmental Model Determining Whether a Treatment Is Actually Implemented," *American Educational Research Journal* 14 (1977): 263-276.

4. Ben-Zion Dinaburg, "Sechel eno mikzoa shemelamdim oto" ["Wisdom Is Not a Subject Taught in School"] (Lecture at the Symposium on Teaching in Secondary School, February, 1952). Quoted in *Mashehu*, No. 53, Bulletin of the Ministry of Education and Culture, Department of History of Education, Ministry of Education and Culture, Jerusalem, Israel, 1991.

5. Quoted in Egil Johansson, "Literacy Campaigns in Sweden," in *National Literacy Campaigns: Historical and Comparative Perspectives*, edited by Robert J. Arnove and Harvey J. Graff (New York: Plenum Press, 1987), p. 74.

6. Sixten Marklund, personal notes, 1992.

7. Lothar Jegensdorf, "Lernzieltaxonomie und Schulerleistung: Zur Kritik und Rezeption einer Pädagogischen Idea" ["Taxonomy of Educational Objectives and the Achievement of Students: About the Criticism and the Acceptance of a Pedagogic Idea"], in *Leistung in der Schule*, edited by Hans K. Beckmann (Braunschweig: Westermann, 1878).

8. Dietrich Lemke, "Lernzielklassifikation/Didaktische Uberlegungen zur Verwendung der Lernzieltaxonomien fuer die Unterrichtsplanung" ["Classification of Educational Goals: Didactic Considerations about Using Taxonomies of Educational Objectives in Planning the Teaching"], in *Lehrenzieldisskussion und Unterrichtspraxis*, edited by Kuno Diener, Klaus Fuller, Dietrich Lemke, and Gert-Bodo Rinert (Stuttgart: Klett, 1979).

9. Charles Lindblom and David Cohen, *Usable Knowledge: Social Science and Social Problem Solving* (New Haven: Yale University Press, 1979).

10. See, for example, Maria Bratanic, Ivan Furlan, Zlata Godler, Vladimir Juric, and Nedjelniko Kujundzic, *Osnovni Problemi Visokoskolske Pedagogije* [Basic Problems in Higher Education Pedagogy] (Zagreb: Skolska Knjiga, 1987); Ivan Furlan, "Ucenje kao komunikacija: Usvajanje znanja, vjestina i navika" [Learning as Communication: Knowledge, Abilities, and Habits] (Zagreb: Pedagosko-Knjizevni Zbor, 1967); Ahno Hujala, "Oppimiselle luotava tavoitteita: Peruskoulussa kaeytetty B. S. Bloomin kehittaemae malli tavoiteoppimiskokeilussa" [Learning Objectives to be Developed: The Model Developed by B. S. Bloom in Mastery Learning Experiments], *Lapset ya Yhteiskunta* 45, no. 9 (1986); Durmus Ali Oezcelik, *Okullarda oelcme ve degerlendirme* [Measurement and Evaluation of School Learning] (Ankara: OSYM Egitim Yayinlari 3); Barika Pozarnik-Marentic, *Pomen operativnega oblikovanja vzgojnoizibrazelvalnih smotrov za uspesnejsi pouk*, [Contains a Slovene translation of the Taxonomy] (Ljubljana: Zavod SR Slovenije za Solstvo, 1976).

162   IMPACT IN EUROPE AND THE MIDDLE EAST

11. Cesar Birzea, *Rendre operationnells les objectifs pedagogiques* (Paris: Presses Universitaires de France, 1979).

12. Kimmo Leimu, personal notes, 1992.

13. Klaus Fuller, "Lernzielklassifikation in Fach Music" ["The Classification of Educational Goals in Music Teaching"], in *Lernzieldiskussion und Unterrichtspraxis*, edited by Diener et al. (Stuttgart: Klett, 1979).

14. Eugen Noveanu and Ligia Pana, *Didactica Limbilor Moderne* [Didactics of Modern Languages] (Bucaresti: Editura Didactica si Pedagogica, 1981).

15. Olof Magne and Kerstin Thorn, *En Kognitive Taxonomi for Matematikundervingen* [A Cognitive Taxonomy for Mathematics Teaching] (Stockholm: Pedagogical-Psychological Institute, School of Education, 1987).

16. Peter Szebenyi, "A tarsadalmi es polgari ismeretek cel es kovetelmeny renszerenek vizsgalati modszerei" ["Methods of examining systems of objectives and achievement requirements in social studies and civic education"], *Pedagogiai Szemle* 22, no. 5 (1972): 506.

17. Shevach Eden, *Al Tochnioth Limdim Chadshoth* [New Curricula] (Tel Aviv: Maaloth, 1971).

18. Johan van Westrhenen, *De Toesting van Onderwijsdoelen* (Groningen: Wolters-Noordhoff, 1977).

19. Gerhard Schaefer, "Informationstheoretische Bemerkungen zur Ableitung von Unterrichtszielen" ["Information Theory Related Notes about Derivations from Educational Goal Definitions"], *Praxis der Naturwissenschaften* 22, no. 1 (1973): 1-7.

20. Arieh Lewy and Shmuel Shye, "Dimensions of Attitude Towards Higher Mental Function Curricular Objectives, HMCO," *Quality and Quantity* 24 (1990): 231-244.

21. See, for example, Bruno Santini, "Taxonomien" ["Taxonomies"], in *Handbuch der Curriculumforschung*, edited by U. Hameyer, K. Frey, and H. Haft (Weinheim: Beltz, 1983).

22. Urs Isenegger, *Versuch einer Funktionsanalyse von Taxonomien* [An Attempt in Function Analysis of Taxonomies] (Freiburg: Pädagogisches Institut, 1969).

23. Heinrich Roth, *Pädagogische Antropologie*, vol. 2: *Entwicklung und Erziehung* [Pedagogical Anthropology, vol. 2: Development and Education] (Hannover: Schrodel, 1970).

24. Ioanne G. Koystakos, *Synchronos Didaktike* [Contemporary Didactics] (Nikosia: Pedagogical Institute, 1980).

25. Zoltan Báthory, *Tanitas es Tanulas* [Teaching and Learning] (Budapest: Tankonyvkiado, 1985).

26. Volodar Viktorovits Kraevskii and Isak Jankolovits Lerner, *Teoreti ceskie osnovy soder zaniya ob shego srednego—obra zovaniya* [Theoretical Basis of the Contents of General Basic Education] (Moscow: Pedagogika, 1983).

27. Guilbert DeLandsheere and Vivianne DeLandsheere, *Definir les objectifs de l'education* (Paris: Presses Universitaires de France, 1974).

28. Vivianne DeLandsheere, "On Defining Educational Objectives," *Evaluation in Education* 1, no. 2 (1977): 77-190.

29. Louis D'Hainaut, "Une model pour le determination et la selection des objectifs pedagogiques de domaie cognitif," *Enseignement Programme* 11 (1970): 21-38.

30. Erik DeCorte, *Onderwijsdoelstellingen* (Lueven: Universitaire Pers, 1973).

31. Alfred De Block, *Taxonomie van leerdoelen* [Taxonomy of Educational Objectives] (Uitgereij, Amsterdam: Standard Wetenschappelijke, 1975).

32. Kimmo Leimu, personal notes, 1992.

33. Vivianne DeLandsheere, "Taxonomies of Educational Objectives," in *International Encyclopedia of Education*, edited by Torsten Husén and T. Neville Postlethwaite (Oxford: Pergamon Press, 1985).

TRANSLATIONS OF BLOOM'S *TAXONOMY OF EDUCATIONAL OBJECTIVES* INTO EUROPEAN LANGUAGES

Taxonomie van een aantal in het onderwijs en de vorming gestelde deelen. Dutch translation by A. van Marten (1971). Rotterdam: Universitaire Pers; Antwerpen: Standaard Wetten-Schappelijke Uitgeverij.

Taxonomie des objectifs cognitif. French translation by Marcel Lavallee (1969). Montreal: Education Nouvelle.

Taxonomie von Lehrzielen im kognitviven Bereich. German translation by Eugen Fuener and Ralf Horn (1972). Weinheim: Beltz Vrl.

Taxonomia didaktichon stochono. Greek translation by Alexandra Lamprake-Paganou (1986). Athens: Kodikas.

Tassonomia degli obiettive educativi. Italian translation by Mario Laeng (1983). Castellato: Giun et Lisciani.

Taxionomia de objectivos educacionais. Portuguese translation by Flavio Maria St. Anna and J. A. Cunha (1976). Porto Alegre: Globa.

Taksonomija ili klasifikacija obrazovnih i odgojnih ciljeva. Serbo-Croatian translation by Ivan Furlan (1970). Beograd.

Taxonomia de los objectivos de la educacion. Spanish translation by Marcelo P. Rivas (1971). Buenos Aires: El Ateneo.

Taxonomica de los objectivos de la educacion. Spanish translation by Isaias Accareta (1972). Acoj: Edit Marfil.

Taxonomia de objectivos educacionales. Spanish translation by Mario L. Soto (1968). Santiago: Centro Perfeccinamiento.

CHAPTER X

The Taxonomy in the Republic of Korea

BOM MO CHUNG

The Taxonomy was introduced to Korean education very soon after its publication in the United States. Quotations from and references to the *Handbook* became standard entries in textbooks and syllabi used in courses on educational evaluation and curriculum development. Since colleges of education all over the country offered the required professional courses on curriculum and evaluation and since scholars in education were frequently called upon to teach in-service education programs, it is safe to conclude that the thinking of the authors of the *Handbook* was quickly propagated among Korean teachers in elementary and secondary schools. This awareness of the Taxonomy occurred well before the Korean version of the *Handbook* appeared in 1966.[1]

There are several possible reasons for the immediate and wide acceptance of the Taxonomy. First, there had been for some time a craving for some kind of systematic model or guide to thinking about educational objectives. Although many philosophical systems were available, an operational system was needed to help teachers understand what was really meant by the term "educational objectives." Second, there was a need for a mechanism by which lower-order educational objectives could be differentiated from the higher-order, the simple could be differentiated from the complex, the extrinsic from the intrinsic, and the stimulus-bound from the ego-bound. Third, there was a strong desire to know whether what we were teaching and measuring was really in line with what we intended to teach and measure (that is, the degree of consonance of the objectives with instructional and evaluational practices). All of these needs are substantially met by the Taxonomy.

The fact that the *Handbook* is still often cited, referenced, and used as a model in many areas of educational research and development attests to its lasting impact on the educational thinking in Korea. In

Bom Mo Chung is President of Haliym University, Choonchun, Korea.

this chapter, I discuss how the Taxonomy was introduced to the Korean academia in education, as well as how it stimulated the improvement of school examinations, facilitated curricular and instructional improvement projects, and has been critically examined in educational discussions.

The Taxonomy as a Model for Examinations

Historically, achievement examinations for admission to higher levels of schooling (called entrance examinations) have been the focus of keen public concern and a major educational problem. Traditionally, advancing to higher levels of schooling (i.e., from elementary to secondary and to tertiary) is taken as a prerequisite to upward social mobility, hence the keen public concern. Since the main practical "goal" of teaching and learning is passing the entrance examinations, the contents of examinations in effect determine the direction of teaching and learning. This examination-driven approach to teaching and learning presents itself as a major educational problem.

In the late 1950s, when there was keen competition to enter into secondary schools from elementary schools, there were efforts in Korea to develop entrance examinations which would be administered uniformly in each region. This approach would replace the practice of having individual secondary schools construct and administer their own examinations. The rationale for the change was that regional efforts, by mobilizing testing expertise, would ensure achievement tests of higher quality and tests that would measure higher mental processes instead of rote memory. It was hoped that this in turn would "redirect" the viciously meaningless learning by rote memorization and stimulate learning activities involving higher mental processes.

The Taxonomy was both timely and important in this effort. It supplied the needed conceptual framework and exemplary items for testing higher mental processes. Testing specialists were well accustomed to the two-dimensional test specifications (content and behavior) proposed by Ralph Tyler. However, the Taxonomy provided the needed rationale for further behavioral specifications of educational objectives. The condensed version of the Taxonomy was quickly translated, distributed, and used as the manual among test construction teams.

The Taxonomy was also used as a model for ascertaining the educational validity of teacher-made achievement tests and official tests like entrance examinations. In 1960, for example, a study was conducted for the purpose of examining the reliabilities and predictive and educational validities of entrance examinations (mostly achievement tests) of Seoul National University.[2] To determine educational validities, test items in Korean, English, mathematics, and social studies were judged by thirty graduate students majoring in educational measurement and psychology in terms of fifteen subcategories of the Taxonomy. The categories and percent of items in the 1956 examinations judged as belonging to the specified categories are shown in table 1. As expected, there was a preponderance of "knowledge" items. Interestingly, however, the percent of items judged as measuring knowledge showed a decrease from 62.1 in 1956 to 59.1, 47.7, and 47.5 in the following three years. Did this represent an effort on the part of test writers to include more items involving higher mental processes?

TABLE 1

PERCENTAGE OF TEST ITEMS ON 1956 ENTRANCE EXAMINATIONS
IN SPECIFIED CATEGORIES AND SUBCATEGORIES OF THE TAXONOMY

CATEGORIES/SUBCATEGORIES	PERCENT OF ITEMS
Knowledge	
of specifics	41.8
of ways and means of dealing with specifics	15.4
of universals and abstractions	4.9
Comprehension	
translation	7.4
interpretation	8.0
extrapolation	1.2
Application	8.6
Analysis	
of elements	2.8
of relationships	2.7
of organizational principles	1.3
Synthesis	
production of a unique communication	2.2
production of a plan or proposed set of operations	1.3
derivation of a set of abstract relations	1.7
Evaluation	
judgments in terms of internal evidence	.8
judgments in terms of external criteria	.0

In the late 1960s, entrance examinations to secondary schools were abolished as these schools began enrolling nearly all children in the age cohort. College and university entrance examinations became the major concern. Since 1968, the Ministry of Education (more specifically its annex office, the Central Educational Evaluation Institute [CEEI]) has been responsible for annually developing the College Entrance Achievement Examinations (CEAE). The actual test items are constructed by a team of invited subject matter professors, teachers, and test specialists. One of the professed reasons for such central control of the CEAE for all these years has been to ensure that the examinations measure achievement beyond rote memory. It has also become a standard practice among item writers to start test construction with the two-dimensional classification table specifying the content and type of behavior to be measured. Although the classification and terminology of the Taxonomy have not been used verbatim, they have served as the model for differentiating among educational objectives and among test items.

In a seminar report of the Central Educational Evaluation Institute, it was noted that a large number of elementary and secondary schools in Korea had developed and were operating their own "item banks."[3] For example, 96.3 percent of schools in Inchon Province and 43.7 percent of schools in Kangwon Province operate individual item pools. It is interesting to note that in classifying the items in the banks the six taxonomic categories were used. In addition, the Tylerian two-dimensional content-by-behavior classification table is presupposed in the actual test construction.

However, a few cautionary remarks are necessary. First, even though the Taxonomy was nominally taken as the model, a perusal of test items of many large-scale examinations causes one to doubt if really serious efforts were made to incorporate higher mental processes in the test items. More often than not, an "application" or "analysis" item is closer to a "knowledge" item. Second, in a highly competitive situation with an extraordinary interest at stake (as is true with the college entrance examinations), it is questionable if test items of higher mental processes can validly "survive" for long. After its release, each test item comes under close scrutiny by both the students and the teachers who prepare them for the examinations. Not only the content of the test items but also their modes, formats, and styles become objects to be memorized and examined in a search for useful "clues." Third, many people doubt the wisdom of central control of entrance examinations. They suggest that innovations in the evaluation of higher mental processes may better be left to the initiatives of individual colleges and universities.

The Taxonomy as a Model for Curricular
and Instructional Improvement

Traditionally, curricular objectives have been stated in terms of a triad of "understandings," "skills," and "attitudes," which together roughly represent the cognitive, psychomotor, and affective domains. Any further subdivisions of each domain were rarely made in curricular and instructional designs.

In the early 1970s, the Korean Institute for Research in the Behavioral Sciences (KIRBS) launched the Mastery Learning Project, an ambitious instructional program for the middle schools. This project intended to put into practice Bloom's theory of mastery learning.[4] This theory asserts that with appropriate instructional strategies, more than 80 percent of the students can attain the level of mastery typically achieved by 20 to 30 percent. After the initial experimental program, nearly 80,000 middle school students participated for nearly three years in the project at its peak. The project was eminently successful. One of the strategies was that, prior to every unit of learning, the objectives of the study were to be clearly stated and understood both by the students and by the teachers. Here again the Taxonomy was the frame of reference and became the manual used in preparing the learning objectives and materials.

The interest in improving instructional program aroused by the KIRBS Mastery Learning Project led to the development in 1972 of the Korean Educational Development Institute (KEDI), which was sponsored and financed by the Ministry of Education. The major initial project of KEDI was the Elementary and Middle School Project, the aim of which was similar to that of the Mastery Learning Project. Launched after a few years of experimentation, the project lasted for more than ten years and included the more than 2,000 elementary and the middle schools in Korea. The project mobilized nearly all conceivable instructional strategies that had been shown to be workable, including a national network of instructional television. For the purpose of constructing curricular and instructional programs and materials and also for the purpose of sensitizing classroom teachers to the objectives of the units of learning, a rather elaborate "Manual of Educational Objectives" was prepared, the lists of educational objectives being arranged and classified by grade levels, subject matter areas, and learning units. The Taxonomy was naturally used as the model once again. We may even dare say that the Taxonomy provided the momentum for the birth of KEDI, which is now a comprehensive national center covering instructional research, educational policies, and curriculum development.

The following is an example from the "Manual of Educational Objectives for Fifth Grade, Elementary School," which contains 277 pages. The science section includes four "General Objectives": (1) to understand basic concepts in science and to be able to observe correctly, (2) to be able to perform methods of exploration in science and to find regularities in nature, (3) to understand that the basic concepts in science are the products of human thoughts and are, therefore, developing constantly, and (4) to develop interest, joy, and desire in the process of scientific inquiry into nature. Four units of learning are also included: (1) energy and its change, (2) circulation of air and water, (3) molecules, and (4) force and movement. Altogether, one hundred specific educational objectives are grouped under thirty subunits of learning. Some samples of the behavioral components of the objectives are that the student is able to explain, show evidence through experiment, tell the relationship, cite examples, tell the difference, present the evidence, interpret the graph, cite reasons, predict, reason, compare, use, ascertain, tell conditions for, anticipate, make graphs, tell the meaning, identify, tell the order, measure, tell the process, apply, calculate, design experiments.

While the terms used in the Taxonomy do not appear verbatim, the writers of the objectives were told to encompass the entire range of taxonomic objectives and to specify them to the extent possible in behavioral terms. The appendices of the manuals include a section, "Examples of Evaluational Items," in which particular objectives are paired with illustrative test items. Other sections include sample questions and suggestions for creating a classroom environment that will improve the climate for learning.

Using a manual of objectives based on the Taxonomy, however, does not necessarily mean that the teachers have valid operational understandings of the differential meanings of the taxonomic terms. Nor does it mean that curricular and instructional realities are in fact "linked" to the stated objectives. In general, the linkage between the professed objectives and the instructional realities is notoriously tenuous, sometimes outright nonexistent.

Thus, there is a need for training elementary and secondary school teachers as well as curriculum specialists in thinking about and applying the Taxonomy. So far, taxonomic thinking in relation to curriculum and instruction has not been a reality in the Korean teacher education system, although, as mentioned earlier, the Taxonomy has been referred to and "taught." Korean teacher education has been dominated, as in many countries, more by subject-matter specialists than by the thinking of specialists in education.

Critical Observations

Despite the wide acceptance of the Taxonomy by researchers and curriculum specialists as a useful conceptual guide, there is in Korea no shortage of critical studies and observations on the Taxonomy. Eisner's advocacy of "implicit objectives"[5] has had a good number of sympathizers. Yong Whan Lee set out to expose the "inconsistencies" of the Tyler-Bloom-Mager model of curriculum where explicit behavioral objectives are the starting point of thinking.[6] For example, he states that "though Tyler proposes the learner, the society, and the subject-matter as the sources of educational objectives, no mention is made as to how objectives are derived from these sources." Similarly, he asserts that the Tylerian thinking of strict dichotomy of ends and means goes counter to the thinking that ends and means are inseparable." He attacks the behavioral approach saying that the neglect of content in thinking about educational objectives is detrimental and that "we call the process of learning a behavioral trait training rather than an education."

Cho directly challenges the validities of the major classification principles of the Taxonomy.[7] Though the Taxonomy presupposes that the same taxonomic categories should apply to the different subject matter areas and to different levels of schooling, Cho questions the extent to which this would be valid. Although the importance of communicability among the test makers was stressed, the evidence shows marked decrease in their ability to communicate about the Taxonomy as the number of workers in evaluation increased. The principle of complexity presents a problem in that the cumulative "simplex" structure cannot be equated with the increasing levels of difficulty as is often erroneously assumed. The principle of neutrality, too, is violated by the Taxonomy in that only observable behavioral outcomes are listed, the internal rational processes are of no concern, and the "content" side of the Tylerian "behavior and content" formula is left out.

Jong Seong Lee summarizes major criticisms leveled against the Taxonomy by some Korean observers.[8] First, learning outcomes resulting from dynamic and complex learning processes include a variety of behavioral changes that far surpasses the specifications of the "content and behavior" formula. Second, the feasibility of attainment of objectives as well as the subdivisions of objectives are bound to be different in different subject matter areas. In science, for example, a high degree of subdivision of objectives is both feasible and desirable; in music, on the other hand, it is both impossible and undesirable. Third, the notion that the specified list of educational objectives should be the criteria for evaluation assumes that only directly observable behavior should be the object of evaluation and so neglects objectives that are not measurable. Finally, statements of objectives should not necessarily precede the selection and organization of educational content.

Response to Critics

As a student of Bloom and one of the major advocates of the Taxonomy in Korea, I must confess a bit of aversion to these critical remarks about the Taxonomy. However, this aversion does not mean that I am totally blind to their partial cogency.

Understandably, most critical comments come from the philosophers and humanists. To the educational philosophers whose conventional inclination is to look for something "fundamental" and for some "comprehensive" picture, the taxonomic categories are too behavioristic and emphasize only the superficial and analytically observable. To humanistic educators, the taxonomic categories are too mechanistic and deprive human learning of its rich aura that is not amenable to behavioristic, analytic, and even verbalistic expressions.

I would respond to such criticism of the Taxonomy by asserting that it does not negate the possible existence of a fundamental layer or comprehensive pattern which lies underneath a system of educational objectives. Likewise, it does not preclude the existence of the not easily identifiable learnings. The Taxonomy is simply one way to systematize things in chaos. It encourages other ways of systematizing, Eisner's and others', that would let us meaningfully touch upon something fundamental, something comprehensive.

Another set of criticisms states in effect that educational objectives are in the minds of teachers, inextricably interwoven and resisting any effort to verbal or analytic identification. Therefore, they are to be left totally to the educational wisdom and conscience of the teacher. Obscurantist remarks such as these are not worthy of serious attention.

There are studies prompted by taxonomic thinking that try to formulate classification systems different from those of the Taxonomy. For example, Huh examined the classifications of cognitive learning outcomes proposed by Tyler, Bloom, Gagné, and others and derived a classification system consisting of four main intellectual abilities: the abilities to perceive, to understand, to remember, and to apply.[9] He then argues that Bloom's "Knowledge" category corresponds with the ability to remember, "Application" to simple application, and "Synthesis" to complex application.

It is possible to develop a taxonomy of educational objectives that employs totally different principles and terms of classification to fit the needs of particular educational settings. A different sociocultural setting may require classification principles and terms different from those used in the Taxonomy simply because of different modes of thinking and different languages. It is interesting to note a paper by Eiichi Kajita, a professor at the Faculty of Human Sciences, Osaka University, Japan.[10] He replaces the categories of the Bloom Taxonomy with concepts derived from a Buddhist conception of teaching ("Kai, Si, Go, and Nya"), which he translates roughly into "Open, Show, Comprehend, and Internalize." In this conception the teacher first seeks to have the learner be able to "open" his mind, then to "show" the truth, then to "comprehend" its meaning, and finally to "internalize" the truth.

It is important also to note that in one of the basic Buddhist scriptures there is a phrase describing human mental operations in four categories: "receiving, thinking, behaving, and cognizing"—a kind of taxonomy of the human mind. Though the expression of this phrase is simple and terse, each term is often given an elaborate and extended interpretation. Thus, for example, receiving connotes also sensing, perceiving, and feeling; thinking connotes imaging and wanting; behaving connotes judging and decision making; and cognizing connotes knowing, understanding, and reasoning. We can safely assume that different cultural settings may need different sets of categories, although there is reason to believe there will be much commonality among them.

There are other criticisms of the Taxonomy that should attract our continuous attention. Critics suggest that the taxonomic terms are not readily understood by teachers and that the psychological presupposition of the cumulative "simplex" structure cannot be sustained by the formula "complexity equals difficulty." Critics have also doubted that the educational process is linear, going from objectives to content to methods to evaluation; instead they propose that the process may be recursive, coming and going between various points. These and other problems need further study.

A final source of criticism is a pragmatic one. Pragmatic critics say that unless the use of the Taxonomy makes a difference in the classroom it will be of little value. However, if teachers are not well acquainted with the Taxonomy and its practical significance for them, this may be in part a problem for teacher education. Teacher educators may not have given sufficient attention to explaining the practical values of the Taxonomy for dealing with problems of curriculum, instruction, and evaluation.

The *Handbook on Formative and Summative Evaluation of Student Learning* clarifies much of the practical significance of the Taxonomy for evaluators.[11] Similar work may be needed to demonstrate to teachers how the Taxonomy can be helpful to them as they deal with problems of curriculum and instruction.

Despite all such efforts to readjust, refine, and redo the Taxonomy, it stands as a towering monument. From this monument taxonomies of various forms and orientations can be built. Without the Taxonomy this building would be difficult, if not impossible.

Notes

1. Eui Do Rim, Yul Jong, and Se Ho Shin, trans., *The Taxonomy of Educational Objectives, Handbook I: Cognitive Domain* (Seoul, Korea: Baeyoungsa, 1966).

2. Committee for the Study of Student Selection Examinations, *A Study of Seoul National University Entrance Examinations* (Seoul, Korea: The Committee, 1960).

3. Central Educational Evaluation Institute, *Present Status and Further Directions of Development of Item Bank Operations* (Seoul, Korea: Central Educational Evaluation Institute, 1988).

4. Benjamin S. Bloom, "Mastery Learning," *UCLA Evaluation Comment* 1, no. 2 (1968): entire issue.

5. Elliot W. Eisner, *The Art of Educational Evaluation: A Personal View* (Philadelphia, PA: Falmer, 1985).

6. Yong Whan Lee, "Critique of the *Taxonomy of Educational Objectives*," *Educational Research* 8 (1982): 89-107.

7. Hui Hyung Cho, "The Nature of Bloom's *Taxonomy of Educational Objectives*," *Forum of Science Education* (Korean) 12 (1984): 67-82.

8. Jong Seong Lee, "Specification and Classification of Educational Objectives," *Journal of Educational Research and Development* (Korean) 11, no. 1 (1990): 33-53.

9. Kyung Jo Huh, "An Analysis of Learned Intellectual Traits," *Research Bulletin on Students* (Korean) 13 (1989): 47-63.

10. Eiichi Kajita, "A Framework of the Classification of Educational Objectives and Activities" (Unpublished paper, Osaka, Japan, 1986).

11. Benjamin S. Bloom, J. Thomas Hastings, and George F. Madaus, *Handbook on Formative and Summative Evaluation of Student Learning* (New York: McGraw-Hill, 1971).

CHAPTER XI

Validity vs. Utility: Personal Experiences with the Taxonomy

T. NEVILLE POSTLETHWAITE

Despite concerns expressed by Bloom himself,[1] the Taxonomy has become a kind of dogma in many educational circles. It has often been used blindly and sometimes written about as though it had become some kind of cast-iron reality.[2] This understanding and use of the Taxonomy is in direct contrast to the intention of its developers. As they clearly state, the Taxonomy was submitted "in the hope that it [would] help stimulate thought and research on educational problems."[3] The developers of the Taxonomy had very limited ambitions and were acutely aware of the many shortcomings of their product.

Despite these shortcomings, however, the Taxonomy has been and continues to be used throughout the world by test developers and curriculum practitioners. Both the initial acceptance and continued use of the Taxonomy was perhaps best explained by DeLandsheere when she wrote: "As practising teachers and evaluators, Bloom and associates' modest ambition was a step towards clarification. The enormous influence exercised by their imperfect tool proves that it answered a deep and urgently felt need."[4]

With the wide use and misuse of the Taxonomy, criticisms are expected. In this chapter, I shall address some of the major criticisms of the Taxonomy and describe some of my personal experiences with it.

Major Criticisms of the Taxonomy

Among the many criticisms of the Taxonomy offered over the years, three appear most frequently. They can be summarized as follows.

T. Neville Postlethwaite is a Professor in the Department of Comparative Education, University of Hamburg, Germany.

1. The distinctions between any two levels of the Taxonomy may be blurred.

2. The Taxonomy is not hierarchical; rather it is just a set of categories.

3. The lockstep sequence underlying the Taxonomy based on any one dimension (e.g., complexity or difficulty) is naive.

The clarity of the categories. Many studies of the classification of intended behaviors by different raters or judges have been undertaken to test the clarity of the categories and the distinctions between and among them. Despite the fact that, as Wood has noted, such an exercise "is like asking people to sort fruit into apples, oranges, bananas, etc. without giving them more than the vaguest ideas of what an apple or banana looks like,"[5] the results of such studies have been quite positive. In general, 40 to 80 percent of behaviors are placed into the same category by different raters (with chance agreement being between 16 or 17 percent); furthermore, the interrater reliabilities range from .63 to .85.

As noted in chapter 5 of this volume, a student's response to a test item is at least partly a function of the student's previous knowledge and experience. For example, the solving of an intended application problem for one student may be a rote activity for another student who has encountered this problem previously in a direct or very similar way. For a student not familiar with such problems, this experience may require an increasing level of "mental activity." Thus, differences among independent raters in the placement of items into taxonomic categories may be partially explained by the different assumptions they make concerning the student's prior knowledge and experience.

The hierarchical structure of the Taxonomy. Failure to reach high levels of agreement among independent judges or raters will necessarily cause problems when one attempts to examine the validity of the hierarchical structure of the Taxonomy. If the same behavior or test item can be placed into two or more categories, the possibility of achieving a clear hierarchy is lessened substantially.

The several empirical studies conducted to test the hierarchical structure of the Taxonomy have been summarized in chapter 5. It is instructive to point out that in none of these studies was a hierarchy found for all six taxonomic categories. At the same time, however, all of the studies supported the hierarchy of the Taxonomy to some extent. In one case, the "knowledge" through "application" categories were found to be hierarchical with a branching to "analysis" on one side and "synthesis" and "evaluation" on the other. In another case, "knowledge" was found not to fit the hierarchical structure, but the "comprehension" through "evaluation" categories were found to be hierarchical.

The greatest support for the hierarchical structure of the Taxonomy was found when the data analysts used LISREL, a computer program designed to examine causal models. Using LISREL, both Ekstrand and Hill produced a hierarchical structure somewhat similar to that suggested by the authors of the Taxonomy.[6] Even though Wood stated that the taxonomic structure was found wanting, he also pointed out that the radex approach used in many studies required interitem correlations of at least .70, with some likely approaching .80 to .90.[7] Interitem correlations of this magnitude are seldom found in practice.

The existing data make it quite clear that the Taxonomy is not perfectly hierarchical in structure. At the same time, however, it still remains to be known whether deviations from the hierarchical structure are the result of the sheer number of items used in studies, the largest number of combinations of such items (e.g., knowledge-comprehension, knowledge-application, knowledge-analysis), the analytic approach used to test the hierarchical structure, or the fact that the Taxonomy itself is not fully hierarchical.

The naiveté of the structure of the Taxonomy. The third major criticism of the Taxonomy is that the lockstep sequence of the six categories assumed by its authors is naive (see chapter 3). The argument of these critics can be summarized as follows: Educational objectives are multidimensional. Thus, to plot objectives in a two-dimensional form (content and behavior) is insufficient. Furthermore, because content influences learning, certain demands for knowledge are more complex than some demands for analysis or evaluation. Finally, some critics argue against the use of knowledge as a category since the acquisition of knowledge requires intellectual skills and abilities.

All of the criticisms regarding naiveté are theoretical in nature. They have not been tested empirically as have the taxonomic categories and classifications. As the results summarized above and in various chapters throughout this volume suggest, there can be classification problems and the complete hierarchical structure of the Taxonomy has not been verified empirically. Nonetheless, to dismiss the Taxonomy out of hand because of naive assumptions on the part of its authors seems itself to be a bit naive.

Personal Experiences

Over the past thirty years, I have used the Taxonomy in my work with teachers, curriculum developers, and test designers. In this section, I shall reflect on some of these experiences.

Experiences with teachers. It was not until 1962 that I first heard of or saw the Taxonomy, quite likely because it took a few years for it to cross the Atlantic. Shortly thereafter I had the opportunity of working with a group of primary school teachers in London. They were struggling with the "new mathematics" and the problem of constructing test items in that subject.

At a very basic level, the idea that different items were needed to test rote addition, to test students' understanding of the principle of addition, and to test students' ability to solve a novel problem helped to make explicit for these teachers what heretofore had been implicit. In a sense, it was an "Aha" experience for us all. We suddenly realized that there were different aspects of something as apparently simple as addition.

Of course, this realization did not guarantee perfect use of the Taxonomy in solving the problems the teachers faced. They experienced difficulties in classifying some of the intended behaviors and test items. Nonetheless, they reported finding the notion of explicitly different "parts" or "categories" of a theme (e.g., addition) to be of great use in their actual teaching.

Experiences with curriculum developers. One critical component of curriculum development is the decision as to which themes should be taught and learned at various grade levels. Another is the writing of textbooks, chapters, or modules to be used by the students in learning these themes. Those of us who have had to undertake content analyses of existing textbooks have often experienced great difficulty in trying to classify the material included on a page. Am I looking at a definition of photosynthesis, an example of photosynthesis, or an explanation of the principle of photosynthesis? Nor did it help to go back to the course syllabus. All that appeared in it was the word "photosynthesis."

In my work in several countries, the idea of different "aspects" of a theme was once again useful. It enabled curriculum teams to determine what a particular chapter or module they had written was trying to teach the students. These teams were not at all interested in whether the taxonomic categories were hierarchical. They were interested in ensuring that important aspects of a theme were in fact covered sufficiently in the chapters or modules.

The *Handbook on Formative and Summative Evaluation of Student Learning* was quite useful to the curriculum development teams.[8] It was not something that was followed blindly. In fact, the matrix on science education included in Leopold Klopfer's chapter frightened most of us. But many ideas were gained from reading this book. And before writing the first draft of a chapter or module, we were able to list the objectives to be addressed (sometimes even in a matrix form).

When we were struggling with the problem of how specific a learning objective should be, it was Ralph Tyler who provided leadership at the Gränna curriculum seminar. (See chapter 1.) Tyler warned against the overspecification of objectives in terms of content, behavior, conditions, and standards. He made it quite clear to the curriculum development teams that it is possible to concentrate on the number and positioning of commas and periods in statements of objectives to the extent that you forget what the objective is meant to communicate in terms of desired student learning.

Experiences with test designers. When I have been working with different national evaluation and assessment teams, the Taxonomy once again proved useful. These teams received the list of objectives or the content-by-behavior matrix for each chapter or module prepared by the curriculum development teams. The task of the evaluation and assessment teams was to design tests that provided valid and reliable information about student learning relative to these objectives.

The Taxonomy and the way it was used provided several insights to the members of the evaluation and assessment teams. First, the curriculum determines the content of the examinations; it is not the other way around. Second, the use of the taxonomic categories increases efficiency in writing test items. That is, being able to place an objective into a particular category enables the test designer to know what types of items are likely to be (or not to be) appropriate.

In all these *practical* situations the Taxonomy was useful. It made us think about what we were really trying to teach and test. We were not concerned with the hierarchical structure of the Taxonomy. Nor were we unduly worried about whether one category was more difficult or more complex than another.

We did worry about the prior knowledge and experience that students would need to be able to begin to learn the objectives included in the chapters and modules. Occasionally, we argued about what we meant by knowledge. But there was wide acknowledgement that, above all, the Taxonomy had given us ideas.

We did look at other approaches for classifying objectives and writing test items.[9] However, either they were too complicated because they had too many categories or were quite difficult to use because of the fine degree of discrimination among the categories. Bloom's Taxonomy had six major categories that could be held in the head and the distinctions among those categories were more obvious.

In Retrospect

The *Taxonomy of Educational Objectives, Handbook 1: Cognitive Domain* is probably the all-time "best seller" in the field of education. The five authors, thirty-four scholars, and the many educators who commented on the initial draft certainly produced a work that is well known, much used, and frequently cited.

Quite clearly, the Taxonomy is not without its problems and flaws. Equally clearly, however, it has prompted both thought and discussion about the purpose of education, ways of accomplishing this purpose, and methods of evaluating its accomplishment.

Prior to the availability of the Taxonomy, practitioners throughout the world produced curricula and tests that emphasized factual information. Content analysis of numerous textbooks and standardized tests conducted during the 1960s and early 1970s support this contention. That the Taxonomy offered easily understandable guidelines for expanding both curriculum and evaluation beyond simple knowledge is perhaps its greatest legacy.

The Taxonomy is not perfect. Hence, it should neither be reified nor used blindly. When used to stimulate thinking about curriculum and evaluation, however, it has few peers. Consequently, curriculum developers, test designers, and educational systems throughout the world owe Bloom and his colleagues a debt of gratitude.

NOTES

1. Benjamin S. Bloom, personal communication, 1972.

2. Robert Wood, *Assessment and Testing* (Cambridge: Cambridge University Press, 1991).

3. Benjamin S. Bloom et al., *Taxonomy of Educational Objectives, The Classification of Educational Goals, Handbook I: Cognitive Domain* (New York: David McKay, 1956).

4. Viviane DeLandsheere, "On Defining Educational Objectives," *Evaluation in Education* 1 (1979): 105.

5. Robert Wood, "Multiple-Choice: A State of the Art Report," *Evaluation in Education* 1 (1979): 205.

6. Judith M. Ekstrand, "Methods of Validating Learning Hierarchies with Applications to Mathematics Learning" (Paper presented at the Annual Meeting of the American Educational Research Association, New York, 1982), ERIC ED 216 896; Peter W. Hill, "Testing Hierarchy in Educational Taxonomies: A Theoretical and Empirical Investigation," *Evaluation in Education* 8 (1984): 179-278.

7. Wood, *Assessment and Testing*.

8. Benjamin S. Bloom, J. Thomas Hastings, and George F. Madaus, *Handbook on Formative and Summative Evaluation of Student Learning* (New York: McGraw-Hill, 1971).

9. See, for example, Robert Gagné, *The Conditions of Learning* (New York: Holt, Rinehart and Winston, 1965) and Joy P. Guilford, *The Nature of Human Intelligence* (New York: McGraw-Hill, 1967).

CHAPTER XII

Reflections on the Taxonomy:
Its Past, Present, and Future

DAVID R. KRATHWOHL

Although many of us did not realize the importance of what we were working on, it is clear that Benjamin Bloom had high hopes for the Taxonomy from the very beginning. Consider these excerpts from his unpublished introductory remarks to the Allerton Conference of 1949, the first meeting devoted solely to work on the *Taxonomy of Educational Objectives, Handbook I: Cognitive Domain*. Following his description of an empirically built "examiners' taxonomy" designed to facilitate the exchange of test items (an early approach to item banking), he ended with this lofty challenge:

However, there is a larger task which we may wish to consider. . . . A taxonomy of educational outcomes could do much to bring order out of chaos in the field of education. It could furnish the conceptual framework around which our descriptions of educational programs and experiences could be oriented. It could furnish a framework for the development of educational theories and research. It could furnish the scheme needed for training our teachers and for orienting them to the varied possibilities of education. . . .

Superficially such a taxonomy would resemble the one we might set up for the purpose of communicating among examiners. However, where the examiners' taxonomy would be developed on an empirical basis, this one would have to start with some psychological theory as its base. Where the examiners' taxonomy depended on logical consistency, this one would depend on psychological consistency. Where the examiners' taxonomy would be validated by the convenience with which it could be used, this one would have to be validated by the findings on the "real" relations among the parts. . . . It would make possible a science of education. . . . I am sure the final product will be one of the most powerful tools in the study and improvement of education.[1]

David R. Krathwohl, Hannah Hammond Professor Emeritus of Education at Syracuse University, was a member of the Committee of College and University Examiners that wrote the *Taxonomy of Educational Objectives, Handbook I: Cognitive Domain*. He was also the senior author of *Taxonomy of Educational Objectives, Handbook II: Affective Domain*.

The Taxonomy as a Heuristic Framework

Aiming high, Bloom foresaw many of the uses that were eventually attempted, uses that result from its serving as a heuristic framework. The cognitive domain's most important role has been to highlight the importance of objectives involving skills and abilities as differentiated from memorized knowledge. More specifically, it provided a framework for analyzing the relative emphasis given various levels of behavior in a test or curriculum. It showed the possible dependency of certain goals on the prior learning of others. It provided a panorama of goals broader than might otherwise have been considered. While the Taxonomy was a framework often used as a heuristic without modification, individuals could and did change it to fit their particular situation.

Webster's *Third New International Dictionary* defines "heuristic" as "providing aid or direction in solving a problem but otherwise unjustified or incapable of justification." Webster's *Seventh New Intercollegiate Dictionary* changes the definition slightly to "serving to discover or reveal; specifically: valuable for empirical research but unproven or unprovable." Certainly the Taxonomy was unproven at the time it was developed and, as we shall see later in this chapter, may well be "unprovable." Kaplan argues that such frameworks are a kind of weak causal explanation.[2] By finding a goal's placement in the structure, one attains a better definition of the behavior involved and learns of its relation to other behaviors. All the above are uses that might be expected of a heuristic framework. Heuristic frameworks are valued for the thought they stimulate, often leading to new insights and understandings. Frameworks, theories, and points of view often serve heuristic purposes.

Heuristic frameworks are usually developed by individuals who enjoy dealing with the abstract. Piaget's work is "an example of a theorizer's writing that had considerable impact. . . . In it the alternation between the theoretical explanation and example is obvious and compelling."[3] Theorizers may also do empirical work, and they certainly are careful observers. Finding a perspective on the mass of detail that daily confronts them is likely to be their style of work. In this context, the Taxonomy is clearly a theorizer's product. Bloom and I used sample objectives to test the structure ourselves, and we involved the staff of the University of Chicago's Board of Examiners in doing so. In the yearly taxonomy meetings, we provided sample objectives so others could do so as well. But these were only small-sample data as to how well such objectives could be classified and there were no data at all showing the validity of the hierarchical structure.

"Theorizer's ideas are not always on target and their ideas must often be modified by other researchers. But their captivating suggestions contain enough of the germ of reality that their conceptualizations are tenacious."[4] Theorizers drive analyzers (those who deductively determine the consequences of presumed relationships from past research and theorizing) crazy with their extravagant claims which analyzers feel compelled to test empirically. Interestingly enough, Bloom anticipated this in the final statement of his introductory remarks to the 1949 Taxonomy Conference: "Our work as a group might end once the tentative formulations have been set up. From there on we would probably turn the taxonomy over to other groups and to individual workers to refine, study, and test."[5]

In 1967 I received a letter from Robert Sinclair, a Staff Associate with the Institute for Development of Educational Activities (IDEA), who wrote: "I recently inquired into the scientific process for developing taxonomies. Scientific validity of the taxonomies of educational objectives is largely dependent, I think, upon research that contributes to their correction and expansion."[6] Deciding that Sinclair was at least on the correct track, I replied:

I'm not sure I understand your letter but let me try a response. . . . I suppose in a strict sense you are right, although the term "validity" attributes more meaning to a taxonomy than I think it ought to be given and perhaps obscures an important issue. The Taxonomy is a model which may or may not have a close correspondence to "reality." It is the correspondence with reality with which I think you are concerned. I would argue that, while this is an important feature, perhaps still more important is the extent to which a taxonomy, as a model, has heuristic value. The more research of various kinds which it stimulates and provides a useful basis for, the better the taxonomy. In a very real sense, whatever validity a structure or model holds is a secondary consideration to the value of the research which it stimulates.

Interpret the word "research" inclusively and clearly the Taxonomy has been a structure that has stimulated considerable thought and writing. Reprints of the framework, often with sample objectives, test items, comment, and critique, have appeared in nearly all measurement and curriculum books, and probably have brought it to the attention of many more individuals than use of the book itself. Judging from the many references in this book to work based on it, and the fact that we are aware of twenty-one foreign-language translations,[7] the Taxonomy has indeed been a useful heuristic framework. The value of that writing is in the eye of the beholders. But since interest in its use has continued over so many years, it seems unlikely that the Taxonomy has been entirely without merit.

Given this, for the remainder of this chapter, let us briefly look at the past, present, and future of the Taxonomy. We will seek to learn from the *past*, using the Taxonomy as a case study of a heuristic framework. By reviewing the process of developing and disseminating it, we can reveal what might contribute to a heuristic's success and what generalizations we can draw from this experience. Sinclair also inquired about "the scientific process" of building taxonomies. So, looking at research right up to the *present*, we can ask "Regarding its 'scientific validity,' what is the best interpretation of these data"? Lastly, in terms of the *future*, we can ask "Where, if anyplace, do we go from here"?

The Past: Learning about Heuristic Frameworks from Experience with the Taxonomy

The authors of frameworks and theories hope that their work will prove to have explanatory and heuristic value, but not all do. Indeed, most efforts sink without a trace. But as the work of Durkheim, Erikson, Freud, Kohlberg, Maslow, Redfield, Riesman, and of others like them amply attests, such efforts are extremely influential when found useful by others. What distinguishes the proportionately few frameworks that found favor from those equally sincerely advanced but which received little attention and application? Can we learn by using the Taxonomy as a case study of a successful heuristic framework? What of its process of development and its characteristics are instructive? To probe these, let us examine its history.

As indicated in previous chapters, the Taxonomy, Bloom's idea, was proposed to a group of college and university examiners at the 1948 American Psychological Association Convention and discussed again at the next year's meeting. Since I had the good fortune to be Bloom's graduate assistant in the University of Chicago's Board of Examiners at the time, we worked at developing a structure that would be illustrative of what was intended. We tentatively laid out subcategories of the "knowledge" category and sketched in the major categories above it in the "arts and skills" and "intellectual ability" categories. Thanks to the crucial and strong support of the project by

Ralph Tyler, Director of the Board at the time, we involved many of its staff such as Christine McGuire, Edgar Friedenberg, and Leo Nedelsky in the process, getting them to critique material and suggest examples of both objectives and relevant sample items.[8]

In the Fall of 1949 I took a position assisting J. Thomas Hastings, Director of the Unit on Evaluation at the University of Illinois. Hastings proposed to Bloom and me that, using funds from his budget, we host a two-and-a-half-day meeting at the University's Allerton Conference Center near Monticello, Illinois, devoted solely to developing the structure. Interested persons were invited to what was to be our largest meeting and the beginning of collaborative work on the project outside Chicago's Board of Examiners. The preliminary structure we had developed was furnished as an example of what the Taxonomy might become. We hoped that the analysis and criticism of this tentative framework would enable us to develop more quickly a classification scheme we could all approve.[9]

The Allerton meeting was extremely fruitful. The discussions were lively and very much task oriented; all ideas were welcomed and carefully considered. The conference members agreed on the major categories of the cognitive domain with a variety of suggestions for subcategories. Responsibility was given to a small committee consisting of Bloom, Max Engelhart, Edward J. Furst, Walker Hill, and me, to carry on the work of the group and prepare material for their critique. We took individual assignments: Bloom—Knowledge and Evaluation; Engelhart—Comprehension; Krathwohl—Application; Hill—Analysis; and Furst—Synthesis. Bloom wrote the draft of the material at the beginning of the *Handbook* and I added to and edited it.[10] We received helpful criticism of the various drafts in successive conferences hosted by Bloom at the University of Chicago in 1950, by Herman Remmers at Purdue University in 1951, and by Walker Hill and Paul Dressel at Michigan State University in 1952. The planned 1953 meeting never materialized, but work was far enough along on the cognitive taxonomy so that it was not necessary. The preliminary edition was finalized for distribution.[11]

A symposium on "A Taxonomy of Educational Objectives" was presented at the American Psychological Association Convention in Chicago in September, 1951. Bloom described work on the "Intellectual Domain" and I the "Affective Domain." Discussants were O. K. Buros, O. H. Mowrer, and J. M. Stalnaker. The symposium was chaired by Herman Remmers who confessed in his introduction: "When I was first invited to attend a meeting of the group, I went with considerable skepticism and even cynicism as to the possibility of devising a useful system. I have mellowed considerably and now think that the probability is rather high that we shall be able eventually to achieve a rather complete classificatory system." All three discussants were critical, however. Mowrer and Stalnaker disliked the jargon of the Taxonomy and Buros believed that the group had dealt with behavior at such an abstract level as to make the Taxonomy meaningless. The point, however, is that, even as it was being developed, the Taxonomy was being exposed to critique by a broad audience even to the extent of inviting criticism from some of the top people of the day. This also served, simultaneously, to provide early awareness of the Taxonomy and anticipation of its availability.

The contract with Longmans Green called for a preliminary edition of 1000 copies to be distributed for comment. The distribution list is interesting. In addition to those who had worked on it and their colleagues, a deliberate attempt was made to place the preliminary edition in the hands of persons who might have further interest in it as well as those whose comments might improve it. Thus it went to 31 leaders in education screened from a list solicited from the U.S. Office of Education, 62 members of the Association for Supervision and Curriculum Development (ASCD) suggested by the Association's Director, 155 persons screened from the membership roster of the National Society for the Study of Education (NSSE), 87 directors of statewide testing programs and their staffs, 36 Illinois curriculum workers suggested by the Illinois State Department of Education, 162 selected persons in the testing field screened from the mailing list for the Invitational Conference of the Educational Testing Service and the membership list of the Division of Testing, Measurement, and Evaluation of the American Psychological Association, and 135 names selected from those suggested by other relevant professional associations.

Did this net many helpful comments? Not too many. But it enlarged the base of individuals who were aware that the Taxonomy existed so that when they or their colleagues needed it, they knew where to find it. It increased anticipation of the final edition. "Awareness" is the first stage in dissemination in nearly every theory of how dissemination proceeds.

After the final edition was published in 1956 further dissemination came from presentations by Bloom and me at various groups and conferences. Furst brought out a textbook on testing that helped introduce the Taxonomy.[12] Then in 1971 Bloom, Hastings, and Madaus published the *Handbook on Formative and Summative Evaluation of Student Learning* to show how the Taxonomy might be used in a variety of different educational areas.[13]

The Taxonomy came on the scene when there was considerable talk about the "knowledge explosion" after World War II. At the same time, there was considerable interest in what was termed a "general education"—the production of well-educated adults. Most colleges were developing a required core of courses to provide such an education. The continuing problem of defining what constitutes a "liberal education" in the face of this knowledge explosion gave heartburn to those constructing the courses. This Gordian knot was cut by an alternative to cramming in all the new knowledge—the alternative of teaching higher-order skills with an emphasis on "learning to learn." The student was to be equipped to seek out and understand knowledge as needed. The Taxonomy clarified this distinction between knowledge and intellectual abilities and skills and it provided a useful smorgasbord of the latter from which one could choose.

The most extensive international dissemination was that done by Bloom, as described in chapter 1 of this volume. In his efforts to assist the growth of curriculum and testing in developing countries, he traveled extensively overseas and sought federal and foundation funds to support the training of individuals at the University of Chicago. These students became disciples for the Taxonomy. Undoubtedly this very impressive achievement led to many of the translations into foreign languages.

Taking also into account the material in the preceding chapters, what can we learn from this case study about the development and dissemination of a successful heuristic? Experience with the Taxonomy suggests the following possibilities.

1. *In the process of developing a heuristic it is important to:*

● Target a potentially important use from the beginning.

● Use the best persons possible for critiquing the product. It undoubtedly helps if they have prominence in their profession since such persons are typically active in a network of similar persons. Therefore, reaching one very likely reaches many other possibly interested persons.

● Create an atmosphere in which genuine criticism is welcomed and personal threat is minimized. Make it apparent that criticisms are to be of ideas, not persons.

• Establish clear responsibilities for the developmental work. Have a single individual and/or a small cadre take ultimate responsibility for the total project.

• Spread development over a sufficient period of time so that careful thought can be given to criticisms, resistance to suggestions can dissipate, and flexibility can take its place.

• Provide extensive trials and revisions of the framework to incorporate the best available thinking at each stage of the development.

2. *In the process of disseminating a heuristic it is important to:*

• Arrange for wide distribution of prepublication copies for comment by strategically selected individuals who might find it useful. This very effectively creates awareness of the heuristic as well as arousing curiosity about the final product when it is released. Ask for comments. This increases readership, provides investment in the framework, and may garner useful suggestions.

• Disseminate the heuristic beyond its field of obvious use. This provides a broad base of colleagues who may suggest its use to inquirers even when they may not themselves find the product useful for their purposes.

• Take advantage of professional association meetings to obtain helpful critiques as well as to create awareness even before the heuristic is released in final form.

• Develop a network of students who continue to work in the area of the heuristic, use it, possibly develop it further, and, especially important, publish their own projects involving it.

• Provide for institutionalizing of the framework.[14] The literature on dissemination tells us this is the final step in adoption. In the case of a heuristic, this refers to its continued use after adoption. At first, it might seem there is little the author of a heuristic can do at this step; it is either successful or it is not. In that sense we were lucky with the Taxonomy. Its reproduction in textbooks, continuing even to this day, is both a sign of its institutionalization and has furthered the institutionalization. But it also seems likely that building a network of students around the world, as Bloom did, aided substantially in completing this final step. His students were persons working in curriculum, usually in important positions in the education structures of their several countries. They were familiar with the Taxonomy and used it in their work. A staff member of the World Bank told a friend of mine "Wherever you go in the world, you can count on their knowing the Taxonomy."

• Consider the timing of the dissemination of the heuristic. Timing the arrival of a heuristic may be somewhere between difficult and impossible, yet timing may be critical to its acceptance. In the retail business it is said that there are three characteristics of a successful business: (1) location, (2) location, and (3) location. This could be said as well for heuristics: timing, timing, and timing. The demand for a heuristic is somewhat dependent upon context. As Airasian indicates in chapter 6 of this volume, the value of a heuristic is greater at certain times than at others.

3. *Characteristics of the Taxonomy that contributed to its usefulness.* The literature on dissemination tells us that adoption is more likely to occur if the product fits easily with what is already there, is easily understood, easy to use, and the rationale seems sound and acceptable. Certain characteristics of the Taxonomy contributed to its usefulness. Its major categories are relatively easy to understand even when one finds their subdivisions more difficult. In providing a panorama of kinds of objectives and test items that could be useful in a course, the Taxonomy is relatively easy to use. By providing an underlying hierarchical structure that was easily comprehended (complexity and abstractness increase between adjacent categories from "knowledge" to "evaluation"), the Taxonomy lent scientific respectability to the structure even as others attempted to validate it. Furthermore, users of behavioral objectives could readily adopt the framework. Those not using such goals often found the concept of behavioral objectives itself was a new and important contribution to their thinking. The adoption of objectives in various faddish systems such as PPBS (Planning, Programming, Budgeting System) and its successors added a timely aspect to their use since the Taxonomy fit the then prevailing developmental model. Finally, the design of the framework with the distinctions and vocabulary of teachers in mind added considerably to the ease with which the Taxonomy could be understood. Even where stipulative definitions were used, they were applied to common terms and neologisms were avoided.

Providing an interesting and arresting name ("Taxonomy") seems likely to have been a contributing factor in its success. There are now many taxonomies. At the time, however, Bloom's unique use of this then unfamiliar term aroused curiosity among social scientists and educators who might otherwise have put the book aside as another "freebie" to look at when there is time. There never is.

So there are generalizable aspects in the development and dissemination processes, in the timing, and in the characteristics built into the Taxonomy itself. But if such a structure is solidly undergirded, it will be considerably more attractive. Thus we are led to the question of the "scientific validity" of the Taxonomy.

The Present: What Can We Learn from the Evidence Regarding the Validity of the Taxonomy?

In some respects, considering the lack of an evidential basis for the Taxonomy, it is surprising how seriously it has been taken. For one thing, most discussion of the Taxonomy takes the major category levels as discrete steps in a progression. Yet, as the introductory material in the *Handbook* indicates, these are arbitrary points on what was presumed to be a continuum of increasing complexity and abstractness. The levels corresponded to the distinctions that teachers and educators seemed to make and so were identified for pragmatic reasons because of their use in educational parlance. Further, in many instances, the common meanings, as in the case of "application," had to be "cleaned up" in order to enable distinctions to be made between behaviors fitting in one category and those belonging in another. So, in many respects, distinctions between categories were made more real than we had intended.

Our experience with the Taxonomy suggests that the framework has been most useful as it is extended and/or modified to fit the purposes for which it is being used. For example, in the context of medical education, Christine McGuire determined that distinctions in the "knowledge" category were too fine while those in the "application" category were not fine enough.[15] Therefore she developed the following modification of the Taxonomy in which she reversed the order of the two highest categories:

1.1 Items testing predominantly the recall of isolated information

1.2 Items testing recognition of meaning or implication

2.0 Generalization: Items requiring the student to select a relevant generalization to explain specific phenomena

3.0 Problem solving of a familiar type

    3.1 Items requiring the student to make simple interpretations of data

    3.2 Items requiring the student to apply a single principle or a standard combination of principles to a situation of a familiar type

4.0 Problem solving of an unfamiliar type

    4.1 Items requiring the analysis of data

    4.2 Items requiring the student to apply a unique combination of principles to solve a problem of a novel type

5.0 Evaluation: Items requiring the evaluation of a total situation

6.0 Synthesis: Items requiring synthesis of a variety of elements of knowledge into an original and meaningful whole

In their *Handbook on Formative and Summative Evaluation of Student Learning*, Bloom, Hastings, and Madaus include a variety of examples provided by instructors and test developers from different subject matter areas who adapted the Taxonomy to their purposes. For example, Moore and Kennedy's chapter on the language arts showed the "application" category divided into "functional application" and "expressive application,"[16] whereas James Wilson's chapter on evaluation in mathematics divided "application" into the abilities to "solve routine problems," "make comparisons," "analyze data," and "recognize patterns, isomorphisms, and symmetries."[17] "Evaluation" was divided into "objective evaluation" and "subjective evaluation" by Moore and Kennedy[18] and into "empirical evaluation" and "systemic evaluation" by Brent Wilson in the chapter on art education.[19] In his chapter on social studies, Orlandi invented new categories dealing with problem solving for skills and abilities,[20] as did Klopfer in the chapter on science.[21]

In addition to those who have used the Taxonomy there are those who have studied it. Those studies typically address two questions. First, is there a single dimension underlying the ordering of the major categories? Second, are the major categories hierarchically arranged? (Little effort has been expended on examining the subcategories and probably justifiably so; unless the grosser distinctions can be validated there is little point in looking at the finer ones.)

Generally these two issues have been attacked as a single problem using one of two major approaches. As Kreitzer and Madaus note in chapter 5 of this volume, one approach is to examine the difficulty level of items that measure the various categories to see if they increase in difficulty from lower to higher levels. The second approach relies on correlational techniques to see if the matrix of intercorrelations among the categories can be hierarchically arranged and accounted for by a single underlying dimension. Let us examine these two approaches separately.

DIFFICULTY-LEVEL APPROACHES TO THE STUDY OF
THE TAXONOMY'S STRUCTURE

As noted in Kreitzer and Madaus's chapter, but to reinforce the point, item difficulty is not necessarily related to the taxonomic level of the behavior tested by an item. Thus, one can create very simple intellectual skill and ability items that nearly every one can answer correctly (e.g., a "synthesis" test item: Describe your face as you see it in a mirror.) and "knowledge" items that deal with trivia to which few have paid attention (e.g., On what date did Bloom address the Allerton Conference?).

To argue that item difficulty and the taxonomic level behavior the item evokes are related requires several assumptions. The first is that the items representing each taxonomic level sample the same portion of the possible range of item complexity and abstraction (e.g., they are the most complex and abstract items possible at each level). The second is that the items are hierarchically related so that achievement of lower-level items is required for achievement of upper-level ones. This can be verified if the sampling of items at each level includes the behaviors necessary for achievement at the next higher level.

The first assumption seems not to be recognized in the cited studies; any items appropriate to the taxonomic level are deemed appropriate. They could be more complex ones at one level and simple ones at the next higher one, thus leading to no apparent differences in difficulty between levels. I know of only one study that built the test items so as to assure fulfilling the second assumption; all others simply assumed it was true.[22] Thus this body of evidence does not lead to a convincing conclusion for or against the hierarchy.

CORRELATIONAL APPROACHES TO THE STUDY OF
THE TAXONOMY'S STRUCTURE

Until I was preparing this chapter, I had not realized that the correlational evidence for a hierarchy seems to depend almost entirely on the Kropp and Stoker data.[23] I had assumed that at least several independent sets of data might be available and that a meta-analysis of their intercorrelation matrixes for the major categories might throw some additional light on the matter. Judging from the sources cited in this volume, this appears not to be the case. Kropp and Stoker have generously provided their data for numerous reanalyses, each of which, while more sophisticated than the previous ones, leaves the issue still in doubt. It would be inappropriate to do a meta-analysis of these studies based almost entirely on the same data set. With samples of over 1400 students in each of four grade levels (9-12), and with four carefully constructed tests that sample all the major taxonomic categories and use both science and social sciences content (two tests each), the Kropp and Stoker database is extremely impressive. Despite the fact that Seddon, in a 1973 review of the data available to that date,[24] raised many questions that might account for the ambivalent results, the difficulty of getting new comparable data may have dampened any other intent to mount an independent corroborating study. Funding for data that even begins to match it would be most difficult to come by.

But there is still another generally unrecognized problem: if the categories are hierarchical, then they are in contingent relation with one another. That is, achievement at a lower level is considered necessary, but not sufficient, for achievement at the upper level.[25] Another way of saying this is that the lower-level behavior is an "entry level behavior" for the upper-level one. This means, for example, that the scatterplot for the achievement of a class of students on application-level geometry items, when plotted against their scores on knowledge-level items, would appear as a triangle instead of the usual ellipse. With the application score plotted along the vertical axis, a typical high positive correlation would have cases in the upper right and lower left hand corners but the upper left and lower right corners would be almost clear of cases. A contingent relation, on the other hand, would also have cases in the lower right hand corner, converting the oval into a triangle. This occurs because some persons who master the knowledge-level items, the lower-level skill, do not master the application items, the upper-level one. Mastery of the knowledge-level items is necessary but not sufficient for (i.e., does not guarantee) mastery of the application items. It follows from this also that persons who had not mastered the lower-level knowledge items, *could not master* the higher-level skill, "application." Therefore, the upper left hand corner would be clear and the shape of the scatterplot would be triangular.

It should be obvious that neither the Pearson product-moment correlation coefficient nor any other statistic that assumes a linear relationship would yield a good estimate of a relationship displayed as a triangular scatterplot. For that matter, statistical estimates of nonlinear relationships also fail. The nonlinearity is not the problem; it is that the cases cluster only at one end of the scatterplot and diverge at the other. At the present time, I know of no measure that will estimate this relationship. Thus, one must ask whether any correlational approach, including all the research on the Kropp and Stoker data from their original analyses to those using the latest, most sophisticated statistical techniques for analyzing linear relationships, can accurately assess the underlying structure of the Taxonomy. Are not all affected by this curious characteristic of these scatterplots?

Although there are no independent estimates to make possible a meta-analysis of intercorrelational studies, such an analysis of those studies of item difficulty probably could be made. It might be more enlightening than interpreting each study individually. Most studies looking for a pattern among the difficulty indices for items testing the major categories of the Taxonomy used a different sample of items, so merging them in this fashion would be appropriate. But, because the authors employed very different ways of presenting results, integrating them will not be as easy as it first appears.

In terms of currently available findings then, we are left with the dilemma of having to rely on a kind of global assessment of the evidence on the validity of the structure of the Taxonomy: its logical consistency, its usefulness in its present form, the extent of agreement and disagreement (statistical and nonstatistical) with the placement and arrangement of the various categories, and the potential agreement on alternative placements and arrangements. It is interesting that, having reviewed the literature on the properties of the Taxonomy in 1973 and having done a very careful job of dissecting the problems with the then available data, Seddon also ascertained that "it is fairest to say that the picture is uncertain." In concluding this same final paragraph he hoped "solutions will be found before another twenty-two years elapse!"[26] Twenty already have! With only two years to go, it seems quite possible his hopes, and ours as well, may not be realized. Yet, even without definitive data that indicate how the structure should be changed, modifications have been suggested. We turn next to an examination of the future of the Taxonomy.

The Future: Should the Taxonomy Be Revised?

As the years have passed, there have been calls to revise the Taxonomy, especially to add test items more typical of elementary and secondary school levels to supplement those of higher education already included. As empirical studies seemed to suggest that one or another of the highest level categories was out of place, the development of a revised structure more in keeping with the data was

proposed. Conservationist and major revisionist points of view have
emerged with respect to next steps in the Taxonomy's development.
The conservationists argue that the "examiners' taxonomy" that was
developed has accrued certain advantages: the extensive familiarity
with the structure, the large body of work that has been built on it,
and the fact that it still serves useful purposes of communicating about
objectives worldwide. Therefore, the main structure should be left as
is with minor adjustments to subheads, a broader range of examples,
and a revised introductory text to take note both of the large body of
research and of its many uses. (This volume would serve as a superb
base for revising the introduction.) This point of view gains support
from the chapter in this volume by Postlethwaite as well as from the
work covered in chapters 6, 7, and 8.

The major revisionist point of view is that a new effort should be
mounted to try to find the stronger structure beyond the "examiner's
taxonomy" which more satisfactorily meets the criteria such a
framework implicitly invokes. In this final section of the chapter, I
recount a revisionist effort that was aborted so those interested in this
second approach can sense what they are up against. Further, I suggest
some criteria which should be considered by those seeking a stronger
structure.

In 1965, Bloom and I invited individuals interested in the Taxonomy to a meeting at the annual convention of the American Educational Research Association to consider the research previously undertaken with respect to the Taxonomy and to look at what might be
required for a revision.[27] A sample from the report of the meeting, prepared by Sarah Hervey, is instructive of the kinds of tough issues that
arose.

Several participants raised questions regarding the nature of the Taxonomy
itself. [Howard] Stoker pointed out the difficulties in measuring the cognitive
processes implied in the Taxonomy . . . [such as] problems in interpretation
which result from measuring the "product response" in place of the
"process." . . . While the Taxonomy specifies processes as educational goals,
evaluation typically focuses upon the product, leaving the teacher or
researcher to speculate about the process which led to the particular product.
There is a need for new item formats to study processes of problem
solving. . . .

The relationship of the Taxonomy to other taxonomies or classification
systems is an area to be explored. Gagné's, Stolurow's, and R. B. Miller's
frameworks and the categorization suggested in Melton's *Categories of Human
Learning* were among those proposed for study. . . .

John Ginther pointed out that any classification scheme is an arbitrary structuring of reality of which the Taxonomy is only one of many. . . . Thus efforts to test its "reality" make the dangerous assumption that only one proper way of structuring "reality" exists.

In addition there were some specific suggestions such as altering or omitting the "extrapolation" subcategory from comprehension, rethinking the ordering of analysis, synthesis, and evaluation (noting that Christine McGuire reordered the last two), and doing a facet analysis of the kind Louis Guttman advocated. It was also proposed that an annotated bibliography of the research be assembled. This proposal led to publications by Cox and Unks[28] and later by Cox and Wildeman.[29] Although plans were made for additional meetings, only one materialized. My own sense is that there were not enough realistically operational and captivating ideas floated to capture time from other more promising projects that everyone was already pursuing.

QUESTIONS TO BE ADDRESSED BY THOSE UNDERTAKING REVISION

Before the Taxonomy is revised, one must be clear as to wherein it is lacking. In addition to the process-product problem voiced above, among the most persistent has been the call for a taxonomy that brings goals and learning exercises more closely together so as to provide more adequate guidance for instruction, a complaint echoed by Sosniak in chapter 7. As she notes, what is needed by teachers is a framework that facilitates the transition from goals to learning strategies and thence to activities which lead to those goals. Can a framework be developed which is more facilitative than those now available? Obviously this is an empirical question. To be widely useful, however, such a framework would have to embrace both the abstract language of goals and the detailed description of student behavior, not an easy task.

Central to useful educator-to-educator communication and to the translation of goals into classroom activities is a solution to the problem of curriculum generality-specificity. In a fascinating review of the literature, Alexander established a continuum which extends from general knowledge and skills (which includes general problem solving) to discipline knowledge and skills, and thence to domain knowledge and skills—each level being more subject-matter specific.[30] She provides a clarifying discussion of the distinctions between the latter two levels, and notes that the domain level has been the focus of research on differences between experts and novices. One can argue that, as one progresses from kindergarten to post-graduate study, at each higher level, education focuses increasingly more tightly on the domain level and, as well, on developing the knowledge and skills of the expert. Will a single set of taxonomic categories serve all levels? Does not the present set of categories best serve the general knowledge and skills level? Are more specific taxonomies required for improved communication in the disciplines? Are still more specific ones needed in domains? The evidence in the *Handbook on Formative and Summative Evaluation* suggests that the most useful taxonomy for the general education level may differ, not only in terms of where one divides one category from another along a taxonomic continuum, but also, at least for certain domains, both in terms of the nature of the continuum itself, and the kinds of categories.[31]

Another persistent concern has been the division of the Taxonomy into cognitive, affective, and psychomotor domains. This division was found useful despite the fact that nearly all goals overlap both the cognitive and affective domains if they are stated in all of their aspects. Further, many goals extend to all three of these domains. The division has served to enforce the isolation of the domains from one another, to make it more difficult to unite all the aspects of a behavior into a single goal statement, and to emphasize cognitive goal aspects at the expense of others, especially the affective. Efforts to overcome this division have been found in the creation of an "action" domain by Elena Sliepsevich in a physical education curriculum.[32] Others have used this device as well. Clearly, this is a problem which will need to be considered by those who attempt the next advance of the Taxonomy.

Although it would be awkward, the possibility exists of thinking about all objectives in multidimensional space. As was noted in the introductory material to *Handbook II: Affective Domain*, there is a parallelism in structure between the cognitive and affective domains.[33] Such similarity could be enhanced by integrating the psychomotor domain taxonomies developed by Harrow[34] and by Simpson[35] into a single structure more parallel to the affective domain than theirs were originally. Jeffrey Stewart and I developed such a structure:[36]

0.0 Basic Movements. (Although not really part of the taxonomy this category of Harrow's is included for work with very young children or the handicapped.)

    0.1 Nonlocomotor movements

    0.2 Manipulative movements

    0.3 Locomotor movements

1.0 Readiness

   1.1 Cue sensitivity

   1.2 Cue and behavior selection

   1.3 Set

      1.31 Mental set

      1.32 Emotional set

      1.33 Physical set

2.0 Movement skill development (emphasis on technique and skill)

   2.1 Translation of mental images into kinesthetic sensations

   2.2 Production of the correct behavior

3.0 Movement pattern development (emphasis on integrating the movement pattern and perfecting the outcome)

   3.1 Production of the movement pattern

   3.2 Perfection of the movement pattern

4.0 Adapting and originating movement patterns

   4.1 Adapting movement patterns (emphasis on automaticity and responsiveness to context as in team sports)

   4.2 Selecting and adapting of movement patterns (emphasis on originality and creativity)

This structure starts with awareness and continues through conscious control and integration of response to automaticity of movement combined with artistic expression at the upper levels. In this respect, it parallels that of the affective domain which begins with receiving (attending), continues through responding and valuing to organization (where the emphasis is on conscious integration of the response), and then to characterization by a value or value complex which involves an automatic response by the individual. All three domains thus provide a structure which runs from the simple to the complex, and from the concrete to the abstract. All three also assume a kind of automaticity of response at the upper levels which can be consciously modified for aesthetic or problem-solving purposes.

Such parallelism could make it easier to remember and use the structure and possibly also to think of it in a three-dimensional space. We currently describe curricula with two dimensional tables of specifications for the cognitive domain: a subject matter dimension and a behavioral one. Using three dimensions for the behavioral aspects plus a fourth for the subject matter extends the dimensions beyond what is possible to visualize unless we collapse a couple of them. Each of the previously cited subject-matter chapters in the *Handbook on Formative and Summative Evaluation* contains a typical two-dimensional table of specifications for objectives, many of which extend into the affective domain simply by adding columns for affective objectives. One could do the same thing for psychomotor objectives. While this gets around the difficulty, it fails to indicate the interrelationship among the domains.

As indicated in the affective domain volume, achievement in the cognitive domain is often used as a means of achieving goals in the affective domain: "Cognitive behavior may be used to indoctrinate points of view and to build attitudes and values. Indeed, we do this shamelessly in the aesthetic fields where we want our students to learn to recognize 'good' poetry, painting, architecture, sculpture, music, and so on."[37] And the opposite path is also sometimes used: "Obviously motivation is critical to learning and thus is one of the major ways in which the affective domain is used as a means to the cognitive. The large number of interest objectives indicates the importance of this aspect of the learning situation. The influence of hedonic tone on memory and learning is also important: children are more likely to learn and remember material for which they have a positive feeling."[38] Similarly, we often use achievement in psychomotor skills as a means to teach sportsmanship and, vice versa, achievement of goals in the cognitive domain may be important in teaching, for example, the physiology of dance. So, objectives may relate to more than one domain at a time, and some kind of interrelationship of the three domains in a pattern would be a useful aspect of any revision. But no simple solution presents itself.

Finally, there is the relationship to some kind of widely accepted, meaningful, and useful psychological structure. Despite the success of reinforcement theory, Gagné's structure, for example, which builds on a Skinnerian base, would not be acceptable to many. Can one find another theory of learning that might serve? In this regard, it is perhaps instructive to mention a chapter that I never included in the affective domain handbook. It was a chapter designed to relate the dimension around which the affective domain is built, "internalization," to a variety of psychological theories of learning from Skinnerian to gestalt to the "TOTE" units of Miller, Galanter, and Pribram.[39] I could not get the chapter to "jell," feeling that, in order to make them match, I distorted either the definition of internalization or the technical terms of the theory to which I was relating it. As a result of circulating the chapter to friends and colleagues, Milton

Rokeach, a colleague at Michigan State, wrote back to the effect: "Dave, why do you think that you can relate all these theories to internalization when the very best minds in psychology have been trying to develop a single integrating theory for decades and have failed?" Gratefully I accepted his perspective and deleted the chapter from the manuscript. There is a lesson here that may not be lost on those who try the next version of a taxonomy.

In summary, the new framework should make progress in solving the process-product relationship, facilitating the translation of goals into learning experiences and activities, finding the right level of discourse to communicate with the classroom teacher, test constructor, and educational psychologist, finding a structure that encompasses and facilitates the description of education goals in all three domains and clearly interrelates them, and finding a structure that has a clear relationship to a widely accepted psychological base. That is a large order! No doubt, any new effort will solve only some of these problems and, as did the present Taxonomy, finesse the rest. But solving some additional ones would be a useful accomplishment. And perhaps whoever is involved can benefit from the experiences of those who developed the original version and create a new heuristic structure that is even more successful and useful than this one has been. Bloom's hope, quoted on the opening page of this final chapter, of something more than an "examiners' taxonomy" is still waiting to be fulfilled.

NOTES

1. Benjamin S. Bloom, "A Taxonomy of Educational Objectives" (Opening remarks at a meeting of examiners, Monticello, IL, November 27, 1949), in David R. Krathwohl, "Summary Report, College and University Examiners' Taxonomy Conference," mimeographed (Champaign, IL: Unit on Evaluation, Bureau of Research and Service, College of Education, University of Illinois, 1949), p. 4.

2. Abraham Kaplan, *The Conduct of Inquiry: Methodology for Behavioral Science* (San Francisco: Chandler, 1964), p. 148.

3. David R. Krathwohl, *Methods of Educational and Social Science Research: An Integrated Approach* (White Plains, NY: Longman, 1993), p. 637.

4. Ibid.

5. Bloom, "A Taxonomy of Educational Objectives" (Opening remarks at a meeting of examiners), p. 5.

6. Robert Sinclair, letter to author, 14 March 1967.

7. In addition to those listed by Lewy and Báthory in chapter 9, we are aware of translations into Chinese, Korean, Malaysian, Telegu, and Thai.

8. Ralph Tyler, as Chair of the Committee on Personality Development in Youth of the Social Science Research Council, also helped us obtain a small grant from the Council to finish work on the affective domain taxonomy.

9. In structuring the conference, Bloom, Hastings, and I had anticipated that discussion of the material prepared on knowledge, skills, and abilities would occupy the bulk of the discussion. As indicated by the report, however, two and a half pages were devoted to what became the cognitive domain, and seven pages to what became the affective area where no conceptualization was presented. This pattern of heavy discussion of the affective area tended to be repeated in what became a series of annual meetings. A tentative draft of the affective area was presented to the 1952 meeting.

10. It may seem strange that these attributions were not made in the manuscript, but the project had a group spirit about it. Since it was impossible to identify all the contributions, no single part was attributed to an individual.

11. The meetings resumed on a smaller scale devoted to the affective domain in 1956 with meetings at Chicago hosted by Bloom and at Louisiana State by Ray Loree.

12. Edward J. Furst, *Constructing Evaluation Instruments* (New York: David McKay, 1958).

13. Benjamin S. Bloom, J. Thomas Hastings, and George F. Madaus, *Handbook on Formative and Summative Evaluation of Student Learning* (New York: McGraw-Hill, 1971).

14. My colleague Donald Ely suggested adding this step in the process.

15. Christine McGuire, "A Process Approach to the Construction and Analysis of Medical Examinations," *Journal of Medical Education* 38 (1963): 556-563.

16. Walter F. Moore and Larry D. Kennedy, "Evaluation of Learning in the Language Arts," in Bloom, Hastings, and Madaus, *Handbook of Formative and Summative Evaluation of Student Learning*, pp. 399-446.

17. James W. Wilson, "Evaluation of Learning in Secondary School Mathematics," in Bloom, Hastings, and Madaus, *Handbook of Formative and Summative Evaluation of Student Learning*, pp. 643-696.

18. Moore and Kennedy, "Evaluation of Learning in the Language Arts."

19. Brent G. Wilson, "Evaluation of Learning in Art Education," in Bloom, Hastings, and Madaus, *Handbook of Formative and Summative Evaluation of Student Learning*, pp. 499-558.

20. Lisanio R. Orlandi, "Evaluation of Learning in Secondary School Social Studies," in Bloom, Hastings, and Madaus, *Handbook of Formative and Summative Evaluation of Student Learning*, pp. 449-498.

21. Leopold E. Klopfer, "Evaluation of Learning in Science," in Bloom, Hastings, and Madaus, *Handbook of Formative and Summative Evaluation of Student Learning*, pp. 561-641.

22. In 1965, Dr. Sara Blackwell's student at Cornell University, Alice Thomas Miller, completed a Master's thesis, "Levels of Cognitive Behavior Measured in a Controlled Teaching Situation," that tested the same science principles of heat and light at the knowledge, comprehension, and application levels of the Taxonomy. Given that the items tested the Taxonomy level intended (she used two judges to assure this), this made it more certain that lower-level knowledge or skill was required for achievement at the higher level. She analyzed the data for a Guttman simplex and found partial support. Further, assuming that higher-scoring students at a given level are more likely to achieve at the next higher level than low-scoring students (a method of analysis used by Roberta Jacklin in "An Exploratory Study of Secondary Pupils' Depth of Understanding of Selected Food and Nutrition Principles" [Ph.D. dissertation, Cornell University, 1964]), there should be higher correlations between achievement at adjacent Taxonomy levels than between those more distant. Her data confirmed this in three out of four instances. Miller's careful methods are worth replicating with more Taxonomy levels and a larger student sample.

23. Russell P. Kropp and Howard W. Stoker, "The Construction and Validation of Tests of the Cognitive Processes as Described in the Taxonomy of Educational Objectives," Cooperative Research Project No. 2117 (Tallahassee, FL: Institute of Human Learning and Department of Educational Research and Testing, 1966). ERIC ED 010 044.

24. G. M. Seddon, "The Properties of Bloom's Taxonomy of Educational Objectives for the Cognitive Domain," *Review of Educational Research* 48 (1978): 303-323.

25. Krathwohl, *Methods of Educational and Social Science Research*, p. 257.

26. Seddon, "The Properties of Bloom's Taxonomy of Educational Objectives for the Cognitive Domain," p. 321.

27. Other persons present were Louis Bashaw, Sara Blackwell, Milton Collins, Richard C. Cox, William Crawford, Robert Follett, Edward Furst, John Ginther, John M. Gordon, Hulda Grobman, Walker Hill, Bertram Masia, Christine McGuire, Helen Nelson, Norris Sanders, Richard Smith, Howard Stoker, and Karl Zinn.

28. Richard C. Cox and Nancy J. Unks, "A Selected and Annotated Bibliography of Studies Concerning the Taxonomy of Educational Objectives: Cognitive Domain," Working Paper 13 (Pittsburgh, PA: University of Pittsburgh, Learning Research and Development Center, 1967).

29. Richard C. Cox and Carol E. Wildeman, *Taxonomy of Educational Objectives: Cognitive Domain, An Annotated Bibliography*, Monograph no. 1 (Pittsburgh, PA: University of Pittsburgh, Learning Research and Development Center, 1970).

30. Patricia A. Alexander, "Domain Knowledge: Evolving Themes and Emerging Concerns," *Educational Psychologist* 27 (1992): 33-51.

31. Bloom, Hastings, and Madaus, *Handbook on Formative and Summative Evaluation of Student Learning*.

32. Elena M. Sliepsevich, *Health Education: A Conceptual Approach to Curriculum Design* (St. Paul, MN: 3M Company Educational Services, 1967).

33. David R. Krathwohl, Benjamin S. Bloom, and Bertram B. Masia, *Taxonomy of Educational Objectives, The Classification of Educational Goals: Handbook II: Affective Domain* (New York: David McKay, 1964).

34. Anita Harrow, *A Taxonomy of the Psychomotor Domain: A Guide for Developing Behavioral Objectives* (New York: David McKay, 1972).

35. Elizabeth J. Simpson, "The Classification of Educational Objectives, Psychomotor Domain," *Illinois Teacher of Home Economics* 10, no. 4 (1966): 110-144.

36. David R. Krathwohl and Jeffrey A. Stewart, "The Psychomotor Domain of the Taxonomy of Educational Objectives," unpublished manuscript (Syracuse, NY: School of Education, Syracuse University, 1973).

37. Krathwohl, Bloom, and Masia, *Taxonomy of Educational Objectives, The Classification of Educational Goals: Handbook II: Affective Domain*, p. 56.

38. Ibid., p. 57.

39. George A. Miller, Eugene Galanter, and Karl H. Pribram, *Plans and the Structure of Behavior* (New York: Holt, 1960).

Name Index

Abramson, David A., 122, 125
Accareta, Isaias, 163
Airasian, Peter W., 82, 100, 101, 102
Alexander, Patricia A., 196, 202
Alexander, William M., 123
Alschuler, Marjorie D., 76, 80
Anderson, Beverly, 101
Anderson, Gordon V., 3
Anderson, Linda M., 144
Anderson, Lorin W., 8, 9, 126, 131, 142, 143, 144, 145
Andre, Thomas, 133, 141, 143, 144
Anscombe, G. E. M., 38
Apt, Leon, 39
Arnove, R. J., 161
Atkin, Myron J., 101
Ausbel, David P., 145
Austin, George A., 62

Baker, Eva L., 102
Barker, Douglas, 144
Bashaw, W. Louis, 79, 202
Báthory, Zoltán, 146, 156, 157, 162, 200
Beckmann, Hans K., 161
Berlak, Harold, 101
Berliner, David C., 124, 128, 131, 142, 143
Biddle, Bruce J., 131, 142, 143
Birzea, Cesar, 152, 162
Blackwell, Sara, 201, 202
Block, James H., 142
Bloom, Benjamin S., 1, 8, 9, 10, 36, 37, 38, 39, 40, 52, 57, 61, 63, 66, 67, 68, 69, 78, 79, 100, 103, 112, 113, 117, 123, 126, 127, 129, 141, 142, 143, 145, 147, 157, 158, 161, 168, 170, 171, 172, 173, 174, 179, 180, 181, 182, 183, 184, 185, 186, 187, 188, 189, 191, 192, 195, 200, 201, 202
Blumberg, Phyllis, 76, 80
Blyth, William A. L., 111, 112, 120, 121, 123, 125
Bobbitt, Franklin, 116, 124
Bolin, Frances, 124
Bolton, Dale L., 67, 79
Bratanic, Maria, 161
Bremer, Neville H., 142
Brophy, Jere, 144
Broudy, Harry S., 30, 38

Brown, Ann L., 63
Bruner, Jerome S., 41, 42, 58, 62, 63, 100
Burns, Robert B., 142
Buros, O. K., 4, 185, 186

Calder, J. R., 67, 79
Calfee, Kathryn, 133, 143
Calfee, Robert, 133, 143
Campbell, Ernest Q., 101
Carlsen, William S., 133, 143
Carter, Kathy, 138, 140, 144, 145
Case, Robbie, 58, 59, 63
Cazden, Courtney B., 124
Chambers, Barbara, 138, 145
Chawhan, A. R., 129, 142
Chi, Michelene T. H., 63
Chipman, Susan F., 63
Cho, Hui Hyung, 170, 173
Chung, Bom Mo, 164
Churchill, Ruth, 3
Clark, Christopher, 145
Clark, Dwight, 115, 121, 124, 125
Cohen, David K., 100, 151, 161
Cohen, Ronald, 76, 80
Cole, Nancy S., 113, 124
Coleman, James S., 92, 101
Collins, Milton, 202
Coolidge, Susan W., 144
Court, Stephen, 82
Cox, Richard C., 196, 202
Crawford, William R., 80, 202
Cronbach, Lee J., 3, 91, 101
Crooks, Terence J., 126, 141, 142, 143
Cunha, J. A., 163

D'Hainaut, Louis, 158, 162
Dahnke, Harold L., Jr., 3
Dale, Edgar, 87, 100
Dante (Alighieri), 71
Davis, O. L., Jr., 144
DeBlock, Alfred, 159, 162
DeCorte, Erik, 37, 40, 159, 162
DeLandsheere, Guilbert, 162
DeLandsheere, Viviane, 39, 40, 78, 79, 81, 158, 162, 163, 174, 179
Detchen, Lily, 3
Dewey, John, 17, 113, 116, 124
Diener, Kuno, 161, 162
Dinaburg, Ben-Zion, 161

203

Subject Index

Allerton Conference (1949), 181, 183, 185
American schools, decline of test scores in, 94
Analysis (category in the Taxonomy): description of, 21-23; types of, 23
Application (category in the Taxonomy): description of, 20-21; problem-solving processes in, 22 (figure)

Behavioral objectives: opposition of National Council of Teachers of English to, 90-91; risks of, 29-30
Behaviorism, dominance of, in 1950s, 41
Brown vs. *Board of Education of Topeka*, 88

Central Educational Evaluation Institute (Korea), responsibility of, for developing college entrance examinations, 167
Classification systems, comparison of, with taxonomies, 14
Cognitive developmental perspectives on learning, 57-59: development as the centerpiece of, 58; generalization of intellectual abilities in, 59; hierarchical relationship of developmental stages in, 58; novice-expert distinctions in, 59
Cognitive and affective domains, artificiality of distinctions between, 32
Cognitive domain: omission of important objectives in, in the Taxonomy, 33-44; reasons for beginning the Taxonomy with, 2
Cognitive psychology, current dominance of, 41, 42
Cognitive-science perspectives on learning, 59-62: domain-specific objectives required by, 61-62; methods and features of, 59-60; view of expert-novice differences in, 61
Coleman Report (*Equality of Educational Opportunity*), 92
Comprehension (category in the Taxonomy), types of, 19-20
Comprehensiveness, as a feature of the Taxonomy, 33-34
Conditions of Learning (Gagné), 42, 55-59, 87

Cumulative-hierarchical structure (of the Taxonomy), 34-37: criticism of, 66-67; critique of linear assumption in, 34-36; simple-to-complex principle as basis for, 65-66; studies of, 67-77; uncertain conclusions from research on, 77-78
Curriculum evaluation movement: expansion of, 91; impact of, on uses of objectives in testing and evaluation, 92; new modes of evaluation as products of, 91-92
Curriculum literature, scant attention in, to ways of using the Taxonomy, 110-112
Curriculum planning, Tyler model of, 30

Education, changing views of, 7
Elementary and Secondary Education Act, Title 1, 88-89: call for accountability in connection with, 89; opposition to evaluation mandate in, 89; promise of, 89
Evaluation (category in the Taxonomy), 24-25
Expertise, nature of, 49
Experts and novices, different perspectives on distinctions between, 49-50, 59, 61

Florida Education Accountability Act (1976), 95

Gränna seminar, 5, 147, 178

Handbook of Formative and Summative Evaluation of Student Learning (Bloom, Hastings, Madaus), 5, 7, 173, 178, 187, 191, 197, 199
Head Start, 88
Heuristic: definition of, 182; important considerations in development and dissemination of a, 187-89
Higher mental processes, prime importance of, 1, 187
Higher-order skills: generalizability of, 48-49; present-day emphasis on, in testing, 90

208

INFORMATION ABOUT MEMBERSHIP IN THE SOCIETY

Membership in the National Society for the Study of Education is open to all who desire to receive its publications.

There are two categories of membership: Regular and Comprehensive. The Regular Membership (annual dues in 1994, $30) entitles the member to receive both volumes of the yearbook. The Comprehensive Membership (annual dues in 1994, $55) entitles the member to receive the two-volume yearbook and the two current volumes in the Series on Contemporary Educational Issues.

Reduced dues (Regular, $25; Comprehensive, $50) are available for retired NSSE members and for full-time graduate students *in their first year of membership*.

Membership in the Society is for the calendar year. Dues are payable on or before January 1 of each year.

New members are required to pay an entrance fee of $1, in addition to annual dues for the year in which they join.

Members of the Society include professors, researchers, graduate students, and administrators in colleges and universities; teachers, supervisors, curriculum specialists, and administrators in elementary and secondary schools; and a considerable number of persons not formally connected with educational institutions.

All members participate in the nomination and election of the six-member Board of Directors, which is responsible for managing the affairs of the Society, including the authorization of volumes to appear in the yearbook series. All members whose dues are paid for the current year are eligible for election to the Board of Directors.

Each year the Society arranges for meetings to be held in conjunction with the annual conferences of one or more of the major national educational organizations. All members are urged to attend these sessions. Members are also encouraged to submit proposals for future yearbooks or for volumes in the series on Contemporary Educational Issues.

Further information about the Society may be secured by writing to the Secretary-Treasurer, NSSE, 5835 Kimbark Avenue, Chicago, IL 60637.

RECENT PUBLICATIONS OF THE NATIONAL
SOCIETY FOR THE STUDY OF EDUCATION

1. The Yearbooks

Ninety-third Yearbook (1994)
Part 1. *Teacher Research and Educational Reform.* Sandra Hollingsworth and Hugh Sockett, editors. Cloth.
Part 2. *Bloom's Taxonomy: A Forty-year Retrospective.* Lorin W. Anderson and Lauren A. Sosniak, editors. Cloth.

Ninety-second Yearbook (1993)
Part 1. *Gender and Education.* Sari Knopp Biklen and Diane Pollard, editors. Cloth.
Part 2. *Bilingual Education: Politics, Practice, and Research.* M. Beatriz Arias and Ursula Casanova, editors. Cloth.

Ninety-first Yearbook (1992)
Part 1. *The Changing Contexts of Teaching.* Ann Lieberman, editor. Cloth.
Part 2. *The Arts, Education, and Aesthetic Knowing.* Bennett Reimer and Ralph A. Smith, editors. Cloth.

Ninetieth Yearbook (1991)
Part 1. *The Care and Education of America's Young Children: Obstacles and Opportunities.* Sharon L. Kagan, editor. Cloth.
Part 2. *Evaluation and Education: At Quarter Century.* Milbrey W. McLaughlin and D. C. Phillips, editors. Paper.

Eighty-ninth Yearbook (1990)
Part 1. *Textbooks and Schooling in the United States.* David L. Elliott and Arthur Woodward, editors. Cloth.
Part 2. *Educational Leadership and Changing Contexts of Families, Communities, and Schools.* Brad Mitchell and Luvern L. Cunningham, editors. Paper.

Eighty-eighth Yearbook (1989)
Part 1. *From Socrates to Software: The Teacher as Text and the Text as Teacher.* Philip W. Jackson and Sophie Haroutunian-Gordon, editors. Cloth.
Part 2. *Schooling and Disability.* Douglas Biklen, Dianne Ferguson, and Alison Ford, editors. Cloth.

Eighty-seventh Yearbook (1988)
Part 1. *Critical Issues in Curriculum.* Laurel N. Tanner, editor. Cloth.
Part 2. *Cultural Literacy and the Idea of General Education.* Ian Westbury and Alan C. Purves, editors. Cloth.

Eighty-sixth Yearbook (1987)
Part 1. *The Ecology of School Renewal.* John I. Goodlad, editor. Paper.
Part 2. *Society as Educator in an Age of Transition.* Kenneth D. Benne and Steven Tozer, editors. Cloth.

Eighty-fifth Yearbook (1986)

Part 1. *Microcomputers and Education.* Jack A. Culbertson and Luvern L. Cunningham, editors. Cloth.

Part 2. *The Teaching of Writing.* Anthony R. Petrosky and David Bartholomae, editors. Paper.

Eighty-fourth Yearbook (1985)

Part 1. *Education in School and Nonschool Settings.* Mario D. Fantini and Robert Sinclair, editors. Cloth.

Part 2. *Learning and Teaching the Ways of Knowing.* Elliot Eisner, editor. Paper.

Eighty-third Yearbook (1984)

Part 1. *Becoming Readers in a Complex Society.* Alan C. Purves and Olive S. Niles, editors. Cloth.

Part 2. *The Humanities in Precollegiate Education.* Benjamin Ladner, editor. Paper.

Eighty-second Yearbook (1983)

Part 1. *Individual Differences and the Common Curriculum.* Gary D Fenstermacher and John I. Goodlad, editors. Paper.

Eighty-first Yearbook (1982)

Part 1. *Policy Making in Education.* Ann Lieberman and Milbrey W. McLaughlin, editors. Cloth.

Part 2. *Education and Work.* Harry F. Silberman, editor. Cloth.

Eightieth Yearbook (1981)

Part 1. *Philosophy and Education.* Jonas P. Soltis, editor. Cloth.

Part 2. *The Social Studies.* Howard D. Mehlinger and O. L. Davis, Jr., editors. Cloth.

Seventy-ninth Yearbook (1980)

Part 1. *Toward Adolescence: The Middle School Years.* Mauritz Johnson, editor. Paper.

Seventy-eighth Yearbook (1979)

Part 1. *The Gifted and the Talented: Their Education and Development.* A. Harry Passow, editor. Paper.

Part 2. *Classroom Management.* Daniel L. Duke, editor. Paper.

Seventy-seventh Yearbook (1978)

Part 1. *The Courts and Education.* Clifford B. Hooker, editor. Cloth.

Seventy-sixth Yearbook (1977)

Part 1. *The Teaching of English.* James R. Squire, editor. Cloth.

The above titles in the Society's Yearbook series may be ordered from the University of Chicago Press, Book Order Department, 11030 Langley Ave., Chicago, IL 60628. For a list of earlier titles in the yearbook series still available, write to the Secretary, NSSE, 5835 Kimbark Ave., Chicago, IL 60637.

2. The Series on Contemporary Educational Issues

The following volumes in the Society's Series on Contemporary Educational Issues may be ordered from the McCutchan Publishing Corporation, P.O. Box 774, Berkeley, CA 94702-0774.

Academic Work and Educational Excellence: Raising Student Productivity (1986). Edited by Tommy M. Tomlinson and Herbert J. Walberg.

Adapting Instruction to Student Differences (1985). Edited by Margaret C. Wang and Herbert J. Walberg.

Aspects of Reading Education (1978). Edited by Susanna Pflaum-Connor.

Choice in Education (1990). Edited by William Lowe Boyd and Herbert J. Walberg.

Colleges of Education: Perspectives on Their Future (1985). Edited by Charles W. Case and William A. Matthes.

Contributing to Educational Change: Perspectives on Research and Practice (1988). Edited by Philip W. Jackson.

Early Childhood Education: Issues and Insights (1977). Edited by Bernard Spodek and Herbert J. Walberg.

Educational Environments and Effects: Evaluation, Policy, and Productivity (1979). Edited by Herbert J. Walberg.

Educational Leadership and School Culture (1993). Edited by Marshall Sashkin and Herbert J. Walberg.

Effective School Leadership: Policy and Prospects (1987). Edited by John J. Lane and Herbert J. Walberg.

Effective Teaching: Current Research (1991). Edited by Hersholt C. Waxman and Herbert J. Walberg.

From Youth to Constructive Adult Life: The Role of the Public School (1978). Edited by Ralph W. Tyler.

Improving Educational Standards and Productivity: The Research Basis for Policy (1982). Edited by Herbert J. Walberg.

Moral Development and Character Education (1989). Edited by Larry P. Nucci.

Motivating Students to Learn: Overcoming Barriers to High Achievement (1993). Edited by Tommy M. Tomlinson.

Psychology and Education: The State of the Union (1981). Edited by Frank H. Farley and Neal J. Gordon.

Radical Proposals for Educational Change (1994). Edited by Chester E. Finn, Jr. and Herbert J. Walberg.

Reaching Marginal Students: A Prime Concern for School Renewal (1987). Edited by Robert L. Sinclair and Ward Ghory.

Research on Teaching: Concepts, Findings, and Implications (1979). Edited by Penelope L. Peterson and Herbert J. Walberg.

Restructuring the Schools: Problems and Prospects (1992). Edited by John J. Lane and Edgar G. Epps.

Rethinking Policy for At-risk Students (1994). Edited by Kenneth K. Wong and Margaret C. Wang.

Selected Issues in Mathematics Education (1981). Edited by Mary M. Lindquist.

School Boards: Changing Local Control (1992). Edited by Patricia F. First and Herbert J. Walberg.